Indiana Legends

Famous Hoosiers
From Johnny Appleseed
To David Letterman

NELSON PRICE

GUILD PRESS OF INDIANA
CARMEL, INDIANA

GUILD PRESS OF INDIANA, INC.
435 Gradle Drive
Carmel, Indiana 46032

Library of Congress
Catalog Card Number
97-75132

ISBN 1-57860-006-5

Printed in the United States of America

Text designed by Sheila Samson

To Mom and Dad—
my favorite Hoosiers

Contents

~

Legends of Our Own Day

~

Other Legends

Acknowledgments

In putting this book together, a typical response from a famous Hoosier when informed he or she was going to be featured in a book called *Indiana Legends* was: "I am not worthy."

Those words—or a variation of them—came from people such as Herman B Wells, unquestionably one of the shining lights in higher education as well as a campus folk hero, and sports figures such as Ara Parseghian. These people may protest; the rest of us know they are certainly legends.

Their modesty is another example, albeit an endearing one, of the collective Hoosier inferiority complex—something that even affects legendary figures.

Writing about legends involves dangers, of course. Often, particularly with frontier characters such as Johnny Appleseed, Tecumseh, and Frances Slocum, accounts of the legends' lives differ, sometimes markedly.

When possible, I have attempted to reconcile the differing versions or offer two and even three alternative interpretations of events. When forced to choose, though, Guild Press of Indiana and I have opted for the Indiana Historical Society's interpretation.

Speaking of Guild Press, I want to say here that more than anyone else, Nancy Niblack Baxter—my publisher, editor, and valued friend—helped me shape this book. Her expertise in pioneer life and the Civil War complemented my knowledge of famous contemporary Hoosiers based on my fifteen years as a profile writer and columnist at *The Indianapolis Star* and *The Indianapolis News*.

Among those who helped us along the way were Kent Calder, editor of *Traces of Indiana and Midwestern History* magazine and Susan Sutton, the historical society's photo coordinator and the supplier of more than two dozen of the photos included in this book.

My gratitude also goes to history experts interviewed for this book.

They include: Mike Bailey, former curator of the Eugene V. Debs Home in Terre Haute; Jennifer Capps, curator of the Benjamin Harrison Presidential Home; Douglas Clanin, editor for the Indiana Historical Society; James Cole, Peru resident, lawyer, and cousin of Cole Porter; Steve Cox, historian at Conner Prairie Settlement; Richard Day, Vincennes historian; James Eber, research assistant for The Lincoln Museum in Fort Wayne; Hank Fincken, Indianapolis playwright-performer; Nancy Gerard, Indianapolis civic leader and expert on May Wright Sewall; Glory-June Greiff, Indianapolis historian, and Catherine Gibson, manager of adult services at the Indianapolis-Marion County Public Library.

I also interviewed—and would like to thank—Val Holley, author of *James Dean: The Biography*; Saundra Jackson, secretary-treasurer of the Levi Coffin House Association; Kenny Jagger, Indianapolis pianist and cousin of Dean Jagger; the late Bill Lutholtz, author of *Grand Dragon: D. C. Stephenson and the Ku Klux Klan*; Barbara Olenyik Morrow, author of *From Ben-Hur to Sister Carrie: Remembering the Lives and Works of Five Indiana Authors*; Bob Motz, Indianapolis actor-singer and Hoagy Carmichael interpreter; the late Adeline Mart Nall, former drama teacher and speech coach at Fairmount High School, and dozens of residents of Fairmount.

Thanks also to Judy Vale Newton, author of *The Hoosier Group: Five American Painters*; Jim Powell, executive director of the Writers' Center of Indianapolis; Wil Shriner, comedian and son of Herb Shriner; Andrea D. Smith, curator of T. C. Steele State Historic Site; Donald Spoto, author of *The Life and Legend of James Dean*; Mark Thomas, board member of the Levi Coffin House Association and nephew of the home's former owner; the staff at the Auburn-Cord-Duesenberg Museum in Auburn, and the library staff at *The Indianapolis Star* and *The Indianapolis News*.

Special thanks must go to two people who have been particularly helpful in gathering information for and writing several of the profiles of famous Hoosiers included in the "Other Legends" section. These two people are my research assistants Paul Glader and Deborah Rinker.

Finally, I'm indebted to George Hanlin of the Indiana Historical Society. He fact-checked the "Legends of History" profiles and often unearthed fascinating anecdotes that had not been brought to my attention. I borrowed some of George's gems and included them in the profiles.

Suffice it to say that writing *Indiana Legends* has taken me to every corner of my home state. I've also been "transported" to every era—from the wilderness explored by French fur traders and frontier characters such as Frances Slocum, through the literary and cultural Renaissance in Indianapolis at the turn of the century, to the diverse, pulsating state that about five and a half million of us call home today.

Whether my trip to meet a legendary Hoosier was one of distance or of time, I have tried in each journey to take you, the reader, with me.

Introduction

Myth-making about charismatic men and women existed long before Tecumseh organized hundreds of admirers in the wilderness or Johnny Appleseed showed up in the Indiana Territory with his seedlings and scriptures. And the creation of legends about famous people shows no signs of diminishing in our own era, when Hoosier entertainers like David Letterman and athletes such as Reggie Miller captivate thousands of us.

Only the process of myth-making has evolved. Instead of relying primarily on word of mouth about the exploits of frontier characters and war heroes, we turn to newspapers, television, magazines, movies, and Internet chat rooms in our quest to know more about the legends of today. But they continue to fascinate us.

What kind of person qualifies as an Indiana legend?

Tough choices had to be made with *Indiana Legends*. In our era, just as in Tecumseh's, there is no scarcity of famous Hoosiers. Rather than having to hunt for legends to include, my dilemma was who to leave out because of space constraints.

And I confronted another question early on: Who qualifies as a Hoosier? Someone merely born here, but who left Indiana as a child, seldom to return? A person who enjoyed international glory as an athlete while attending one of our universities, but who wasn't born here and didn't settle in Indiana as an adult?

For advice, my publisher, Nancy Niblack Baxter, and I turned to the Indiana Historical Society's Tom Krasean and Bob Taylor. They helped us choose the "Legends of History" profiled in this book.

During the two years I have devoted to traveling around the state to interview relatives of historic legends, curators, historians, and other experts, the question I have been asked most frequently has been, "What do legendary Hoosiers have in common?"

For example, what possible links exist between James Whitcomb Riley, a poet who was known for his sentimental depictions of rural childhood, and James Dean, a movie star who became an international symbol for anguished youth?

Well, at least one. We Hoosiers seldom have thought of ourselves as the stuff of legend. Quite the contrary, for much of the history of the nineteenth state, Indiana residents have seemed to suffer from an inferiority complex.

Famous people? *Legends?* Surely they only come from New York City, Boston or Philadelphia. Baloney. They are right here, too—by the shores of the Wabash and Ohio rivers and in the shadow of the RCA Dome.

Legendary people have come from the Hoosier cities of Peru, Kokomo, Terre Haute, and Seymour. Those towns have produced the sophisticated composer of music associated with Fred Astaire and Ginger Rogers, a teenage crusader who taught the country tolerance, the founder of the Socialist Party in the United States and one of today's most acclaimed rock stars.

From astronauts to auto racers, artists, tycoons, Olympic athletes, and movie stars, Indiana has spawned dozens of famous Americans.

Sometimes, though, Hoosiers who become folk legends are not a source of pride. Notorious examples in this book are gangster John Dillinger and Ku Klux Klan leader D. C. Stephenson. They are included because to overlook those legendary figures would be to deny parts of our past.

In addition, accounts of how despicable people reap fame and power are instructive, serving as cautionary tales about whom we choose to glorify. And let's face it, the lives of notorious characters often are just as fascinating as the lives of virtuous ones.

At any rate, read on and meet the Hoosier legends. Here's to Indiana as the home of the cream of the crop!

Legends of History

*The death of François-Marie Bissot, Sieur de Vincennes Jr., in 1736,
as depicted in a drawing by famous Hoosier artist Will Vawter.*

*"Your very humble and very obedient servant . . ."
Jean Baptiste Bissot, Sieur de Vincennes Sr. (Drawing
by Richard Day.)*

Vincennes Sr. & Jr.

Jean Baptiste and François Marie Bissot —
Traders

The first legendary Hoosiers actually were French Canadians.

Beginning in the 1600s, the French sent priests and explorers to colonize the middle part of America. These early visitors encountered American Indian tribes who ranged from friendly to hostile. The French founded Detroit, St. Louis and New Orleans. They also came to Indiana and established the fort of Vincennes on the Wabash River in 1732.

Many French nobles and common people came over to farm, settle and develop the colony they called "New France." Two memorable French citizens were the Sieurs de Vincennes Sr. and Jr., a free-spirited father who endeared himself to a tribe of Indians and a loyal son who followed in his footsteps—but met disaster.

Born in Quebec in 1668, Jean-Baptiste Bissot, the first Sieur de Vincennes, was educated at a seminary in New France—specifically, Quebec. He died during the winter of 1718-19. The second Sieur de Vincennes, François-Marie Bissot, was one of his seven children. Born in 1700, he founded the Hoosier town that bears his name, one of the oldest cities in the Midwest.

Life could often be short and brutal in this ruthless land. Two cultures were in conflict in the woods of the Midwest, and they would fight it out until only one survived. Vincennes was caught up in that conflict, and it resulted in his own death in 1736. This, unfortunately, was often the story when Indians and whites met.

Flames crackle. The Chickasaw Indians chant and sing hymns.

Prisoners of war are on display at the Indian village, which has swelled to four hundred or five hundred Chickasaw warriors, many times its usual size. The village is in an isolated part of present-day Mississippi. The prisoners are white men, invaders from the north who sought the Chickasaws' seed corn and other provisions.

Among the prisoners are three Frenchmen of distinction—a Jesuit priest; the commandant of Illinois forces, and thirty-five-year-old Sieur de Vincennes Jr., a lieutenant from what is now southern Indiana.

As the Chickasaw push them toward a roaring fire, Vincennes and his Catholic companions cross themselves, pray, and prepare for a gruesome death. They are about to be burned in a public execution.

Did they deserve this fate? And how did an early Hoosier like Sieur de Vincennes Jr. find himself so far from his frontier home on the Wabash River in what was then called New France?

In the spring of 1736 he had plunged into the wilderness with all of the French soldiers and Indian braves he could muster. Although he did not realize it, Vincennes would never again see his wife and two young daughters, or his home at Fort Vincennes on the Wabash.

His destination was western Tennessee. Vincennes and the Illinois commandant of the French post had been ordered to gather their forces and rendezvous in March with the governor of Louisiana near what is now Memphis. The governor planned to make war against the Chickasaw, who were hostile to New France.

The hitch: The governor and his soldiers never showed up, delayed in New Orleans by a lack of supplies. A courier explained to the Northerners that the governor's men would not be able to join them until April.

Alarmed, several Indian chiefs aligned with Vincennes warned that the group didn't have provisions for such a long wait in enemy territory.

But scouts reported seeing an isolated Chickasaw village. They insisted it would be easy to take and would supply the needed provisions. The decision to attack was made—but it failed disastrously and resulted in Vincennes' horrific death by fire.

And it was all so ironic. Vincennes had spent most of his life beloved by other Indians, particularly the Wea and the Miami. His father, Sieur de Vincennes Sr., also had been adored. (The title *sieur* was common shorthand for *monsieur*, the French equivalent of *mister*.)

Vincennes Sr. had encouraged friendly fur trade among the Miami and urged them to become Catholics. After his death, Vincennes Jr. had continued his work among the Miami, helping them in the trade they so much desired.

The French established Fort Ouiatenon, an isolated outpost among the Wea near what is now Lafayette; it was the first permanent white settlement in Indiana. In 1722 Vincennes Jr. was put in charge of the outpost.

Because of his outstanding record there, Vincennes Jr. earned the right to build a third fort, Post Vincennes. Construction began in the early 1730s. Slowly, the village of Vincennes sprang up, complete with rough cottages, fur traders drinking in taverns and pigs in the streets. Vincennes Jr. constantly lobbied for more supplies and complained that, because they often had more supplies to trade, the English hauled away most of the furs in the area.

Fur trading with the Indians was the staple of many people's lives. But with France so far away, it wasn't easy to get pots, pans, silver crosses, and wool blankets, which the French settlers needed for trading.

"On account of the nearness of the English," Vincennes Jr. wrote in 1733, "it has been impossible for me to bring together all these [five Indian] nations because there always has been a lack of merchandise in this place."

Vincennes Jr. was able to celebrate two joyous events: He was promoted to lieutenant and he married his wife, Marie. But daily life remained a struggle.

"In this post we lack everything," Vincennes Jr. wrote in 1733. "I am obliged to borrow from travelers and to give the little that I have myself to take care of all the affairs which come up daily."

Hundreds of miles away, the governor of Louisiana was planning the massive attacks against the Chickasaw. The disastrous effort in 1736 sometimes is known as "Indiana's first war," even though Hoosiers were involved only in a secondary way.

The French governor needed help from his fellow colonial settlers in Indiana and Illinois. Both Vincennes Jr. and the Illinois commandant obeyed the summons to western Tennessee. But the decision to attack the Chickasaw village was ill-considered.

It was no wonder the Indians were infuriated enough to order the death of Vincennes and his companions. The Frenchmen were robbing the village of the corn that would supply the tribe through the winter, taking the food of women and children. Besides, many Indians resented whites intruding on their lands and feared they would break their promise to compensate the Indians for the land they took.

Alerted to the movements of the French, about four hundred or five hundred Chickasaw fell upon the northerners in a fury; the French were forced to retreat with the Chickasaw in hot pursuit.

The Chickasaw also took prisoners—including Vincennes Jr., the Illinois commandant, and the Jesuit priest. According to many accounts, the prisoners were taken to a village in present-day Mississippi, tortured, and burned at the stake. Richard Day, a Vincennes historian, suspects their deaths might have been slightly different. A survivor who was nursed back to health claimed the Chickasaw sang hymns around a bonfire. Instead of being burned at the stake, the prisoners may have been tossed into the blaze.

As news of the disaster spread north to the French forts and Indian villages along the Wabash River, people were devastated. The new little village of Post Vincennes had lost its commandant and many of its adult men.

Vincennes Jr. was survived by his widow, daughters, and grieving friends, both French and Indian. Six years later, a large group of Wea traveled to Montreal and told the French governor-general they continued to "weep" for Vincennes Jr.

"You do rightly in weeping for the death of Monsieur de Vincennes," the governor replied. "I had given him to you because I knew he loved you, and you loved him greatly."

He might have loved them, but it was war—and it was destined not to get better for a long time.

John Chapman was indeed a somewhat eccentric individual. The illustration at left shows what he probably looked like. However, countless children's first impression of Johnny Appleseed is the saucepan-capped character depicted below in Walt Disney's "Melody Time." Experts doubt that he actually wore a pan.

Johnny Appleseed
John Chapman — folk hero

Did he stroll around barefoot with his saucepan atop his head? Was he a bit . . . well, "touched"? Did his wanderings take him as far as Nebraska? No other legendary Hoosier is the subject of as many myths as footloose folk hero Johnny Appleseed.

Among the few irrefutable facts: He was born John Chapman in Leominster, Massachusetts, in 1774. His mother died when he was two years old, then his father remarried. John Chapman grew up to become a preacher of the Swedenborgian (Church of the New Jerusalem) faith. He died in the Fort Wayne area, probably in 1845. But the rest of his story is shrouded in mist. A few aspects of his life we know—or think we know.

Yes, he was eccentric—even for the American frontier of the eighteenth and nineteenth centuries, which was full of eccentric characters.

Johnny Appleseed was a vegetarian. He never married. A pacifist, he respected the American Indians. In a fire-and-brimstone era, Johnny told jokes when he preached.

He also wandered around the frontier, distributing not apple seeds but seedlings. Johnny predicted where immigrants would settle and planted seeds in the area. A year or two later, he distributed the seedlings to the pioneers as they arrived.

Following the defeat of the French in the 1760s, English traders and settlers filtered into Indiana, Ohio, Illinois and Michigan. After the Revolutionary War, they came in a rush. John Chapman was ready to welcome these hardy pioneers.

Chapman—or Appleseed—had a rationale for the apple plantings that he distributed. Settlers could buy land in the Midwest for a pittance. But to keep the property, they were required by the government to show development within five years. Apple trees usually produce fruit in four to five years; with Johnny's seedlings, the pioneers enjoyed a two-year head start.

His fruit-related distribution probably was an offshoot of Johnny's deep spiritual faith. In addition to apple seedlings, he distributed books such as the Bible and Swedenborg's writings to Midwestern pioneers—actually, chapters of books since lugging around entire volumes would have been burdensome.

"I have news straight from heaven!" Johnny sometimes proclaimed as he distributed the "chap-books," planting his seeds of faith.

Tales about the eccentric wanderer spread across the frontier. Many stories—such as accounts that vegetarian Johnny would douse his campfire and eat his dinner cold so flames would not even harm a mosquito—probably were exaggerations. Some accounts probably were observations about other unusual frontier characters that were attributed to the legendary "Appleseed."

Nobody doubts, though, that Johnny displayed heroism during a dramatic episode before he even reached Indiana.

During the War of 1812, many Indians sided with the British. Several settlers in northern Ohio were slaughtered in a massacre; the survivors, including Johnny, took refuge in a blockhouse in Mansfield.

The group decided someone would have to slip out and travel thirty miles south, past the Indians, to Mount Vernon to summon help. Johnny volunteered and made his way through the wilderness, sounding warnings about the Indians to settlers as he traveled—rather like a latter-day Paul Revere. Thanks to Johnny, reinforcements saved the terrified Mansfield group.

During the 1830s Johnny was in Indiana, distributing seedlings. And the Hoosier state, particularly its northern part, is the area in which he spent most of his last years. Reliable accounts about his wanderings put him only as far west as Illinois and as far north as Michigan.

To this day, in many northern regions of Indiana, old-timers point to ancient, gnarled trees and say, "My great-grandpa said, 'This was originally planted by Johnny Appleseed.' "

Where did his passion for apples come from?

His grandfather in New England apparently had an apple orchard. Also, at least at some point around the time of the Revolutionary War, Johnny's father was a farmer.

What did he contribute to our state's history?

Johnny established a sense of neighborliness and religious faith that lonely people cherished. He also brought the latest news and, of course, the apple—the fruit whose sauces and pies added to the comfort, happiness and health of people on the Hoosier frontier.

Johnny Appleseed: One view

Johnny Appleseed is the most requested character in the repertoire of Indianapolis playwright-performer Hank Fincken, who portrays the folk hero at schools, festivals and civic gatherings across the country.

"People are captivated by Johnny's basic humanity," says Fincken, who thoroughly researched his amiable Hoosier character.

"Johnny would preach for his supper. Because he was an eccentric—but also because he used humor in his sermons—people would laugh with and at him in equal measure."

Although he grows a beard before a series of performances ("Johnny doesn't strike me as the kind of fellow who would shave every day"), Fincken never sticks a pot or saucepan on his head.

"Only two eyewitnesses described him that way," Fincken explains. "How come so many other people who wrote about seeing Johnny never mentioned it? If you wore a pot on your head, it would be the first thing everyone would report.

"My gut feeling is he didn't because it's so impractical and uncomfortable. It's sweltering in the summer, and it won't warm your ears in the winter."

The fact that Johnny has become a folk hero is a tribute to an aspect of our character, Fincken says. "Here's a simple guy doing kind work for no egotistical gain or profit. Doesn't it say something endearing about American and Hoosier culture that a guy like Johnny would become heroic to us?"

George Rogers Clark

Frontier fighter

To some, he is a hero—the father of the Northwest Territory, a desperado, an early naturalist and a brilliant military strategist partially responsible for the initial shape of the new country known as the United States. To others, he is a controversial figure—a self-promoter, a debtor and a ruthless conqueror given credit that rightfully belongs to General "Mad" Anthony Wayne and others.

Born in 1752 in Virginia, George Rogers Clark grew up in a family destined for fame. A brother, William, with whom he lived briefly later in life, became one of the American West's best-known explorers as half of the Lewis and Clark duo.

With little formal education, Clark was hired at nineteen as a surveyor and spent three years charting the Kentucky frontier. His military achievements during the Revolutionary War—particularly his historic march on Fort Sackville at Vincennes in the winter of 1779—made him a legend.

In 1784 the city of Clarksville, the first Indiana town founded after Vincennes and the first American settlement in the Old Northwest Territory, was settled on land granted to Clark and some of his militia as a reward for their valor.

George Rogers Clark's life after the war, however, was marred by frustrated ambition, debts and loneliness. His reputation even was tattered by whispers of treason because of an interlude with the French army. Felled by a stroke, a bitter Clark died at his sister's home near Louisville, Kentucky, in 1818.

Tall and red-haired, the twenty-six-year-old frontiersman and major in the ragtag Kentucky militia was astonished by the news. George Rogers Clark had thought the town of Vincennes was in friendly hands.

It was 1779, and the Revolutionary War was winding down, at least in the northern American colonies along the East Coast. Less than a year earlier, in 1778, Clark had captured Vincennes and Kaskaskia, a town in the Illinois country, without firing a shot. He won over French residents of both towns by informing them that France was allied with Virginia and the other American colonies. Plus, the British commander of the garrison at Vincennes had returned to Quebec before Clark arrived, so there wasn't even token resistance.

But now, in January 1779, a Piedmont-born trader named Francis Vigo was describing to Clark the details of how Vincennes had been lost.

Captured and released by the British, Vigo was a fount of information. He reported that Colonel Henry Hamilton, the English lieutenant-governor at Detroit, recaptured Vincennes (population 621) with a force of British redcoats, American Indians and many French volunteers. The group had marched down and seized the Vincennes garrison, which the British called Fort Sackville.

Right away, Hamilton destroyed billiard tables and confiscated every drop of liquor because, he wrote, they were "the source of immorality & dissipation."

(Above) "Through icy streams and primeval forests 'The Hero of Vincennes' "—George Rogers Clark—led his men"—from a mural by F. C. Yohn in the George Rogers Clark Memorial in Vincennes, Indiana. (Right) The hero later in his life.

And that wasn't all. Vigo reported that Hamilton planned to muster his troops to attack the Illinois settlements and vanquish the pesky Clark once and for all. But the British were waiting until spring to attack because unseasonably warm winter weather was causing massive flooding around Vincennes.

That was all Clark needed to hear. Known for his audacity and aggressive self-confidence, Clark determined to strike first—and quickly, freakish winter or not. Plotting a surprise attack, he rallied a hundred and seventy men, about half of them French volunteers, and left Kaskaskia on February 6.

"We must Either Quit the Cuntrey or attact [attack] Mr. Hamilton," he wrote Virginia Governor Patrick Henry. " . . . Great things have been affected by a few men well Conducted . . ."

Their overland journey was a hundred and eighty miles—and arduous. It wasn't just melting snow and ice that caused the February floods. Driving, cold rains exacerbated the thaw around rivers and lowlands. Members of Clark's militia—whom the Indians sometimes called "long knives"—waded through cold waters that rose to their waists.

By the time they reached the overflowing Wabash River, the men were exhausted, wet, hungry, and nearly out of supplies. Alternating between discipline and encouragement, Clark pushed his troops onward. Even his critics commend his talents as a strategist and his superb intelligence network on the frontier.

Arriving at Vincennes on February 23, Clark sent a message to the French inhabitants, instructing them to stay in their homes or join the British within the fort. Hamilton refused to surrender. So Clark paraded his men in such a way—and at a sufficient distance—that the townspeople and the British would estimate his small force at one thousand.

Then, taking cover behind the houses surrounding Fort Sackville, they started firing. Nearly half of Hamilton's men were French Canadians who refused to fight against Clark. After one night and one day of battle, Hamilton realized the fight was hopeless and gave up.

He agreed to meet in front of Fort Sackville with Clark, who demanded unconditional surrender. Then, to flaunt his advantage, Clark ordered four pro-British Indians brought to the gates of the fort, where his men viciously tomahawked and scalped them. Hamilton surrendered; the Americans' flag was raised over the fort, which Clark renamed Fort Patrick Henry. It was the first major American victory in the West during the Revolutionary War.

The success of Clark's frontier army was described to the British and American peacemakers as they huddled in Paris. Among the issues being debated was the location of the western boundaries of the United States; American negotiators won a major concession in obtaining a boundary at the Mississippi River rather than the Ohio or the Wabash. Historians still debate the importance of Clark's victory on the boundaries and the Treaty of 1783 (officially known as the Peace of Paris), but many believe he won the Midwest for the new United States of America.

After the Revolutionary War, Clark's life was anticlimactic. An alcoholic who was hounded by creditors, he wrote his memoirs in an attempt to restore his reputation. However, they were not published during his lifetime.

Chief Tecumseh (left) and his brother Tenskwatawa, the Prophet.

Tecumseh and the Prophet

Shawnee leaders and warriors

The brothers made a nearly perfect leadership team—and a controversial one. Tecumseh, the most celebrated Shawnee Indian in American history, was a brilliant organizer and strategist—inexhaustible and idealistic, but self-controlled and levelheaded. The Prophet, his brother, was charismatic, flamboyant and creative.

Both brothers were gifted with dazzling mental and oratorical skills. Yet one died in disgrace, shunned by many of his own people. The other was killed in battle, becoming anathema to whites but a folk legend to many Native Americans for his efforts to unify Indian tribes into a Pan-American confederation. The vast Indian nation of Tecumseh's dreams would have stretched from the Alleghenies to the Everglades to the Ozarks, with Tecumseh leading unified tribes in their resistance to encroaching white settlers. It was a dream worthy of one of the greatest leaders America ever produced.

The future leader was born about 1768 in a Shawnee village north of present-day Dayton in western Ohio. Although his father was a revered Shawnee chief, Tecumseh's mother may have been a Creek.

According to legend, a panther, one of the spirit world's fiercest creatures, passed across the sky in the form of a meteor at the moment of Tecumseh's birth; the ferocious cat became his lifelong symbol. Slim, straight, and muscular, Tecumseh stood about five-feet-ten and possessed a proud bearing and piercing, hazel eyes.

His brother, named Tenskwatawa, would achieve fame as a holy man called the Prophett. According to some accounts, Tecumseh and Tenskwatawa were the two surviving brothers of triplets. (Another account says all three brothers lived.) Yet other interpretations of the family history say the triplets, including the Prophet, were Tecumseh's younger brothers. Regardless, all of them had an older brother, Chiksika.

The father of all of the brothers was killed in 1774 when a group of Indians tried to ambush Virginia militiamen. The ambush was a retaliation for a massacre of Indian men, women and children by frontiersmen.

Legend has it the dying father whispered to his eldest son—fourteen-year-old Chiksika—that he must never make peace with white settlers and must oversee his younger brothers' training as warriors.

Described even as a boy as a leader and an excellent shot with both musket and bow, Tecumseh apparently always was fearless and a spellbinding speechmaker, a talent highly valued by the Shawnee.

Often riding alongside Chiksika, Tecumseh became a marauder in small raids against whites across the Old Northwest. According to several accounts, he vigorously de-

nounced the Shawnee practice of torturing prisoners. But his fury at white settlers increased after Chiksika was killed during a battle in 1788.
Tecumseh and the Prophet settled in Indiana about 1808.

The distinguished, thirty-seven-year-old governor of the Indiana Territory and the regal, forty-something Shawnee chief were about to draw their weapons—at each other.

Ironically, William Henry Harrison and Tecumseh, the two great adversaries of the Old Northwest, had much in common. Both were conservative, aristocratic leaders who occasionally acknowledged to confidants their respect for each other. Both were determined to preserve the cultures of their boyhoods. Perhaps inevitably, that led in August 1810 to the clash on the lawn at Grouseland, the governor's plantation-style mansion near Virginia.

Known as "the Moses of his family" because of his commanding leadership, Tecumseh was infuriated by the Treaty of Fort Wayne that Harrison had negotiated with other Indian chiefs in 1809.

Through an interpreter, the buckskin-clad Tecumseh accused Harrison of pitting Indians against one another—and of shrewdly securing "ownership" of three million acres from weak-willed chiefs who lacked the authority to sell them.

"Brother, you ought to know what you are doing with the Indians," Tecumseh told Harrison. "Perhaps it is by direction of the President to make those distinctions. It is a very bad thing, and we do not like it . . .

"Brother, do not believe that I came here to get presents from you. If you offer us any, we will not take [them]. By taking goods from you, you will hereafter say that with them you purchased another piece of land from us."

Land, Tecumseh continued, his voice rising, was like the air and water, a common possession of all Indians, not a single tribe. That's why, he argued, Harrison's "purchase" of land from some Indian chiefs was not a proper transaction.

Harrison argued back, insisting the chiefs had acted responsibly. According to some accounts, Tecumseh called Harrison a "liar" to his face. Other versions say his Shawnee words were deliberately misinterpreted by an Indian chief who sided with the whites.

In any case, Harrison and Tecumseh glared at each other and nearly started to brawl. Alarmed, Indiana militiamen accompanying the governor drew their guns. But the confrontation ended when both leaders realized a tussle between them would solve nothing for the thousands of people who depended on each of them.

Harrison ordered his men to lower their weapons. Then he told the Shawnee they were free to leave peacefully, turned on his heel and walked out of the grove, trailed by his entourage.

Initially, Harrison hadn't even expected to talk with Tecumseh. The governor had instead invited the Shawnee leader's better-known, flamboyant brother—Tenskwatawa, the holy man called the Prophet—to Washington to meet President James Madison.

In part, Harrison hoped the new capital would intimidate the Shawnee and make him realize that Indian resistance was hopeless against such a flourishing new country. Tecumseh went to Vincennes on behalf of his brother to deliver the answer to the governor's invitation. The near-fight occurred, the invitation to Washington was declined, and the Prophet never visited the nation's capital.

A unique figure in American history, the Prophet had a reputation among his people as an alcoholic. But in 1805, after he slipped into a coma and recovered, he claimed he had seen "visions" during a near-death experience. He proclaimed himself the messenger of the "Great Spirit." He began to travel, preaching his "gospel" of mistreated Indians to tribes in the Midwest. Meanwhile, his brother traveled throughout the Midwest and into the Deep South, urging the Chickasaw, the Choctaw and other tribes to band together against whites.

Did Tecumseh believe his brother's mystical "visions"? Scholars still debate that. Certainly, however, the brothers worked closely for several years—and Tecumseh recognized the power of the Prophet's sermons to help draw Indians together.

The Prophet's downfall came in 1811 at Tippecanoe River near Lafayette. Harrison and an army of about a thousand men marched up the Wabash River and camped on the Tippecanoe a few miles from Prophetstown, a village built by the Shawnee brothers. Ever tireless, Tecumseh was away on one of his frequent trips, visiting tribes in the Deep South to recruit them to the confederation of his dreams. During his brother's absence, the Prophet unwisely decided to attack.

At dawn on November 7 at the Tippecanoe River, the Prophet and his warriors surprised Harrison and his army. Although the Americans suffered staggering casualties in the bloody, hand-to-hand combat, they managed to drive off the Indians. Then Harrison and his soldiers marched to the deserted Prophetstown and burned it to the ground.

"It was no surprise there was a Battle of Tippecanoe," says Douglas Clanin, an editor for the Indiana Historical Society. "The die was cast at Tecumseh's meeting with Harrison. The surprise was it didn't happen sooner."

Horrified when told of the defeat—and devastated when he saw the ashes of his village in January of 1812—Tecumseh feared his dream of a confederation had been shattered. Once again, he vowed vengeance on the whites. He also denounced his brother as a disgrace. Tecumseh spared the Prophet death at the hands of outraged fellow Indians, but his compassion stopped there. As the Prophet moaned at his feet, Tecumseh turned and walked away. Broken and homeless, the Prophet lived about twenty-four more years, eventually dying in the West in the mid-1830s.

Always resilient, Tecumseh managed to gather his warriors. Sensing the approach of the War of 1812 between the Americans and the British, he traveled to Canada. An alliance with England seemed the only way to drive the Americans from Indian hunting grounds.

On the Canadian side of the Detroit River, Tecumseh assembled perhaps the most formidable force ever commanded by a Native American—and, along with British troops, captured Detroit in 1812. The next year he joined the British invasion of Ohio.

But the Indians and British were forced by Harrison to retreat to the Thames River in Ontario. In October of 1813 Tecumseh, who directly supervised much of the fighting, was killed during the Battle of the Thames.

Earlier, his longtime nemesis Harrison paid tribute to the fiery Shawnee leader's talents, writing to colleagues in Washington, D.C.:

The implicit obedience and respect which the followers of Tecumseh pay him is really astonishing. . . . [It] bespeaks him one of those uncommon geniuses which spring up occasionally to produce revolutions and overturn the established order of things. If it were not for the vicinity of the United States, he would perhaps be the founder of an Empire that would rival in glory Mexico or Peru.

William Henry Harrison, in a painting done by Rembrandt Peale in 1814. The portrait hangs in Grouseland, Harrison's home in Vincennes.

William Henry Harrison

Governor of the Indiana Territory
and President of the United States

The ninth President of the United States—and the first to die in office—was a youthful twenty-seven when he landed the powerful position that would dramatically advance his career.

That appointment in 1800 was to the job of governor of the Indiana Territory, initially a vast expanse of the country's frontier that even briefly stretched to present-day Iowa and Missouri. (Two years earlier, as secretary of the Northwest Territory, William Henry Harrison helped oversee an expanse that included Michigan, Illinois, and Wisconsin.)

Born in 1773 on a plantation known as Berkeley in Charles City County, Virginia, William Henry Harrison was the youngest son of Benjamin Harrison, a signer of the Declaration of Independence. As such, William Henry considered himself "a child of the Revolution." Raised in the Southern aristocratic style, Harrison hoped to replicate prosperous plantation life in the Old Northwest. That explains his support for slavery in Indiana, but he never succeeded in getting it legalized north of the Ohio River.

Although he was privately tutored and enjoyed a boyhood of affluence on the Virginia plantation, Harrison also endured hard-scrabble periods during his life. After a year studying medicine—probably to please his parents—Harrison's world shattered with the sudden death of his father. As the youngest son, William Henry inherited no property from his family's estate.

Scrambling to support himself, Harrison joined the military. In 1791 he was commissioned an ensign in the infantry. Even though just eighteen, he was able to recruit a company of about eighty men to risk their lives for two dollars a month fighting Indians in the wilderness. Over the next seven years, Harrison rose to the rank of captain. He served as an aide-de-camp to General "Mad" Anthony Wayne during Wayne's campaign against the Indians and was cited for bravery at the Battle of Fallen Timbers in 1794.

The next year he married Anna Symmes, the daughter of a judge who disapproved of Harrison's army life. William Henry and Anna Harrison had ten children. A younger son, John Scott Harrison, became the father of Benjamin Harrison, the twenty-third President and the only one elected from Indiana. Despite his connections to the Hoosier state, William Henry Harrison was an Ohio resident when he captured the presidency in 1840.

The Harrison family moved to Vincennes, the territorial capital, in January 1801, after he became governor. Right away, Harrison began copying the plantation of his boy-

hood. Near the Wabash River on a three-hundred-acre estate, he built Grouseland, a mansion with a ballroom and verandahs similar to those of his birthplace.

He strolled down the semicircular staircase to the first floor of his home, the first brick mansion in southern Indiana.

Built in a Georgian style, Grouseland had four chimneys, thirteen large rooms, hand-carved mantels and wainscotings of polished black walnut.

William Henry Harrison was in his glory at the mansion, from which he governed the Indiana Territory. He paid attention to almost every detail of Grouseland, including the outer walls, which were slit for portholes, and attic windows designed for sharp-shooters.

This was, after all, the frontier—although elegant Harrison was hardly a typical pioneer.

A tall man with a craggy chin, deep-set eyes and a long nose, William Henry Harrison modeled himself after another aristocratic Virginia native—George Washington. Like his idol, Harrison exuded self-confidence, reserve and dignity. Also like Washington, he was rarely introspective, though he occasionally indulged in fiery bursts of temper.

The crude, lawless behavior of many settlers in the Indiana Territory of 1800 stunned and repulsed Harrison. An Episcopalian who considered himself a cultured, well-bred Southerner, Harrison, as the new governor, was taken aback by the widespread, random killings of Indians in the wilderness and in the booming number of Hoosier frontier towns.

Exasperated, Harrison wrote that "many of the inhabitants of the Frontiers consider the murdering of Indians in the highest degree meritorious."

Disagreeing with that view, the new governor hoped to establish order.

"He initially issued warrants for the arrests of whites who killed Indians," noted Harrison expert Douglas Clanin, an editor for the Indiana Historical Society. "The settlers didn't want that. Everyone was going around saying, 'The only good Indian is a dead Indian.' "

The slayings continued. Mobs stormed jails and freed any white man arrested for murdering an Indian. Eventually, Harrison gave up and stopped issuing warrants for Indian murders, meaning whites who killed them went unpunished in the Indiana Territory.

"As an officeholder with a growing family, Harrison was sensitive to the demands of the people," Clanin said. "He was a man of his time—not ahead of it in his thinking, but not behind it either."

Although he at times owned large expanses of land, Harrison often was cash poor. Business savvy was not among his attributes.

His military brilliance and political instincts, though, were unquestioned. Harrison was so skilled at partisan politics that he won appointments as governor of the Indiana Territory from both President John Adams, a Federalist, and Thomas Jefferson, a Democratic-Republican.

Harrison considered himself a strong negotiator with the Indian tribes in the Indiana Territory. In 1809 he negotiated the Treaty of Fort Wayne in which the Delaware, Miami, Potawatomi, and Eel River Indians gave up about three million acres in exchange for a series of annual payments. That treaty enraged Tecumseh, the Shawnee leader who became Harrison's longtime nemesis in the Old Northwest.

A year after a face-to-face confrontation on the lawn of Grouseland, during which Harrison and Tecumseh almost drew their weapons at each other, the governor and his militia marched up the Wabash River. They camped along Tippecanoe River close to Prophetstown, a village built by Tecumseh and his flamboyant brother, the Prophet.

Ignoring the explicit instructions of Tecumseh, who was away in the Deep South, the

Prophet ordered a surprise, dawn attack on Harrison's forces. Harrison's troops, sleeping on their weapons, quickly rallied. Harrison then launched a spectacular counterattack that became the stuff of legend—and known as the Battle of Tippecanoe. "Old Tip," as the governor soon became known, led his troops into the deserted Prophetstown and burned it.

Harrison pulled off more military coups during the War of 1812. As the general in charge of the Northwestern Army, he defeated the combined forces of the British and the Indians in several battles and freed Detroit from their control. In the Battle of the Thames in 1813, Harrison ended the Indian confederation, Tecumseh was killed and the northwestern border of the United States was secured.

After the war, Harrison settled in Ohio, managed a farm and became a U.S. congressman. In 1828, he was appointed minister to Colombia. A persistent office-seeker, Harrison garnered attention with anniversary celebrations of the battles of Tippecanoe and the Thames.

As a Whig running for president in 1836, he carried seven states but lost to Martin Van Buren, a Democrat. Four years later, though, Old Tip, now sixty-seven and ridiculed by his detractors as "Granny," returned to defeat Van Buren and capture the presidency. Ironically, the man with the aristocratic Virginia pedigree ran for the White House as a humble frontier farmer and war hero in a rollicking crusade called "the log cabin campaign."

In March of 1841, Harrison delivered one of the longest inaugural addresses in American history. Exhausted and harried by critics and office seekers, he died a month later of pneumonia.

Frances Slocum—called Maconaquah by the Miamis—chose to stay with her beloved adopted people, rather than return to "civilization" and the family of her birth.

Frances Slocum

also known as Maconaquah, the Lost Sister of Wyoming and the White Rose of the Miami— White captive-turned-American Indian loyalist

Though one of Indiana's most famous women lived most of her life near the Mississinewa River in the northern part of the state, her story begins in Pennsylvania.

The morning of November 2, 1778, began calmly at the cabin of a peace-loving Quaker family. The Slocums had moved from New England and settled in the Pennsylvania frontier near the village of Wilkes-Barre in the lush woods of the Wyoming Valley.

Five-year-old Frances Slocum was barefoot and playing with her younger brother. Her father, Jonathan, and her grandfather were working in the fields. Her mother, Ruth, was doing housework in the cabin. Neighbor boys—two brothers from a family named Kingsley—were turning a grindstone and sharpening a knife near the cabin door; the older Kingsley brother wore an army coat.

In most frontier homes, this was a tense time. The Revolutionary War was underway, and the Delaware Indians in Pennsylvania generally were siding with the British. Several colonist families in the Wyoming Valley had been killed. Many families fled the valley in fear, taking refuge in forts in the Pennsylvania wilderness or even moving back to New England.

But the Slocums felt secure. None of their remaining neighbors had seen Indians around for a while. And as pacifist Quakers, the Slocums assumed they would be free from harassment. William Penn, the beloved Quaker pioneer who helped develop Pennsylvania in the 1680s, had been a loyal friend of the Indians; Quakers had been spared in most Indian raids ever since. As pacifists, the Quakers were not even taking up arms with other settlers against the British.

But little Frances' oldest brother, eighteen-year-old Giles, had disobeyed Jonathan Slocum's order to leave British soldiers and the Indians alone. Determined to protect the homes of white settlers, Giles joined other frontiersmen and fought the Delaware. The Indians felt betrayed and decided to retaliate.

So the serenity on that November morning was shattered. The Slocums and their friends heard a gunshot. The older neighbor boy, the Kingsley brother wearing the army coat, suddenly collapsed—dead. Ruth Slocum screamed to her terrified children to hide in the woods.

Delaware Indians began searching the cabin. They discovered little Frances, desperately trying to hide. The Delaware also discovered one of her brothers, who had crippled feet and couldn't flee. They picked up the children, including the surviving Kingsley brother, took them to the yard and began to carry them away.

Watching all of this from her hiding place in a thicket, Ruth Slocum ran out and tried to stop the Delaware. She pointed out that her son was lame. The Delaware re-

leased him. Then Frances began screaming for her mother. One of the Indians tossed the little girl over his shoulder, and the Delaware disappeared into the woods with the two children.

So began the story of Frances Slocum, whose dramatic, colorful life became one of the most enduring legends of frontier life. Her story often is used to illustrate the differences between white settlers and American Indians. Neither understood the values of the other and tragically the two cultures were eventually unable to coexist.

A young trader named George Washington Ewing often traveled on horseback across Indiana during the 1830s. One night he was bartering with Miami Indians in Deaf Man's Village, a town on the Mississinewa River not far from the Hoosier city of Peru. Ewing was exhausted and cold. Because he was friendly with most Indians, he decided to spend the night with a Miami family rather than return home.

It had been nearly sixty years since little Frances Slocum had been kidnapped by the Delaware. Her distraught mother had devoted her life to searching for her daughter, but Ruth Slocum and most of the family's neighbors in Pennsylvania had been dead for years. Wareham Kingsley, the neighbor boy abducted with Frances, had returned to Wilkes-Barre about six years after the kidnapping. He assured the Slocums that Frances was being treated kindly by the Delaware, but that did little to comfort to the mourning family.

Tales and rumors—but, sadly, no facts—about the lost "little sister" of the Wyoming Valley spread across the American frontier. Gradually, though, people lost interest. After more than fifty-five years, even Frances' brothers and sisters assumed she was dead.

Then Ewing, the Hoosier trader who made his home in Logansport, made that fateful decision to stay overnight at a two-story log house of the Miami family in Deaf Man's Village. He knew a few members of the blended family of Miami who lived in the house. The family included two young women, one the mother of small daughters; the amiable husband of one of the women, and a feeble, dignified widow.

Joining the family circle, Ewing settled near the fireplace and chatted in the Miami language, which he spoke with ease. He enjoyed talking with the Miami man, but mostly was intrigued by the mysterious, elderly widow.

She seemed to run the household. Ewing noticed that everyone treated her with respect, even deference. He also noticed she had auburn hair, unusual for an American Indian. It may be that Ewing had encountered the elderly woman several times before this night and had wondered about her past for some time.

Slowly, all of the other members of the Miami family bade good night to their guest and went to bed. The elderly widow sat still, staring at the open fireplace. Ewing was about to excuse himself to sleep when she asked him to wait. She seemed agitated.

The trader soon learned why. The woman explained that she was ill and might die soon, but wanted to share a secret. She told him an amazing story:

She explained that she had been born to white parents, but was carried away as a child by Delaware Indians. She had forgotten her given first name, but her father's name was Slocum. The Indians called her Maconaquah. They treated her with love and warmth, as if she had been born to them.

She had married twice. Her first husband was a Delaware. Her second, a Miami chief, had gone deaf in his later years—hence the name of the village—and later died. The couple had two sons, also both dead, and two daughters, who were the women Ewing had chatted with earlier in the evening.

The old woman begged Ewing not to reveal her secret. She was terrified that white people—maybe some of her relatives—would force her to abandon her home and her Miami family.

Ewing promised to protect her. But when the trader returned to Logansport the next day, he reconsidered. Her relatives would want to know about her, he concluded, and he decided to track them down. He sent details about the "white Indian" woman named Slocum to the postmaster in Lancaster, Pennsylvania, the town closest to the frontier area that she had described in her story.

The postmaster also served as editor of the Lancaster newspaper. But Ewing's news about the "white Indian" woman was set aside at the newspaper office and forgotten for two years. Finally, a new editor arrived and published Ewing's account.

The news about the "Lost Sister" eventually reached some Slocums. Astonished and anxious to see Frances, two of her brothers and a sister traveled to Peru, Indiana, in 1837. Then, with an interpreter, they went to Deaf Man's Village. Their elderly sister greeted them with indifference.

But the Slocums quickly determined that she was indeed Frances. During the siblings' childhoods, one of the brothers had damaged her finger while they were playing in a blacksmith shop. Without prompting, the elderly woman shared details of the long-ago mishap in the shop—and displayed her marred finger.

As she had told Ewing, the elderly woman explained that she had forgotten her first name from childhood.

"Was it Frances?" one of her siblings asked, according to legend.

"Yes—*Franca . . . Franca . . . ,*" she replied.

Her siblings assumed she would want to return to Pennsylvania with them, but Frances declined. She explained that her husband, on his deathbed, asked her always to live with Indians. And the Indians always had treated her with kindness. Besides, she enjoyed her home and her land in Indiana.

The Slocums pleaded with her to return East for at least a visit. Again Frances declined, explaining that she would not know the white people's customs; also, she was frail and might die during the trip. She wanted to pass away among the Miami.

The Slocums spent a few days in Indiana; by the time they left, their relationship with their sister had become warmer. Despite her fears of imminent death, Frances lived several more years—years that brought many more cultural changes in Indiana. By the early 1840s, most of the state's Miami Indians had been relocated west of the Mississippi River.

But a Congressional resolution permitted Frances Slocum and her family to remain in their two-story log cabin near Peru. She died there in 1847 at the age of seventy-four.

Her story, though, has captivated generations of Americans since then. Frances Slocum is the subject of dozens of books, tributes, articles and poems about American frontier life.

Robert Owen

Robert Owen

Social reformer, leader at New Harmony, and utopia-seeker

New Harmony is a small, idyllic-looking village on the Wabash River in Indiana's far-southwestern corner—the state's distinctive "boot." With its shady trees, lush gardens and Midwestern charm, the serene, picture-postcard village looks like the setting for Fourth of July parades, outdoor classical music concerts and Sunday picnics—not social experiments.

But New Harmony was the setting for "utopia seeking," including two historic attempts at communal living. The most significant was led by Welsh/Scottish industrialist Robert Owen, a dreamer who devoted much of his life to persuading politicians and other prominent Americans to a sort of early socialism. His "utopia" in New Harmony during the 1820s didn't last, but it became part of the Hoosier state's legacy.

Earlier, in 1814, New Harmony had attracted a German immigrant named George Rapp, a rebel against the established Lutheran Church. He initially settled in Pennsylvania with a following of about six hundred religious dissenters. Calling their colony Harmonie, they were committed to living by the principles of early Christianity. Although the colony flourished, Rapp traveled west to Fort Vincennes in the Indiana wilderness.

"You will not believe what a rich and beautiful land is found," Rapp wrote to his followers, known as the Harmonists.

Intrigued, they flocked to Indiana and became known as Rappites. For ten years their village of Harmonie thrived, growing to nine hundred residents. They devoted themselves to hard work and self-sacrifice, including celibacy, and prepared for the second coming of Christ.

On flats above the tree-lined Wabash, their most talented craftsmen erected splendid homes, dormitories (to separate the sexes), a flour mill, a brewery, churches and various public buildings. Instead of the primitive cabins of the Indiana frontier, they built impressive brick and stone structures—surrounded by flourishing vineyards, orchards and fields of wheat and other crops.

But Rapp was frustrated. He concluded that Harmonie's prosperity was causing complacency among his devotees. And the town was too far away from consumer markets. Determined to start anew, he planned a new colony in Pennsylvania and, with what historians have called "dramatic suddenness," decided to sell Harmonie.

That provided a certain fifty-three-year-old British industrialist with the perfect "physical plant" for his dreams.

For sale: More than twenty thousand acres of fertile land and a village in the Indiana wilderness.

Robert Owen—a British industrialist, educator, philosopher, and social reformer—was intrigued by that description. He was still bursting with energy at age fifty-three. Some fellow Brits opposed Owen's spiritual views, and he had disagreements with managers at some of his mills. Owen also was impatient with the progress of social reform in England. Weary of labor strife there, he was searching for a new frontier.

The deal for Indiana land offered by one of the Northwest Territory's first real estate agents was too tempting to pass up. Owen agreed to pay $125,000 in 1824 for the New Harmony package; by the time of the closing the next year, he bargained the price down to $95,000. (When livestock and personal property were thrown in, the cost was about $140,000).

Owen, a gentle but opinionated man, was an old hand at seizing opportunities—and at chasing dreams. Born in Wales in 1771, the son of a saddler and hardware merchant, he attended school only until age ten. But after starting as a store clerk, Owen became manager of a large cotton mill in Manchester while still in his teens.

He married elegant Anne Caroline Dale, whose father had started mills in Scotland. In 1794 Owen organized his own textile company. Soon his company bought the Scottish mills founded by his father-in-law. The mills used American cotton and employed about two thousand workers, five hundred of them children from the poorhouses of Edinburgh and Glasgow.

Owen was appalled by their misery, including deplorable living conditions, lack of sanitation and rampant crime. All of that made Owen a crusader. He established better schools and company stores where workers could purchase goods cheaply. During an American embargo in 1806, his Scottish mills were forced to shut down for four months—but he continued to pay full wages to his employees, an unthinkable act at the dawn of the Industrial Revolution. He became known as a pioneer for treating factory workers with dignity.

Rejecting religious views common at the time, Owen decided that education was the key for saving mankind and improving character. "The great secret in forming a man's character," he wrote, "is to place him under the proper influences from his earliest years."

To pursue his vision, Owen wanted a new setting, one not contaminated by the clergy and industrialists. He set his eyes on the new nation across the Atlantic. And when his eyes fell on the Harmonist/Rappite village of Harmonie, he couldn't resist buying it. The sturdy, comfortable homes were blessings compared to the rough cabins elsewhere in the Indiana frontier. Here he could build the perfect society.

Owen wanted his village, which he renamed New Harmony, to be a haven free from poverty and inequality. Science was to be emphasized. New Harmony, he wrote, would become an empire of good sense. He brought distinguished scholars, scientists, intellectuals and educators to the site on a keelboat nicknamed the "Boatload of Knowledge."

None of this, he emphasized, was for self-glorification. "I have not the smallest desire to leave a name to be remembered by men for an hour after my death," Owen said.

He regarded cities as "evil" sinkholes. In his utopia, self-sufficient villages would support five hundred to twenty-five hundred people. Villagers would farm, make goods and run businesses, sharing the cooking and other chores—as well as the profits from their work.

The New Harmony experiment started out well. One of the residents wrote to a son: "Here there are no brawling braggarts and intemperate idlers."

Owen traveled across the country lecturing about his visions for a new social system. His audiences included President James Monroe and President-elect John Quincy Adams and some of their Cabinet members, along with members of both Houses of Congress. Owenite societies were organized in Ohio, New York, and Pennsylvania.

Alas, Owen's utopia didn't last. Within two years, New Harmony residents were beset by personality clashes, schisms and disagreements about religion and the best form of government. They even argued about the nature of happiness and how best to achieve it.

And nobody wanted to do the rough work, such as forking manure. Most residents opted for gentlemanly poetry discussions while potters' wheels and baking ovens lay idle. Human nature triumphed over idealism.

And with Owen away, the unmanaged economy in New Harmony—"the experiment on the Wabash"—struggled. New Harmony finally collapsed in 1827. By that time, almost all of the other Owenite societies had disintegrated, too, and Owen had lost four-fifths of his fortune. He devoted himself to preaching his social reform ideas and, at age eighty-two, became a spiritualist. He died in 1858.

Robert Owen's Legacy

Even though Robert Owen's life as a Hoosier was brief, he left two legacies that have significantly affected the state: his descendants and the spirit of innovation.

His son Robert Dale Owen (1801–1877) was elected as a Democrat to the Indiana legislature, where he successfully pushed for women's property rights. He also became a board member at Indiana University and persuaded the U.S. Congress to provide IU with twenty-four thousand acres of land.

As energetic as his father, Robert Dale Owen helped revise the state constitution in the early 1850s and served in Congress, where he sponsored legislation that established the Smithsonian Institution. At his urging, the Smithsonian was developed as a truly scientific institution rather than a library for scholars.

His younger brother, David Dale Owen (1807–1860), was Indiana's first state geologist and is known as "the pioneer geologist of the Midwest." Regarded as the founder of the Indiana Geological Society, David Dale Owen made New Harmony his home throughout his scientific career, which included a county-by-county examination of Indiana's water, soil and rocks, including the coal and limestone of southern Indiana.

In his pioneering book, *A Geological Reconnaissance and Survey of the State of Indiana in 1837 and 1838*, the first extensive analysis of the state's land and water, David Dale Owen wrote:

The greater part of Indiana must have been, at some period of the earth's history, covered by an ocean; for most of the fossils in the limestones are of marine origin.

None of the precious metals will ever be found in Indiana, unless in minute portions in boulders or in small quantities in combination with other metals; because the primitive and graywacke formations in which alone productive mines of gold and silver ore occur, do not exist in Indiana.

Although his adopted state was not blessed with precious metals, David Dale

continued next page

Owen documented the rich coal formations in such southern and western Indiana counties as Posey, Vanderburgh, Warrick, Spencer, and Perry, as well as the abundant limestone in southern Indiana and the fertile soil in much of the Hoosier state.

Following in David Dale Owen's footsteps, many members of subsequent generations of the Owen family became geologists. Since World War II, a descendant of Robert Owen—geologist Kenneth Dale Owen and his wife, Texas oil heiress Jane Blaffer Owen—have become the patriarch and matriarch of New Harmony historic renovation.

Their efforts have brought about a renaissance in the town, blending its unique history and natural beauty with stunning architecture, including a world-famous roofless church.

All of this has made the village a mecca for cultural and literary groups, particularly when they meet to grapple with spiritual issues. One such gathering is the annual New Harmony Project, a retreat of America's top playwrights, screenwriters, TV writers and actors.

In a way, Robert Owen's "Boatload of Knowledge" still floats.

Indiana
Historical Society

Robert Dale Owen

William Conner

Settler and fur trader

He was a vital link between the American Indians and early white settlers of the Indiana Territory—and for several unusual reasons. William Conner's roots in both cultures ran deep, and he was among the first white settlers of what eventually became the Hoosier state.

Perhaps the ultimate frontier "survivor," Conner was born to white parents in a village in the Ohio wilderness. His mother, Margaret, had been captured as a child during an Indian raid; she was raised by the Shawnee.

Richard Conner, an adventurous frontiersman enchanted by Margaret, had to apply to the Shawnee chief to marry her. According to some accounts, he paid $200, and the couple had to agree that their firstborn son would remain with the tribe. That son, James (born in 1771), was left with the Indians. A second son, John, was born four years later.

By the time William, the third son, came along in 1777, the Conners had reclaimed young James. Although the family settled in a new town built on the Ohio frontier, the Conners joined a church primarily attended by Indians and mingled with various tribes. William grew up as a "white Indian." A fourth brother, Henry, born in 1780, was blond and called "White Hair" by the Indians.

During the Revolutionary War, British troops and their Indian allies brutally forced the Conners to move to Detroit. The Conner brothers grew up in Michigan; William and his second brother, John, began trading furs as young men.

Sensing opportunity in the wilderness to the south, the brothers came to the Indiana Territory in 1800 and established trading posts among Delaware Indians.

John settled in southeastern Indiana and planned the town of Connersville. According to a story told by his granddaughter, John Conner was building his cabin—it didn't even have a roof or floor yet—when a wagon full of immigrants drew up and asked to be directed to Connersville. Laughing, Conner replied, "My friend, you are right in the heart of the town."

William's post was on the White River near Noblesville, one of three towns he planned. His trading post became the stopping point for hundreds of travelers making their way across the Indiana Territory.

Because of their keen knowledge of the Indians, the Conner brothers were hired as scouts and interpreters by William Henry Harrison during the War of 1812. Shuttling between white and Indian cultures, William Conner had two wives (an Indian and a white woman) and two sets of children. He became a prosperous entrepreneur and land speculator, owning approximately four thousand acres in Hamilton County.

Although primarily a frontier businessman, Conner also held several county offices and served three terms in the Indiana General Assembly. He died in 1855. Like his brother, John Conner became a businessman, seizing an opportunity and opening a suc-

William Conner, from a portrait at Conner Prairie Pioneer Settlement.

cessful dry goods store in Indianapolis almost as soon as the new state capital developed. John died a few years later in 1826.

The Conner family was in danger.

So were their neighbors and friends, Moravian missionaries and about four hundred Indians who had been converted to Christianity in the Ohio frontier of 1781.

The Revolutionary War raged. British troops, with the help of hostile Indians, wanted to shut down all of the Christian missions in Ohio. Richard and Margaret Conner would get no special treatment just because they had four young boys. James, the oldest, was ten; tow-headed Henry was just a baby.

Despite their peaceable ways, the Conners were ordered to abandon their home, their crops, their belongings and even their kettle. They were told to march. Quickly.

Richard carried one of his little sons—alternating between William and John—while Margaret carried the baby, Henry, in what later would be known as "Indian fashion." She may have even darkened the infant's blond hair so Henry would look more like an Indian and attract less attention to the fact that the Conners were among the few whites in the group.

Tearing their shoes to shreds, the Conners traveled a hundred and twenty-five miles in twenty days on sore, bleeding feet. Their captors even refused to let Margaret and other new mothers nurse their babies. They marched to a camp on the Sandusky River in Ohio, then were ordered to make a second grueling trip to Detroit. By the time the Conners and their friends arrived in Detroit, they were exhausted and starving.

Even so, four-year-old William Conner and his three brothers survived the journey. For William Conner, the march to Detroit was just the first survival episode in a lifetime of persevering through—and even triumphing over—frontier cultural changes. He simply refused to be vanquished.

When William and John left Michigan as young men in 1800 to set up dual trading posts in the Indiana Territory, there were few white women in central Indiana. Both brothers married Delaware Indians.

William's wife, Mekinges, has been described in some accounts as an "Indian princess." It's doubtful she was a member of any sort of royal family, although her father probably was highly regarded among the Delaware.

Conner's home, a log cabin, became a gathering spot for both Indians and white travelers. The cabin also housed a boisterous young family. With Mekinges, Conner had six children.

As a liaison between whites and Indians, Conner served as an interpreter at the Treaty of St. Mary's in 1818. He also helped persuade Delaware chiefs to accept the treaty, in which the Indians agreed to give up their lands in central Indiana and move to other land west of the Mississippi River. Among the Delaware who moved—first to Missouri, then to Kansas and Oklahoma—were Conner's wife and his six children. It's possible she wanted to remain with her fellow Delaware. In any case, Conner probably had little contact with Mekinges or their children after the move.

Instead, ever the ultimate "survivor," Conner adapted to a new culture. As the Indiana wilderness evolved into a young white society, he married again—but this time to a white woman. Historians suspect his second wife, Elizabeth Chapman, was the only young, eligible white woman in the Noblesville area. With her, he had a second boisterous family—ten children.

In 1820 ten commissioners appointed by the Indiana General Assembly gathered at the Conners' log cabin to plan a new state capital. The commissioners included General John Tipton. Governor Jonathan Jennings eventually joined the sessions as an ex-officio member.

This distinguished group occasionally met under trees because Conner's cabin was too cramped to accommodate everyone. For entertainment, they hunted deer at night in canoes by torchlight.

Chosen as the site for Indiana government because of its central location, Indianapolis officially became the capital in 1825. (Corydon had been serving as the capital since Indiana became a state in 1816.)

By the time Indianapolis was up and humming, Conner's log cabin was gone. He built a two-story brick home overlooking the White River and planned the towns of Alexandria and Strawtown in addition to Noblesville. Then, adapting again to take advantage of new opportunities, Conner invested in general stores, mills, and crafts shops in all of the towns he planned as well as in Indianapolis.

Conner Prairie historian Steve Cox characterizes Conner as "an aggressive and inquisitive frontier capitalist." As such, Conner sensed the dawning of the Industrial Age—and was a key player in getting railroads to come to central Indiana.

By the time he died in 1855, Conner had moved to Noblesville. But his restored brick home along the White River is familiar to generations of Hoosiers and visitors from around the world. The house is part of the grounds of Conner Prairie Settlement, an outdoor living history museum of frontier life.

General John Tipton
and Chief Menominee
Military and political leader and Potawatomi chief

General John Tipton in his own time was respected as a man who knew how to keep law and order on a restless frontier. Today we may see him in a broader light. His father had been killed by Indians and, as was true of most frontiersmen, he distrusted and despised Native American people. He was to be the ruthless instrument used in the forceful removal of the Potawatomi of northern Indiana.

His career, however, is one of considerable scope for the era. Tipton's diaries provide lasting accounts of influential gatherings that permanently affected Indiana, including the meetings to select a state capital. (It was on Tipton's motion that a site was chosen at the mouth of Fall Creek at White River—now Indianapolis.) Later, he was appointed the Indiana commissioner to meet with a counterpart from Illinois and hammer out the boundary line between the two states. He also played a key role in founding Hoosier cities from Columbus to Huntington and Logansport.

Tipton was born in Tennessee in 1786. His father was killed by Indians before Tipton reached manhood and, in 1807, at age twenty-one, he moved with his mother and her three other children to Harrison County in the unsettled Indiana Territory. Two years later, just before the War of 1812, rugged, flamboyant Tipton enlisted in the "Yellow Jackets," a frontier military company organized to fight Indians near his home.

During the famous Battle of Tippecanoe in 1811, Tipton started out as an ensign and carried the colors for Gen. William Henry Harrison's troops. During the battle, Harrison promoted Tipton when all of the officers of the "Yellow Jackets" were killed.

Despite his controversial reputation, Tipton managed to enjoy a political career. A pro-slavery Democrat, he eventually became a close friend of President Andrew Jackson (who also hailed from Tennessee) and frequently visited Jackson at his home, the Hermitage. In 1831, the Indiana legislature named him to the U.S. Senate to fill a vacancy. He was elected to a full term two years later. Tipton also held high offices in the Masonic fraternity, becoming a grand master.

By all accounts, his career in the Senate was unspectacular. Lacking formal education and never a fluent public speaker, Tipton was better suited to the rough-and-tumble of frontier conflicts than to the hallways of the nation's capital. He died in 1839 and is buried in Logansport.

The year before his death, Tipton came into conflict with the leader of the Potawatomi, Chief Menominee. Menominee probably was born in 1791; he became a Roman Catholic and, like other Potawatomi, was known for his colorful apparel. Instead of the buckskin and war paint associated with some tribes, the Potawatomi favored ruffled shirts, jewelry, and ribbon-bedecked pants.

Although a peacemaker by nature, Menominee was determined to hold on to what remained of his tribe's northern Indiana land after a series of treaties with the white settlers. He frequently met with a French priest to study treaty law. Soon he would need to

This statue of Chief Menominee stands near his beloved Twin Lakes.

General John Tipton

Tippecanoe County Historical Association

know that law as settlers, led by Tipton, pressed Indians to give up the last of their lands.

It's known as the Trail of Death.

The tragedy began in the summer of 1838 with a standoff near Logansport between white leaders and Potawatomi chiefs.

Chief Menominee was refusing to leave his village, claiming he had never signed a treaty or sold his land. The chief defied Governor David Wallace's order to abandon the "Twin Lakes" region of the twenty-one-year-old state of Indiana.

The Potawatomi said they didn't want to leave "the graves of our children." At one point, the Potawatomi held practically all of the region north of the Wabash River, nearly one-fourth of Indiana.

As the conflict intensified, Chief Menominee met with President Martin Van Buren. Sympathy began to build in the U.S. Senate for the plight of the Potawatomi in Indiana. Of his visit with Van Buren, Menominee said in a speech to white and Indian political leaders one month before his removal by force:

> *The president does not know the truth. He, like me, has been imposed upon . . . He does not know that you made my young chiefs drunk and got their consent, and pretended to get mine . . . He would not drive me from my home and the graves of my tribe, and my children, who have gone to the Great Spirit, nor allow you to tell me your braves will take me, tied like a dog. When [the president] knows the truth, he will leave me to my own. I have not sold my lands. I will not sell them.*

Indiana leaders hated Menominee for taking his case all the way to the President. In September, a company of soldiers under Tipton's command arrived, determined to force the 859 Potawatomi to leave. A missionary priest near the Indian village assembled his flock in a chapel for a final service. The next day, the Potawatomi paid a final visit to their graveyard.

Then Tipton and his soldiers led the Potawatomi men, women and children on a nine-hundred-mile march to Kansas. At first, Chief Menominee was bound as well as guarded. The trek took sixty-two days and resulted in the deaths of dozens of Indians from disease, exhaustion and the grueling effects of the weather.

Some accounts say Menominee was among the dead; according to other accounts, he died three years later in 1841 after being stricken with typhoid. In any case, those who survived the Trail of Death were ordered to live on a western reservation.

"It was a sad and mournful spectacle," wrote one eyewitness, "to [watch] these children of the forest slowly retiring from the home of their childhood that contained not only the graves of their revered ancestors, but many endearing scenes to which their memories would never recur as sunny spots . . ."

Some Potawatomi remained in the northwest corner of the state, but eventually most of Indiana's Potawatomi were further removed to Oklahoma. Interestingly, several Potawatomi have returned to Indiana to re-establish ties. Their tragic and courageous story is remembered every September in Fulton County, Indiana, in the Trail of Courage Festival.

John Tipton is memorialized by the north-central Indiana county that bears his name, and Chief Menominee by a marker set in a peaceful grove near the Twin Lakes he loved so much.

Motivated by their Quaker beliefs, Levi and Catherine Coffin helped thousands of runaway slaves on the Underground Railroad before the Civil War. Catherine would gather Wayne County women in her sitting room to weave blankets and clothing for the refugees. One of the key Northern homes on the Underground Railroad in the North, the Levi Coffin house is a popular destination for field trips of Indiana schoolchildren. The house is in the Wayne County town of Fountain City, which was known as Newport when the Coffins lived there.

Levi Coffin

Underground railroad leader

His home became known as the "Grand Central Station" of the legendary Underground Railroad before the American Civil War. The reason for the renown is no mystery. With his Newport, Indiana, house serving as a temporary haven, merchant Levi Coffin, a dedicated Quaker, helped an astounding two thousand slaves find freedom as they traveled through the Midwest to new lives in Canada.

Even when Coffin left his Newport home—which by then had become part of Hoosier folklore—and moved to Cincinnati in 1847, it was to pursue his antislavery crusade. Coffin and his wife, Catherine, ran a wholesale warehouse in Cincinnati for "free labor goods"—cotton shirts and other wares not produced by slave labor.

The Coffins' reputation was so extensive that generations of researchers concluded they were the inspiration for a courageous abolitionist couple in Uncle Tom's Cabin, the classic novel written by a fellow Cincinnati resident, Harriet Beecher Stowe. Although Stowe probably didn't base her characters on the transplanted Hoosiers, there is no doubt that the Coffins' antislavery efforts formed the consuming passion of their lives.

Levi Coffin probably saw himself as carrying on the humanitarian legacy of his grandfathers, whose homes were used as hospitals during the Revolutionary War. Both American and British wounded were treated there—as were dozens of victims of smallpox.

Born in a Quaker settlement in North Carolina in 1798, Levi Coffin was the sixth of seven children—and only son—in a farm family. In Reminiscences, a memoir Coffin wrote the year before his death in 1877, he describes one of his first encounters with slavery in North Carolina:

I was about seven years old . . . One day I was by the roadside where my father was chopping wood, when I saw such a gang approaching . . . The slaves came first, chained in couples on each side of a long chain which extended between them . . . My father addressed the slaves pleasantly, and then asked, "Well, boys, why do they chain you?" One of the men, whose countenance betrayed unusual intelligence and whose expression denoted the deepest sadness, replied: "They have taken us away from our wives and children, and they chain us lest we should make our escape and go back to them." My childish sympathy and interest were aroused and when the dejected procession had passed on, I turned to my father and asked many questions . . . In simple words, suited to my comprehension, my father explained to me the meaning of slavery, and, as I listened, the thought arose in my mind, "How terribly we should feel if father were taken away from us."

These unsettling thoughts resulted in a lifelong crusade that eventually involved construction of his Newport house—and of an unusual, second-floor bedroom. In one wall

*of the slanted-roof room, there is a small door about two and a half feet square. In times
of jeopardy, slaves could squeeze through the tiny door and huddle in a triangular crawl
space. Then a bed would be moved sideways a few feet to conceal the entrance.*

It was truly a "full-service" operation—and the "business" of the Levi Coffin house in
the 1840s wasn't even a town secret. Zealous in his antislavery beliefs, Coffin would button-
hole fellow Newport residents on the streets of the Quaker town and recruit them to his
abolitionist crusade. Helping slaves win freedom, he told townspeople, was "God's will."
Many found it difficult to say no to the prosperous merchant and landowner who controlled
much of the town's banking and supplies.

Although less intimidating, Catherine Coffin was just as dedicated as her husband. She
would gather women friends in the sitting room of the family's stately, Federal-style home,
and seated around a spinning wheel near a brick fireplace—in plain view of a large,
streetside window—they would prepare yarn for the weaving of blankets and clothes or
mend garments for runaway slaves. The Coffins also arranged for medical care for the fugitives, who usually slipped into their house at night. All of the different kinds of care and
comfort explain why the Coffin house became known as a full-service stop on this railroad
to freedom.

However, not everyone in Newport supported the Coffins' efforts. Levi's activism dis-
turbed the Wayne County town's Quaker meetings. Although committed pacifists, many
Quakers felt they should adopt a "live and let live" tolerance toward Southern slave owners.
These Quakers were overwhelmed and put off by Levi Coffin's urgent and incessant calls to
help blacks. Frustrated by the inactivity of some of his brethren, Coffin broke from the fellowship in 1843 and founded a rival, antislavery Quaker congregation—or "friends meeting"—on the opposite end of Newport. So began a rift that eventually split Quaker meetings across Indiana.

Like many Quakers in Indiana before the Civil War, Levi Coffin wasn't a native Hoosier.
He spent his first twenty-eight years in North Carolina, where he was a farmer and a teacher
at private Quaker schools. As part of an exodus of Quakers to the Old Northwest in search
of prime farmland, Coffin moved to Newport in 1826.

Shrewd and energetic, he sensed and seized opportunity. Coffin opened the first dry
goods store in Newport. Then, realizing that the big cash farm animal in east-central Indiana was the hog, he opened a pork-butchering business. Next he purchased one of the town's
four mills. Finally, Levi Coffin opened a paint shop and amassed real estate, eventually owning two hundred and fifty acres in four counties.

All of this gave him clout with his "Underground Railroad" activities. In 1839, he built
the brick house on the corner of Mill and Main Cross streets (U.S. Highway 27) which
would become his legacy. The second-floor bedroom, with its tiny, secret door and narrow,
"hideaway" crawl space also served as the bedroom for two maids who helped the Coffins
rear their five children.

Ironically, the house was never searched—despite the fact that about two thousand runaway slaves (primarily from Kentucky and Tennessee) passed through it. There were dozens
of close calls when furious slave owners or slave-catchers (hired "guns"—generally scoun-
drels who were desperate for cash and offered to hunt down fugitives) showed up at the
doorway in pursuit. As many as fourteen slaves could huddle in the crawl space. They usually slept on mats on the brick floor of the Coffins' roomy basement.

Summoning every ounce of his authority as one of Newport's leading citizens, the stern-
faced Coffin always kept the slave hunters at bay by demanding they produce search war-

rants—and after that, slave-ownership papers. No one ever showed up with all of the proper documentation to force entry; by the time they would return with their paperwork, Coffin and his helpers had hustled the escaped slaves to the next haven, usually under the cover of darkness.

Also by the time the fugitives left, Catherine and her friends had mended their torn clothes and woven new garments to keep the shivering slaves warm during the chilly Midwestern nights. Any fugitives who had been injured during their escape or nighttime flights had their wounds treated by the Coffins' friend, Newport physician Dr. Henry Way.

By doing all of this, the Coffins were risking scorn, if not jail. Under the Fugitive Slave Act of 1793, all Americans—even Northerners—were required to turn in runaway slaves. Helping them escape was like being an accomplice to a robbery.

That didn't faze Coffin. In 1844, he even traveled from Indiana to Canada to visit the refugees he had assisted.

"The Bible, in bidding us to feed the hungry and clothe the naked, said nothing about color," he explained in *Reminiscences*.

Partly because of the Coffins' activities, settlements of legally freed blacks popped up across east-central Indiana. By 1840, Wayne County was home to more freed black residents than any other Indiana county. The Coffins helped start and support schools for black children whose families settled in neighboring Randolph County. Famous freed blacks passing through Indiana—including the legendary Frederick Douglass—spent several nights at the Coffin house.

Eventually, Levi Coffin became known by some abolitionists and ex-slaves as the unofficial president of the Underground Railroad. (According to folklore, the nickname for the escape route came about when an exasperated pursuer complained that slaves were so elusive as they fled through several states that they must have been booking passage on a silent "underground railroad.") A common route of the Railroad wound from Kentucky through Cincinnati or Jeffersonville and Rising Sun, Indiana, with a stop in Newport before heading toward northern Indiana, Michigan and, at last, freedom in Canada.

In the decades after the Coffins moved to Cincinnati, much changed for both Levi and for the town of Newport. Because there was another Newport in Indiana (in Vermillion County), the town changed its name to Fountain City. Meanwhile, the Coffins free-labor business faltered; Levi died nearly penniless in 1877. But while living in Cincinnati, he had helped about a thousand more slaves to escape.

Although its name changed, the town of Newport/Fountain City never forgot the fearless abolitionist—or his distinctive house. In the 1910s, the Coffin house became a popular hotel that traded on his legacy and was known as the Underground Railroad Hotel.

Now owned by the state and restored by the Levi Coffin House Association, the Coffin house is a historic site visited annually by thousands of schoolchildren. They invariably ask to "hide" in the crawl space to get a sense of the terror felt by escaped slaves—fugitives helped by a steadfast Quaker friend.

This illustration of young Abraham Lincoln as he probably looked during his days as a Hoosier is a favorite of the Lincoln Boyhood National Memorial in southern Indiana. The artist Lloyd Ostendorf, of Dayton, Ohio, specializes in depictions of Lincoln.

Abraham Lincoln

President

He's considered one of the most remarkable figures of modern times. Yet, despite the exhaustive examination accorded most of his life, Abraham Lincoln's fourteen years as a Hoosier have not been thoroughly credited for the influence they had on him as a boy and as a young man.

The man who would become the sixteenth President of the United States spent one-fourth of his life in Indiana. The Lincoln family settled near Little Pigeon Creek in what is now Spencer County and lived there from 1816 to 1830. It was there that Abe Lincoln went from age seven to twenty-one—the years generally considered to be the most formative.

"I grew up in Indiana," Lincoln said as an adult.

Even so, he usually is associated with two other states: Kentucky, where Lincoln was born February 12, 1809, in Hardin County (now Larue County); and Illinois, where his family moved in 1830 in search of fertile land. It was in Illinois that Lincoln was a state legislator and attorney before being elected to the U.S. Congress. He died at age fifty-six from an assassin's bullet after presiding over his country during its most traumatic period, the American Civil War (1861–1865).

The lanky, eloquent politician who would become "the Great Emancipator" came with his family to the Hoosier state, the same month Indiana became the nineteenth state in the union. Its constitution prohibited slavery.

When the family arrived, the Lincolns had to clear miles of dense frontier and had few close neighbors. After six years, the area contained nine families with forty-nine children within a one-mile radius of the Lincoln cabin.

Likewise, the original four-member Lincoln family that came from Kentucky also was greatly transformed. After three years, their one-room log cabin had become the home of what today would be called a "blended family," combining three sets of children who had lost one or both parents.

During his fourteen years in Indiana, Abe Lincoln was shaped by the rugged frontier and a series of sorrows. Like others before and after him, he found several ways to cope, including the use of humor.

One of Thomas Lincoln's cows began to tremble.

The sign was unmistakable and horrifying to residents of the Little Pigeon Creek settlement in the southern Indiana wilderness of 1818. Cows with the "trembles" suffered from the dreaded milk sickness.

Who would its next human victims be?

Mysterious and deadly, the disease was contracted by people when they drank the milk of cows that had grazed on a poisonous plant, a white snakeroot. Milk sickness almost always meant death within a week or two; whenever it occurred in southern Indiana, it created panic and ravaged entire communities.

Before long, Nancy Hanks Lincoln, a thirty-four-year-old, deeply religious mother of two, was nursing three victims of the illness.

One victim of the sickness and its symptoms—dizziness, intense thirst, excruciating stomach pains, and vomiting—was Mrs. Peter Bonner, a neighbor. The other two were members of the Lincoln household: Nancy's aunt, Elizabeth Sparrow, and her husband, Thomas Sparrow. With their ward, Dennis Hanks, the Sparrows had moved to a campsite near the Lincolns about a year earlier, in 1817. But now Dennis' guardians were dying—and Nancy Lincoln began to experience severe symptoms herself.

The one-room Lincoln cabin suddenly became crowded, with eighteen-year-old Dennis moving in after the Sparrows' deaths and sharing the loft with eight-year-old Abraham Lincoln. Abe's ten-year-old sister, Sarah, slept with the adults below.

Horrified and helpless, the Lincolns and Dennis could do nothing but watch and try to ease Nancy's suffering.

"She knew she was going to die," Dennis Hanks recalled years later. "She called up the children to her dying side and told them to be good and kind to their father, to one another and to the world, expressing a hope that they might live as they had been taught by her to live."

The surviving Lincolns buried her in a family plot on a little hill near their cabin. They could see her grave each dawn as they stepped out the door. Thomas Lincoln made the coffin for his wife, using wooden pegs that young Abe had whittled.

Frontier children grew up as products of their environment, and Abe Lincoln was no exception. The family's cabin stood near forests with huge oak trees, awe-inspiring and extremely foreboding. Extremely hard work was a part of daily life. The gentle and harsh lessons of nature were everywhere, and from those the boy learned lifelong precepts of endurance and practicality, along with the simple faith he had learned from his mother. Looking from the cabin door toward her grave on the gentle slope of rolling grassland, he surely must have felt sadness at life's brevity.

Bouts of melancholy plagued Lincoln for the rest of his life after the death of his gentle, nurturing mother. Visitors to the White House during the period of 1863 to 1864—those dark days when Northern armies were faltering and the war seemed lost—spoke of the sadness which, along with strength, defined the President's nature.

Indications of his mental toughness—and physical strength—were apparent from his arrival in the Indiana frontier. Skinny and unusually tall for his age, seven-year-old Abe had helped his father build the log cabin when the family moved to southern Indiana's unbroken forests of oak, ash, sycamore, and beech. Although he was gawky, Abe could wield an axe. While he chopped undergrowth, his father felled the trees.

By the time the Lincolns arrived and built their cabin, most Indians had left southern Indiana. Young Abe, who had attended school briefly in Kentucky, periodically went to two or three in Indiana. But mostly he learned at home in the cabin, reading the Bible, Shakespeare, and adventure books about Aladdin, Sinbad, and Robinson Crusoe.

A sensitive, introspective boy, Abe was inside one day when he saw a flock of wild turkeys approach the cabin. His father wasn't home, so Abe asked his mother if he could use Thomas Lincoln's heavy rifle. After she gave permission, Abe stood inside, struggled with the cumbersome weapon, aimed it through a crack, pulled the trigger, and killed a turkey.

Abe was excited until he ran outdoors and saw the beauty of the bird he had killed. Recalling the experience as an adult, Lincoln said he was so shaken that he never again "pulled a trigger on any larger game."

Despite its hardships, life in southern Indiana was not all grim. Slightly more than a year after Nancy died, Thomas returned to Kentucky looking for a wife and a mother for Abe and Sarah. He married Sarah Bush Johnston, an Elizabethtown, Kentucky, widow with three children of her own. The whole brood—including her children Elizabeth, John, and Matilda—moved into the one-room Lincoln cabin. Just like his mother, Abe's stepmother encouraged his reading. She considered him a model child.

By the time he was fourteen, Abe was making speeches to his sister, stepbrother, stepsisters, and other youngsters who wandered over. Soon he was telling stories at the fence as other Hoosier farmboys gathered around. Then, often using humor to illustrate points or cope with grim truths, he began storytelling at the general store and blacksmith shop.

His use of droll humor, often involving frontier or rural characters he picked up in the countryside, became a lifelong habit. The frontier yarns Abe Lincoln loved so well were like Aesop's fables: They taught lessons in an interesting way.

As president, he even used frontier humor in political confrontations. When Lincoln decided to select a new Secretary of War, prominent Republican senators seized the opportunity to press Lincoln to overhaul all seven of his Cabinet secretaries.

The President quietly listened to their pleas, then told a story from his days in the Midwest. It concerned a farmer who, in Lincoln's words, was "much troubled by skunks." The farmer's wife demanded that he get rid of them.

"He loaded the shotgun one moonlit night and awaited developments," Lincoln recalled. "After some time the wife heard the shotgun go off, and in a few minutes the farmer entered the house.

" 'What luck have you?' asked she.

" 'I hid myself behind the woodpile,' said the old man, 'with the shotgun pointed towards the hen roost, and before long there appeared not one skunk, but seven.

" 'I took aim, blazed away and killed one. But he raised such a fearful smell that I concluded it was best to let the other six go.' "

Laughing, the senators dropped their demands for the six Cabinet resignations—it would cause far too much trouble.

Lew Wallace

Lew Wallace

Novelist, soldier, diplomat, lawyer, politician

"I am looking to you and Ben-Hur *to keep me unforgotten after the end of life."*

That plea is from a letter that spirited, glory-loving Lew Wallace wrote to his wife, Susan, in 1887. He really didn't need to fret about his posthumous fame—at least as it relates to his spectacular, best-selling novel.

Historians believe that, except for the Bible, Ben-Hur: Tale of the Christ *(1880) was read by more people in its era than any other book. In this century, Hollywood has based two epic movies on the book, a historical romance about Christians in the early Roman Empire and the coming of Christ. The most recent movie, a 1959 blockbuster starring Charlton Heston and featuring a stunning chariot race, won a record-setting eleven Academy Awards.*

Ben-Hur'*s author, Lew Wallace, is most closely identified with Crawfordsville, Indiana. But this adventurous, flamboyant Hoosier, the son of the state's sixth governor, was also associated at various stages of his adventure-packed life with*

  - *New Mexico—President Rutherford B. Hayes appointed Wallace governor of the new territory in the late 1870s. The transplanted Hoosier dealt with Apache Indians, warring cattlemen and notorious gunslingers, including Billy the Kid.*

  - *Turkey—Wallace served as the United States' minister there during the 1880s. He befriended sultans, visited lavish palaces and was considered a highly effective diplomat.*

  - *Mexico—where Wallace was an American soldier—twice. He was just nineteen at the start of the Mexican War in 1846, but Wallace, eager for action, opened a recruiting office in Indianapolis and formed a company of troops. Nearly twenty years later he returned to Mexico; although Wallace didn't see battle this time, he hastened the departure of the French forces of Napoleon III.*

  - *The battlefields of the Civil War—Fighting for the Union forces, Wallace helped capture Fort Donelson in Tennessee—although he suffered a setback with an apparent blunder at the bloody Battle of Shiloh, also in Tennessee. During the Battle of the Monocacy in 1864, Wallace said his vastly outnumbered troops managed to hold off the Confederate Army from Washington, D.C.*

After the Civil War, Wallace sat on the military court that tried the conspirators in the assassination of President Abraham Lincoln. He also presided over the military court which convicted the superintendent of Andersonville Prison in Georgia of cruelty for allowing the death of Union prisoners there.

Aside from all that, Wallace was a Hoosier politician (he was elected to such offices as county attorney and state senator), a lawyer and, of course, the author of historical romance novels.

This jack-of-many-trades was born in 1827 in Brookville, a bustling village in southeastern Indiana. As a youth, his father, David Wallace, had obtained a cadetship at West Point, the prestigious military academy, thanks to Gen. William Henry Harrison.

"Almost the earliest of my recollections is the gray uniform of Cadet Wallace," Lew wrote decades later in his autobiography. "The small tail and shining bullet-buttons of the coat captured my childish fancy. None of the good man's honors exalted him in my eyes like that scant garment."

Regardless, David Wallace did enjoy many subsequent honors. After his return to Indiana, the elder Wallace became a prosperous lawyer. He married Esther French Test, the daughter of a judge and congressman. The couple had four boys. Esther died in 1834 when Lew, the second son, was just seven years old.

About two years later, David remarried. He was elected to the state legislature, and was elected Indiana's lieutenant governor twice in the 1830s. In 1836, David Wallace became governor of the Hoosier state.

Young Lew, meanwhile, was already a thrill seeker. His adventurous spirit was even evident during his first year in school, when the Wallaces were living in Covington, Indiana, on the Wabash River.

"My sixth year was the beginning of a habit of truancy which followed me through my school terms, and has even yet to be struggled against," Wallace recalled in his autobiography. ". . . The Wabash [River] skirted the low ground, swishing the limb-tips of the trees on both shores . . . Since that time, I have seen many of the famous rivers of the earth, among them the Danube, the Rhine, and the Nile; never one of them so impressed me as did the Wabash in that stolen interview . . . It had a coaxing power."

And Lew Wallace could never resist the power of an attractive challenge.

It was a daring move.

Many faithful Christians in America of 1880 condemned novels, regarding works of fiction as worthless—even sinful. Yet Lew Wallace was so bold as to make Christ a character in his epic work.

Wallace had never been particularly religious, nor was he ever a formal member of any church. He hadn't even visited Rome or the Holy Land, the setting for *Ben-Hur*. Thus, many Americans were skeptical that such a man could write an inspiring novel.

"I protest, as a friend of Christ, that He has been crucified enough already, without having a Territorial Governor after him," wrote Joseph Wasson, a California politician who visited the New Mexico Territory in 1879. That's where Wallace, as governor, was dealing with vicious cattle wars, Apache attacks, a nuisance named Billy the Kid—and writing *Ben-Hur* by lamplight at night.

Concerns such as Wasson's were quickly forgotten with the publication of *Ben-Hur*, though. The sweeping novel about a proud, handsome Jewish prince named Judah Ben-Hur mesmerized Americans—churchgoers and nonbelievers, exalted clergymen and humble parishioners, Catholics and Protestants.

Everyone was captivated by the novel about a former galley slave who seeks revenge against Messala, his former best friend. The saga featured chariot races, pirates, pageantry, slaves, sheiks, lepers, camels, and gladiators—not to mention historical figures such as Pontius Pilate and the Three Wise Men. Of the horror surrounding leprosy in ancient times, Wallace described the once-beautiful mother and sister of Judah Ben-Hur:

Slowly, steadily, with horrible certainty, the disease spread, after a while bleaching their heads white, eating holes in their lips and eyelids, and covering their bodies with scales; then it fell to their throats, shrilling their voices, and to their joints . . . at each advance making the sufferers more and more loathsome; and so it would continue till death, which might be years before them.

At first a skeptic, Ben-Hur then watches in awe as Jesus transforms the lepers with a miracle of healing. In writing *Ben-Hur*, Wallace was respectful of the Bible, contrary to some churchgoers' fears. Wallace, an imposing, fiftyish man with a fashionable beard, even announced that he would rather lose his right hand than offend Christian readers.

Among those spellbound by the page-turner was President James Garfield. He stayed up until the wee hours in the White House one night and read for several subsequent days during April of 1881 because he couldn't put it down, according to Wallace biographers Robert and Katharine Morsberger.

"I am inclined to send its author to Constantinople where he may draw inspiration from the modern east for future literary work," Garfield wrote in his journal.

By 1900, *Ben-Hur* had become the best-selling novel of the nineteenth century, exceeding the legendary *Uncle Tom's Cabin*, in which Harriet Beecher Stowe's depicted the evils of slavery.

And whatever his motivations, President Garfield did appoint Wallace as America's minister to Turkey in 1881, thus indeed sending the former Brookville, Indiana, boy to Constantinople (now Istanbul).

Both before and after *Ben-Hur*, Wallace wrote other books, primarily historical romances. They included *The Fair God* (1873), a tale of the conquest of Mexico; *The Boyhood of Christ* (1888); and *The Prince of India* (1893), which is set in and around Constantinople and deals with the Byzantine empire. Despite Wallace's reputation, though, not one of his later books even remotely approached *Ben-Hur* in popularity.

In some circles, Wallace is remembered almost as much for his Civil War exploits. Many Hoosiers consider him the state's most distinguished Civil War veteran, although his role at the disastrous battle near Shiloh Church on the Tennessee River in 1862 continues to spark arguments.

Experts debate whether Wallace, who was commanding troops nearby, or General Ulysses S. Grant is to blame for a tragic mistake made by Union forces on the first day of that bloody fight. Either because of unclear orders from Grant or because of Wallace's bungled response, the Hoosier officer's troops arrived too late to help their comrades that day.

And although Wallace fought valiantly to protect Washington, D.C., from overwhelming Confederate forces in the Battle of Monocacy in July of 1864, contemporary Civil War historians have given his performance mixed reviews.

The soldier-author-diplomat spent the last twenty years of his life in Crawfordsville, lecturing, writing and enjoying his fame. He also built the Blacherne apartments in Indianapolis and kept an apartment there. Wallace died of stomach cancer in 1905.

More than seventy years later, his spacious author's studio and its grounds in Crawfordsville were declared a National Historic Landmark.

"I want," he once told his wife, "to bury myself in a den of books." Truly, he brought himself a piece of eternity through one book.

There were five Studebaker brothers. (Left to right) Seated: Clement, Henry, and John Mohler Studebaker. Standing: Peter and Jacob F. Jacob Studebaker, the youngest brother, was the least involved in the family business. He joined Studebaker Brothers in the late 1860s and died in 1887.

The Studebakers

Clement, John Mohler, and Peter —
Wagonmakers and automakers

For generations, Studebaker Brothers was the biggest employer in South Bend. For a time in the late 1800s, it was the largest vehicle builder in the world. By the mid-1900s, it was America's last independent automaker, competing with the industry's "Big Three": Ford, General Motors and Chrysler.

In Indiana, Studebaker Brothers was one of the premier examples of auto-related industries that shaped the state's economy in the late nineteenth and early twentieth centuries.

All this success was achieved by the hard work and self-discipline of the great-grandsons of a German immigrant.

The Studebaker brothers' story began in 1820, when John Clement Studebaker, the grandson of a native of Germany, married Rebecca Mohler and established a blacksmith shop near Gettysburg, Pennsylvania. In 1835 hard times prompted the family to journey west; saddled with debt, they traveled in a wagon built by John to Ashland, Ohio.

About 1850, more hard times forced another westward move—to South Bend.

"In talking over this disastrous period of his life, he said to us, 'I had just one thing the sheriff could not take, and that was my trade,'" his fourth son, Peter, who was born in 1836, recalled years later.

"'Boys, you must all learn a trade.'"

So in 1852, with sixty-eight dollars, the two oldest Studebaker boys, Henry (born in 1826) and Clement (born in 1831) opened a blacksmith shop in South Bend. Shortly afterward, brother John Mohler Studebaker (born in 1833) left for California and the gold rush.

It was the beginning of a business which would influence the American transportation industry for more than a hundred years.

They called him "Wheelbarrow Johnny."

But before there were Studebaker wheelbarrows, there were Studebaker wagons. And as a nineteen-year-old in South Bend, John Mohler Studebaker built a wagon destined to be historic.

It would be the first Studebaker vehicle to cross "The Plains" and to be used on the West Coast. That's where adventure seeker John Mohler, the third of five Studebaker brothers, was determined to go.

He arrived near Placerville, California, the heart of the mining region, in 1853. Everyone still was caught up in the gold rush craze that had begun four years earlier. John had an advantage. Even though he was full of spirit and wanderlust, John had a level head. The transplanted Hoosier wasn't about to hunt for elusive gold.

Instead, he saw an opportunity and seized it. As the son of a blacksmith and wagonmaker, John turned his attention to the business he knew: making vehicles. Specifically, he made the vehicles needed in every gold-mining camp—wheelbarrows.

Enduring primitive conditions while living in the camps, John set to work. Demand was so intense that John got ten dollars per wheelbarrow, a princely sum. By the time he returned to South Bend five years later, he was wealthy.

His return coincided with the desires of his big brother, Henry, to quit the wagon business that Henry had started with the second brother, Clement. John bought Henry out and invested part of his California fortune.

The only problem was that the hardships of life in the mining camps had weakened John's health. Unable to devote his full attention to the Studebaker Brothers Wagon Works, John went to Europe for a year and a half to recuperate. He returned determined to make his second fortune.

By 1860 annual production at Studebaker numbered in the thousands of vehicles. During the Civil War, the family became a major supplier for the Union Army. Demand for wagons didn't stop with the war's end, either. The westward migration of Americans fueled the need for wagons, and the business thrived because of the Studebakers' reputation for quality.

Not even two disastrous fires in 1872 and 1874 could stop the brothers. Each time, they rebuilt. After the second blaze, their expanded wagon works covered ninety-eight acres. Capacity became an astounding seventy-five thousand vehicles annually.

When the family patriarch, John Clement Studebaker, died in 1877, he had seen his sons' business grow to become the world's largest vehicle builder. Their products included heavy commercial wagons, fancy carriages and sturdy buggies.

His sons never forgot their father's example of hard work and self-discipline.

"I often [knew] him to work from four o'clock in the morning until nine o'clock at night," Peter Studebaker wrote later in life. "I well remember sitting by him at the forge at night when a small lad and having my bare feet scorched from the sparks from his forge and anvil.

"Yet with all this application to severe toil, he found time to read his Bible daily, and lived to the age of seventy-seven years."

By the time his father died, Clement Studebaker was becoming prominent in the Republican Party. Three presidents—Ulysses S. Grant, Benjamin Harrison, and William McKinley—eventually were his friends.

Meanwhile, the brothers entered the automobile era. In 1902 the Studebakers built their first car, an electric—called, naturally, the Electric. (Until the end of his life, John Mohler preferred electric autos. He denounced gasoline cars as "clumsy, dangerous, noisy brutes which stink to high heaven, break down at the worst possible moment, and are a public nuisance.")

The Studebaker Electric kicked off the transition from motorized buggies to the "horseless carriage" years of the early 1900s. Despite John Mohler's dislike of them, gasoline-powered cars were added to the Studebaker line in 1904.

After Studebaker bought the Everitt-Metzger-Flanders Company of Detroit, the new Studebaker-EMF business was the nation's Number Two automaker, behind Ford. (The EMF name was gone within two years.)

Sadly, Clement, who was so alert to the possibilities of self-propelled vehicles, didn't live to see autos really take off. He died in 1901; Peter had passed away even earlier, in 1897. The dynamic and much-admired John Mohler stepped down as chairman of Studebaker Brothers at age eighty-two in 1915.

When "Wheelbarrow Johnny" died in 1917, fifty percent of the company's production was devoted to World War I. Three years later, the last horse-drawn Studebaker vehicle was built in South Bend, and the first car was totally assembled there. (Before 1920, the bodies were built in South Bend but assembled in Detroit.)

Even without the Studebaker brothers at the controls, the company was headed for more successes. Famous models called the Dictator, Commander and President appeared in 1927; the next year, Studebaker bought Pierce-Arrow, one of America's great luxury car makers. (That company was later spun off during a restructuring.)

In 1934 Studebaker introduced the "breath-taking" Land Cruiser model. During World War II, the company built trucks, aircraft engines and "Weasels"—amphibious troop carriers.

The decline came in the 1950s. Studebaker merged with Packard, then closed the South Bend plant in 1963. The end of the line at plants in Detroit and Hamilton, Ontario, came a few years later.

But mention the name *Studebaker*—or bring up the sparkling President model of 1932 that featured a clock, vacuum wiper, and a cigarette lighter as standard features—and aficionados of classic American cars are bound to smile.

*Benjamin and Caroline Harrison at an
Army-Navy reception at White House
during his presidency. (Below) "Benjie's
Ducking Club"—a hunting group of
Harrison and his friends—on an outing in
Maryland in March of 1891.*

Benjamin Harrison

President

The only president elected from Indiana was the nation's twenty-third chief executive—and the grandson of its ninth. William Henry Harrison, governor of the Indiana Territory decades earlier in his political career, died a month after occupying the White House in 1841. Benjamin Harrison was just seven.

Although he may not have enjoyed detailed memories of his famous grandfather, young Benjamin undoubtedly heard dozens of stories about him from "Old Tippecanoe's" widow, Anna. She lived with Benjamin's family on their Ohio farm later in her life.

Descended from a family prominent in American political and cultural life for two hundred years (his great-grandfather, also Benjamin, was a signer of the Declaration of Independence and a governor of Virginia), Benjamin Harrison was born in 1833 on the family farm—actually, a twenty-two-hundred-acre estate in North Bend, Ohio. A chubby, blond boy, he particularly enjoyed hunting.

As an adolescent, Benjamin met the love of his life—Caroline Scott. She was a year older than Benjamin, and her father was his science teacher at Farmer's College in Ohio. Harrison married Caroline when he was twenty years old after graduating from Miami University of Ohio and studying law.

The couple explored opportunities for a law career in several Midwestern cities, including Cincinnati and Chicago. In 1854, a year after their wedding, the Harrisons decided to settle in growing Indianapolis. Benjamin had concluded that the capital of Indiana was full of promise for a young attorney.

They arrived with eight hundred dollars in cash (although Benjamin's father promised the couple another five hundred dollars), and were immediately welcomed by Hoosiers who had known William Henry Harrison. One of Benjamin's first law partners was the brother of Lew Wallace, famous author of Ben-Hur.

The Harrisons became the parents of a son, Russell, born in 1854, and a daughter, Mary, born in 1858; a third child died at birth. Years later in the White House, it was Mary's children—Benjamin and Caroline Harrison's grandchildren—who upset the groundskeeper by having a rambunctious goat, "His Whiskers," as a pet. The goat boarded at the horse stables on the White House grounds.

Advancing rapidly in law—and developing a reputation as a stirring courtroom orator—Harrison served as city attorney in 1857. Three years later, he won election to his first statewide office, reporter of the Indiana Supreme Court.

Then came the Civil War. At the request of Governor Oliver P. Morton, Harrison raised the Seventieth Indiana Regiment and drilled the recruits. Called "Little Ben" by his soldiers (standing between five-feet-six and five-feet-seven, Benjamin Harrison was shorter than almost every president except James Madison), Harrison became a fearless leader in battle. His valor under fire at the Resaca conflict and Peachtree Creek battle in Georgia eventually resulted in his commission as brigadier general.

He returned to Indianapolis a war hero. That, along with his courtroom triumphs, led to his nomination as the Republican candidate for governor in 1876. Although he lost, Harrison became the GOP leader in Indiana after Morton's death. In 1881, he was *elected to the U.S. Senate. There, Harrison became known as the "soldier's friend," in part because of his frequent objections to President Grover Cleveland's vetoes of veterans' pension bills. In private life, Harrison's self-indulgences were few—primarily duck hunting and fine cigars.*

When the Republican Party's most prominent figure, James G. Blaine of Maine, declined to seek the presidential nomination in 1888, Harrison captured the nomination as a "soldier-citizen."

John Scott Harrison was upset. The Ohio congressman, a Whig like his famous father, William Henry Harrison, had just learned that his son Benjamin planned to break with the party. Benjamin, a young attorney in Indianapolis, considered the Whigs a dying breed; the antislavery platform of the new Republicans appealed to him. Republicans in the 1850s wanted slavery forbidden in new states such as Texas and California.

According to a letter Benjamin wrote one of his old college professors, the Republicans' bold antislavery stance was the final reason for him to bolt from the Whigs. Fortunately, the rift with his father—who always claimed to hate politics—didn't last long. An eloquent speaker known for captivating juries, Benjamin was doing much to make his father proud. (John Scott Harrison would go down in history as the only American to be the son of one president and the father of another.)

Despite his oratorical and leadership skills and his famous political pedigree, war hero Benjamin Harrison didn't like traveling as a campaigner—and, for different reasons, didn't even do so during either of his presidential bids. In 1888, he conducted an unusual "front porch" campaign, meaning many of his most important speeches were made in Indianapolis. On election day, he trailed his Democratic opponent, Grover Cleveland, in the popular vote, but by capturing New York, Indiana (then considered a "swing state" in presidential elections) and other crucial states, Harrison won the all-important electoral vote.

Immediately confronted as president with pressing economic and social problems, Harrison oversaw passage of a historic law in 1890—the Sherman Anti-Trust Act. It outlawed trusts and monopolies which were killing competition and stifling small businesses and trade. Under Harrison's orders, the U.S. Navy grew dramatically, becoming a two-ocean operation; the merchant marine also became more efficient.

Known as the "Centennial President" because he was elected almost a hundred years after George Washington, Harrison presided over some of the gala celebrations in the nation's capital and across the country. A devout Presbyterian—at age twenty-eight, Harrison had been an elder at First Presbyterian Church in Indianapolis—he appointed all Presbyterians to his Cabinet. Some analysts criticized Harrison's leadership style as too "hands-off"; his own major disappointment as President was his failure to annex Hawaii. Independent-minded, Harrison severed ties to many GOP bosses in big cities.

"When I came into power," Harrison complained later, "I found that the party managers had taken it all to themselves . . . They had sold out every place to pay the election expenses."

A private person and a devoted family man who wore a beard his entire adult life—both when it was in and out of fashion—Benjamin Harrison vowed not to travel during his campaign for re-election in 1892 because of his wife Caroline's illness. Out of respect for his plight, his opponent—again, Cleveland—didn't take to the stump, either.

In what became a dull campaign, Harrison was hurt because of his independence from Republican bosses. Rather than rally the party faithful in big cities, many of the miffed leaders just brooded. With a Populist candidate, James B. Weaver, capturing one million votes—many from farmers upset with falling prices—Harrison lost to Cleveland.

Lonely and crushed by both his wife's death and the loss of the presidency in a two-week period, Harrison returned to Indianapolis alone to live in his empty, Italianate-style home at Twelfth and Delaware streets.

But he rebounded by starting a writing career, publishing *This Country of Ours*, an explanation of how the federal government works. He also revived his legal work and flourished; Harrison's cases included one that led to an appearance before the U.S. Supreme Court and others in which some legal analysts describe his work as "brilliant."

Four years after returning to Indianapolis, Harrison married Caroline's niece, Mary Lord Dimmick, who was the same age as his daughter, Mary. Although the union didn't cause a national scandal, it upset several family members. According to Benjamin Harrison Home curator Jennifer Capps, the family members were upset not because of the couple's age difference, but because of Mary's relationship to the late Caroline.

In any case, the second marriage apparently was a happy one. Benjamin—at age sixty-three—even fathered another child, Elizabeth. She was just four when her father died in 1901.

Caroline Scott Harrison

A gentle woman who loved to paint with watercolors and grow orchids, Caroline Scott Harrison was the only first lady whose husband was elected from Indiana. She also was the second wife of an American president to die in the White House. (Mrs. John Tyler was the first.)

Caroline Scott was born in Ohio in 1832. Her father, John Scott, was a physics teacher at Farmer's College; his students there included Benjamin Harrison. Caroline attended a private girls' school founded by her father. She also studied music and art at the Oxford Female Institute in Ohio.

After the Harrisons settled in Indianapolis, Caroline, like her husband, became an active member of First Presbyterian Church and taught the children there to sing religious songs. While Benjamin fought in the Civil War, she was a leader in local patriotic groups and women's organizations concerned with the welfare of wounded soldiers.

Because of her husband's "front porch" campaign for the White House, he delivered many of his speeches in Indianapolis, thus placing the national spotlight on the family's home at Twelfth and Delaware streets. So many souvenir hunters snatched parts of the Harrisons' white picket fence that Caroline is said to have quipped, "If we don't go to the White House we'll go to the poor house, with all of the repairs we'll have to make."

Even in the White House, Caroline was concerned about the condition of the home. Convinced the structure had fallen into neglect—and knowing her grown children, grandchildren, and her elderly father would be living with them—she said

continued next page

This portrait of Caroline Scott Harrison hangs in the White House near the China Room as a tribute because she started the china collection.

Indiana Historical Society

it was in deplorable shape for a family, and she vowed to "clean up" the White House.

Some "firsts" resulted: The Harrisons became the first family to live in the White House with electricity. It was installed in 1890, two and a half years after Benjamin's election.

Caroline wanted to expand the presidential living quarters (her suggestions weren't approved, though) and, indulging her love of orchids, made use of the greenhouse at the White House. She also started the White House china collection and made the Harrisons the first family to have a decorated Christmas tree in the White House.

Mrs. Harrison was chosen the first president-general of the Daughters of the American Revolution; her name and leadership instantly brought prestige to the new organization. (An Indianapolis chapter is named for her.)

"It has been said that 'the men to make a country are made by self-denial,' " Mrs. Harrison said in her welcoming address to the first Congress of the DAR. "Is it not true that this society, to live and grow and become what we would desire it to be, must be composed of self-denying women?"

Unfortunately, some of Caroline Harrison's accomplishments have been overshadowed by her tragic illness. As she struggled with tuberculosis, her married daughter, Mary, began substituting for her mother at White House functions. Caroline's lingering illness even affected her husband's re-election campaign; because of her condition, Benjamin Harrison announced he would not take to the campaign trail.

She died two weeks before he lost his bid for re-election in 1892. Thousands of Indianapolis residents watched her funeral procession to Crown Hill Cemetery.

Colonel Eli Lilly

Pharmaceutical company founder,
Civil War hero, and civic leader

It's now a $6 billion, Indianapolis-based pharmaceutical company, manufacturer of the antidepressant Prozac and other drugs distributed around the world. But it once was nearly a one-man show, a small business that opened May 10, 1876, on a side street not much more than an alley.

The owner, a thirty-seven-year-old chemist and Civil War hero, was an idea man. Colonel Eli Lilly dreamed of the day his humble chemical business would become a major pharmaceutical company.

After eight months, sales of quinine and other products totaled $4,470. Two years later in 1879, they had increased more than tenfold to $48,000. That year Colonel Lilly was one of twenty-five business leaders who sponsored a society to coordinate all of Indianapolis' charities, a forerunner of the United Way concept. Soon the Colonel was proposing a new, innovative water supply system for his adopted hometown, initiating what became the Indianapolis Water Company. After natural gas was discovered in Indiana, Colonel Lilly promoted the idea of a publicly held company that would provide inexpensive gas to industries and the general public. In 1887, the city welcomed the Consumers Gas Trust Company, a name suggested by the Colonel.

"Col. Eli Lilly during his active career in Indianapolis did not have a superior among his contemporaries either in the practical achievements of business or in the civic pride and energy which have made Indianapolis a great city," Hoosier historian Jacob Piatt Dunn wrote.

Among the Colonel's ideas—which he executed with masterful skill at community organization—was the Commercial Club of Indianapolis in 1890. Lilly was elected the first president of the club, which changed its name in 1912 to the Indianapolis Chamber of Commerce. The Colonel was among twenty-seven energetic, enthusiastic Hoosier business leaders who met downtown in the Bates Hotel to "beat the drum for progress," as a newspaper of the day put it. Membership quickly grew to nine hundred as Indianapolis rapidly changed from a tranquil Midwestern town to a bustling, vibrant city, with the Colonel and his friends taking command of business and cultural life.

"I see a city with sidewalks smooth and even . . . shaded by trees which may be hacked to pieces by any chance butcher, but kept in order by the city forever," Colonel Lilly proclaimed in a speech to the Commercial Club in 1892. "Roadways are smooth . . . alleys kept clean . . . rust is unknown . . . sewage system complete . . . water is pure . . . the sad and weary streetcar mule has made his last run long since and rapid transit is everywhere."

He might have been peering through a time lens at Indianapolis of the 1990s. If he did, the Colonel would instantly realize the integral part that he and his descendents played in making the Hoosier capital what it is.

Eli Lilly became who he was through trying circumstances and extremely hard work.

Courtesy Eli Lilly and Company Archives

Colonel Eli Lilly in 1885

The line of Eli Lillys began in Sweden in the fifteenth century. The Eli later known as the Colonel was born in 1838 in Maryland. His parents, Gustavus and Esther Lilly, were Methodists who opposed alcohol and slavery. The family moved to Kentucky, but eventually settled in Greencastle, Indiana. Eli studied pharmacy at the Good Samaritan Drug Store in Lafayette; he worked in the drug trade in both Lafayette and Greencastle before the Civil War.

In the war, Lilly organized the Eighteenth Indiana Light Artillery Battery, which eventually became part of John T. Wilder's famed Lightning Brigade. During the war, Lilly was captured and imprisoned by the Confederates, but was eventually released. By the end of the war in 1865, Lilly was a colonel.

After the war he stayed in the South on a cotton plantation with his family—his wife, Emily Lemon Lilly, and their young son, Josiah Kirby (later called "J. K."), born in 1861. A drought in Mississippi caused the crop to fail on Lilly's twelve hundred acres. That setback was followed by a tragedy. In 1866, Emily Lilly died of a mosquito-borne disease, probably malaria. She was eight months' pregnant, and the couple's second son was stillborn two hours after her death.

"The bright and joyous bride I led to the altar under your roof is gone!" a grief-stricken Lilly wrote to his family members in Greencastle. "My precious wife Emily, who you too so dearly loved, is no more. I can hardly tell you so it glares at me so on paper, but it's a bitter, bitter truth, that Emily is indeed dead . . .

"We laid her away in a grove of china trees and cedars in the yard not far from my window, where she will repose 'til cold weather will let me bring her to Greencastle."

The Colonel and little J. K. were also stricken with the illness, but recovered. The Colonel eventually also overcame his sorrow. He married his second wife, Maria Cynthia Sloane, in 1869 and decided to resume his chemical and drug trade in the North. He settled in Paris, Illinois, but later concluded that business opportunities were limited there.

So the Colonel and his family came to Indianapolis.

ELI LILLY, CHEMIST. That was it—the only words on a sign Colonel Eli Lilly hung out in 1876 on an alley known as Pearl Street in the warehouse district of Indianapolis. The laboratory on Pearl Street was in a cramped, two-story brick building.

The Colonel started the business with fourteen hundred dollars and three employees. His first full-time salesman—who joined in 1878—was Colonel Lilly's brother, James. Their cousin, Evan Frost Lilly, was the bookkeeper, and Eli's son, J. K., washed bottles and ran errands. The small business made medicine, syrups, sugarcoated pills, and fruit flavors for sale in Indianapolis and surrounding towns. The Colonel had chosen to launch his business in Indianapolis because the city had abundant water resources and railroads, which would be vital for the major drug center that Lilly already was envisioning.

He had other visions, too. Some concerned the bloodbath of the nation's recent past: the Civil War. About 210,000 Hoosiers fought in the traumatic conflict, with more than 24,000 casualties from Indiana. Colonel Lilly was determined to make sure these people should be remembered forever.

Acting on a suggestion of Governor Oliver P. Morton and others, Lilly devoted much of his spare time to lobbying and raising money for a 284-foot limestone monument to the valor of fallen Hoosier soldiers, many of whom had been Colonel Lilly's friends and neighbors.

Construction began in 1888 on the Soldiers and Sailors Monument, which would become the city's permanent symbol; located in the center of the "Mile Square," the monument was completed in 1901 and dedicated the next year. By then the Colonel had died.

In 1893, nearly thirty years after the Civil War, Lilly organized a huge national reunion in Indianapolis to honor the Grand Army of the Republic, veterans of the Union army. By the time of the reunion, Eli Lilly and Co. was flourishing. In the late 1880s, sales topped two hundred thousand dollars, and about a hundred Hoosiers were working for the Colonel. By this time, he had moved the company to a site on McCarty Street in a southside Indianapolis area that was rapidly becoming an industrial and manufacturing center.

The Colonel—a Democrat before the Civil War, but a Republican afterward—turned down dozens of offers to run for local political office. He refused to allow his name to be entered in the governor's race of 1896. Instead, the Colonel concentrated on his dizzying array of civic activities.

He was so consumed by them that by 1890 his pharmaceutical company for all practical purposes was headed by young J. K. Lilly, his son and former errand boy. Since those errand boy days, J. K. had studied at the Philadelphia College of Pharmacy, a top school. Other management responsibilities at Eli Lilly and Co. were assumed by the Colonel's brother James (the first salesman) and cousin Evan (who started as the bookkeeper).

They guided the company through a severe national depression in 1893. Enormous success in the drug industry followed, although the Colonel lived to see only the first decades of success with what became an pharmaceutical empire. He died of cancer in 1898 at age sixty.

The Lilly Family

Eli Lilly and Co. remained a family-managed enterprise for two generations after the death of its enthusiastic founder, the Colonel. His habit of serious and dedicated philanthropy has continued even longer than has family control of the corporation.

After Colonel Eli Lilly's death in 1898, his son J. K formally succeeded him as president. During J. K.'s presidency, which lasted thirty-four years, he initiated changes in marketing and research and greatly expanded the sales force across the United States and, eventually, internationally.

J. K. Lilly lived in a stately home on the northwest side of Indianapolis that now serves as the residence of the chancellor of Indiana University-Purdue University at Indianapolis. He died at age eighty-six in 1948.

J. K.'s son Eli (born in 1885)—who as a boy had been inspired by his grandfather's Civil War stories—followed his father at the helm. Known most of his life as "Mr. Eli," he is credited with applying the techniques of mass production to drug making.

Like his colorful grandfather, Eli pursued diverse civic, cultural and philanthropic interests far beyond the ever-booming company. In particular, he was a history and archaeology buff. Lilly wrote books about prehistoric Indiana and other subjects of historical interest.

In the last forty years of his life, Eli Lilly gave away millions of dollars, both personally and through the Lilly Endowment, which he helped create in 1937. The endowment is a major benefactor for dozens of Hoosier religious, historical and civic organizations as well as schools and universities.

The company shifted from family management in the 1950s, when a veteran employee, Eugene N. Beesley, became president; Eli Lilly continued as chairman of the board. Public shares of stock were offered beginning in 1952.

"Mr. Eli" died in 1977. The value of his estate, according to James H. Madison's biography, was $165,775,000; the company his grandfather founded continues to dominate Indianapolis' near southside and remains a major global force in the pharmaceutical industry.

Courtesy Eli Lilly and Company Archives

A 1946 family portrait shows four generations of Lillys (left to right): Eli, his father, J. K. Sr., and J. K. Jr. Seated, holding Eli II, is J. K. III.

Courtesy the Propylaeum Club

May Wright Sewall

May Wright Sewall

Sufragette, civic leader, educator

Even if she had lived in an era when women leaders were common, indefatigable May Wright Sewall would have stood out.

She made a name for herself in half a dozen fields, achieving international fame as an organizer of more than fifty women's groups and as a peace activist. In Indiana, Sewall founded an impressive number of civic and social groups, many of which remained influential decades after her death. She also taught the classics to a generation of women from Indianapolis' most prominent families.

On top of all that, May Wright Sewall developed a national reputation for her skills as a hostess. "She was the Martha Stewart of her era," says Indianapolis civic leader Nancy Gerard, a Sewall expert. "If she had not been lecturing around the world on suffrage and peace, she would have been in demand as a speaker on domestic affairs, entertaining and graciousness."

Often referred to as "the leader of 500,000 women" because of her key role in so many women's organizations, she was born Mary Eliza Wright in Wisconsin in 1844. Almost always called "May," she was said to have been a precocious child, reading Milton by age seven. After high school, she earned money for college by teaching at schools in Wisconsin. She enrolled in North Western Female College (which was later absorbed into Northwestern University) and taught in Michigan and as far away as Mississippi. She then married and began to make her mark.

"My country is the world. My countrymen are all mankind."

That was May Wright Sewall's favorite saying—and when she spoke of "countrymen" and "mankind," she certainly was including women and girls. Their worldwide advancement—academically, culturally, and socially—became her life's mission. This was in an era when many assumed that women lacked men's intellectual gifts.

Her activism started on a small scale—and in secret. May Wright Sewall began participating in the suffragette movement from its beginnings in Indianapolis in the 1870s. Because of public hostility, Sewall and her fellow suffrage advocates—many of them the wives of the city's most prominent men—met in secret to form the Equal Suffrage Society of Indianapolis.

Her husband, Edwin, who taught alongside his wife at Indianapolis High School (which later became Shortridge High School), had died of tuberculosis in 1875, only one year after the couple had moved to Indianapolis. At that time, May was teaching English and German at the school.

She joined the faculty at the prestigious Indianapolis Classical School for Boys, an elite private school. Its founder, Theodore Lovett Sewall, had modeled the school after East Coast prep schools such as Exeter and Andover academies.

About the time she joined the faculty, May married Sewall. Two years later, in 1882, she persuaded him to open the Classical School for Girls. The couple ran both schools and, at May's insistence, the curriculum was identical, with an emphasis on Latin, Greek, and the classics of world literature. The girls school even had a gymnasium, highly unusual for a young women's academy then. May took pride in hiring all of the teachers personally.

But the Classical School for Girls was only one of her interests. In 1875, she helped found the Indianapolis Woman's Club. She also was a founder and early officer of the Art Association, the predecessor of the Indianapolis Museum of Art.

The Sewall home at Pennsylvania and Walnut streets became legendary for her glittering soirees. Her guest book read like a Who's Who of distinguished Americans as they passed through Indianapolis. In addition to suffrage leaders like Carrie Chapman Catt, her guests included Clara Barton, Jane Addams, actress Ellen Terry, and journalist William Allen White. They scrawled such effusive tributes to Sewall in her guest book that she finally wrote at the beginning:

TAKE WARNING.
Put no more personal compliments in this book! Friends disobeying this command will not be invited again to sleep under our roof.

May was a stocky, sensible woman, and she began wearing her skirts at ankle-length—a shocker in an era when women's skirts swept the ground. Only a woman as prominent and warmly regarded as Sewall could have gotten away with a major breach of late nineteenth century etiquette.

To her relief, she was also blessed with a supportive husband. Theodore Sewall encouraged his wife's activism and took pride in her successes. There was almost no limit to May's energy or her interests. At her initiation, the Indianapolis Propylaeum was built on North Street in 1890 (it moved to North Delaware in 1923). It was the realization of one of May's dreams: a club and building managed by women on behalf of women.

She also founded the Contemporary Club. And when a dignitary from India visited Indianapolis and told poignant stories about poverty-stricken, unwed mothers in his homeland, May—typically—formed a civic group to help. Called the Ramabai Circle, its mission was to liberate Indian women.

Then she went national: She founded the International Council of Women and served two terms as president. For eight years, May also chaired the executive committee of the National Woman Suffrage Associations; and for most of the 1890s, she served as president of the National Council of Women of the United States.

Meanwhile, in Indianapolis, she presided over a meeting at the Grand Opera House that appointed delegates to attend state political conventions across the country. Their mission was to convince lawmakers to give women the vote.

In the midst of all this, May suffered a heartbreaking loss. In 1895, Theodore died of tuberculosis, as had May's first husband, Edwin. Theodore had closed the Classical School for Boys six years earlier, but May was determined to keep the girls' school going. She didn't shut it down until 1907, when financial difficulties necessitated it; May never was known as an outstanding bookkeeper. (One of her former faculty members in 1902 went on to start Tudor Hall, now part of Park Tudor School, a prestigious private school attended by generations of Indianapolis girls. Ironically, its success contributed to the closing of the girls school.)

Also in 1907 May moved from Indianapolis to New England. Her international speaking engagements and organizing trips—mostly championing women's causes and the peace movement—were easier to handle if she was based on the East Coast.

May traveled around Europe, where women greeted her as a remarkable figure. She rallied women from Scotland to the Netherlands and spoke about peace in the enchanting Eastern European city of Prague, a trip that May called "the most beautiful experience of my life."

President William McKinley chose Sewall as a delegate to a women's meeting in Paris. She also was president of the International Conference of Women Workers to Promote Permanent Peace, a national conference in San Francisco.

But her health began to falter. In 1919, May moved back to Indianapolis, her first love among cities.

Near the time of her death, she decided to go public with a passion that she had kept private for years: her belief in spiritualism. She convinced the Indianapolis-based Bobbs-Merrill Company in 1920 to publish her book on spiritualism, *Neither Dead Nor Sleeping*, in which she described psychic experiences and conversations with her beloved Theodore.

May persuaded one of her Hoosier literary friends, Booth Tarkington, to write the book's extensive introduction. He did so because of his enormous respect for May—but Tarkington carefully avoided endorsing her beliefs on spiritualism.

Soon after the book's publication, May Wright Sewall died in Indianapolis. Sadly, the activist who had spent her life advancing the causes of women—and who had served as president of so many organizations—never cast a ballot in an American presidential election. She died in 1920, a few months before women voted in national elections for the first time.

A portrait of T. C. Steel by a fellow Hoosier artist, Wayman Adams. This was probably painted in 1913.

T. C. Steele

Painter

"The two great qualities that an artist must possess and that are essentially necessary to all who pass the point of mediocrity are first an innate and deep love of the beautiful. Secondly, mechanical skill."

So wrote the most famous and esteemed member of a distinguished group of five American impressionist painters. Known as the "Hoosier Group," the five artists developed a distinctive style of painting that has left an indelible mark on American art. The Hoosier Group included William Forsyth (1854–1935), J. Ottis Adams (1851–1927), Richard B. Gruelle (1851–1914), and Otto Stark (1859–1926).

By far the most famous, however, is the fifth member of the group that coalesced during the "Golden Age" of Hoosier painters: Theodore Clement Steele.

Although acclaimed during his lifetime as a supremely talented artist—many of Indiana's most prominent citizens, including Steele's pal James Whitcomb Riley, sat for T. C. Steele portraits—his lasting legacy comes primarily from the way he captured the fleeting beauty of nature, particularly idyllic Brown County, in landscape paintings.

Born in 1847 in a log house near Gosport, Steele was the son of a saddlemaker-farmer and his wife, a nature lover. At age four, Theodore went with his family from Gosport to Waveland (population six hundred) in west central Indiana. The cultural focus of the town was the Waveland Collegiate Institute, a prep school for the college-bound. At the academy, Steele indulged his passion for art after being given a box of cast-off paints. By age thirteen in 1860, he was teaching drawing to fellow students.

Following graduation, Steele sought portrait work. In 1870 he married Mary Elizabeth "Libbie" Lakin, a Rushville native who frequently sang with Steele for the enjoyment of friends. The sensitive, music-loving couple lived in Battle Creek, Michigan, for three years while Steele honed his portrait-painting talents. They soon became the parents of two children: a son, Rembrandt Theodore Steele, known as Brandt; and a daughter Margaret, nicknamed Daisy.

The family returned to Indiana and eventually settled in Indianapolis. Steele began painting portraits of the city's elite. Sensing Steele's talent, wealthy Hoosier benefactors, including Herman Lieber and members of the Fletcher family of Indianapolis, offered to send the painter and his family to study with master portraitists in Munich, Germany, for two years. (By then, a third Steele child, son Shirley Lakin, had been born.)

Three other members of the Hoosier Group—Adams, Forsyth, and Stark—also were studying in Europe about the same time. The Steeles, who enjoyed Munich, ended up staying for five years.

Returning to Indianapolis in 1885, the family settled in a New Orleans-style house with lush gardens and vines known as Tinker Place. Between commissioned portraits, Steele began painting his yard. He also opened an art school; among his students was a young fiction writer named Booth Tarkington.

Then came the most traumatic event in Steele's life—the death from tuberculosis of his wife and muse Libbie, whom he often called "darling Bessie." Steele told his children, "I owe everything to your mother. It was she who made a landscape painter of me, instead of a portrait painter . . . Your Mother taught me first to see with her eyes and then through my own."

Bereft, T. C. Steele decided to dramatically overhaul his lifestyle . . .

What had gotten into him?

His Indianapolis friends, even fellow artists, were stunned and alarmed by T. C. Steele's behavior in 1907.

The renowned painter, a grief-stricken widower for eight years, was buying more than two hundred heavily wooded acres in Brown County. It might as well have been Mars. Brown County was settled by subsistence farmers, clannish and uneducated. With minimal, rugged dirt roads, Brown County also was isolated; even a trip to Bloomington, twelve miles away, took an entire day.

Why would a prominent portraitist, at age sixty, buy land there?

Well, T. C. Steele not only purchased the hilly Brown County property, he began building a studio home on it. Then he married again—an Indianapolis woman, Selma Neubacher, who was twenty-three years younger than Steele. On the day of their August wedding or the next day, she got her first look at her new home.

Known as "The House of the Singing Winds," the bungalow was accessible only by steep, muddy roads. Steele's priorities in designing the house were clear; the most spacious room, a parlor-living room that consumed nearly two-thirds of the bungalow, doubled as his studio. The kitchen for Selma was small in comparison and chimney-less, which necessitated a winding, overhead stovepipe—and guaranteed sweltering summers as she prepared her husband's meals.

Not only were Steele's Indianapolis friends perplexed by his drastic lifestyle change, the painter's new neighbors in Brown County hardly were welcoming. They were deeply suspicious of the "city artist" and his refined wife. Who was this bearded man who sat around painting all day? And why was his wife planting useless flowers? Why weren't they toiling over crops?

The Brown County residents even initially balked at requests from the Steeles to have their adolescent daughters work as housekeeper-helpmates for Selma. They were afraid their children would get "airs" if they associated with the artist and his wife.

Writing years later about her first impressions of Brown County, Selma recalled:

At the time conditions seemed incredible. Were we not but a few miles removed from a university center? And yet there were obvious reasons why this countryside should have been left untouched by the progress of the world outside. Its people were shut in by bad roads a large part of the year. Travel was slow and very difficult. Thus, but few had contact outside their hills . . . There was no enforcement of compulsory school attendance. Very many were illiterate. Intermarriage had been going on a long time. Child marriages were frequent.

Rising to a challenge, the Steeles set about winning over their neighbors. Captivated by Brown County's beauty, T. C. Steele was determined to put down roots in the rustic area and paint its wonders. He loved the view of Brown County's vistas from his hilltop porches and garden; he could see for twenty miles.

The Steeles intrigued their neighbors by inviting them to "The House of the Singing Winds" to enjoy a novelty for Brown County—"ready-made music," to use the locals' phrase. The Steeles owned a Victrola as well as a player piano. Selma also explained to her neighbors that there was a practical side to the flower gardens that had become her passion, much as landscape painting had become her husband's. After she planted flower beds, her husband painted the blooms, sold his artwork and earned money; nodding, the neighbors said they understood the value of that.

Much as the Steeles loved Brown County, even they didn't want to struggle through winters at The House of the Singing Winds. For several years, the couple returned for the cold months to Indianapolis, where they remained socially and culturally active. In Brown County, the Steeles hired workers to bring up their drinking water from a community well in the nearest town, Belmont. The Steeles began expanding their Brown County bungalow and built guest cottages so their city and university friends could visit. Eventually, they lived in southern Indiana year-round, wintering in Bloomington.

As roads improved, Steele's relationship with Indiana University flourished. He became an artist-in-residence at the university, which gave him a studio on campus. (Steele also built his dream studio—a spacious, open, barn-like structure—next to The House of the Singing Winds.) The famous artist often could be seen sitting on a stool around campus with his easel, canvas and paints.

As the first artist to settle in Brown County, Steele was a pioneer in several ways and made the area famous for its natural beauty. A hard-working, disciplined artist, he produced about fifteen hundred paintings during his lifetime. He died in his beloved House of the Singing Winds in 1926. By then, Selma had long been won over by Brown County's charms; the "city girl" chose to live in the house until her own death nearly twenty years later in 1945. The house is now part of the T. C. Steele State Historic Site.

Above the fireplace in The House of the Singing Winds, Steele had this motto inscribed:

Every morning I take off my hat to the Beauty of the World.

James Whitcomb Riley

James Whitcomb Riley

Poet

Swimmin' holes, jack-o'-lanterns, bullfrogs, bonnets and simple pleasures of carefree childhood—these are the topics immortalized and sentimentalized by the man known as the "Hoosier Poet" or the "Poet of the People." James Whitcomb Riley was a homegrown, international celebrity in an era long before satellite dishes, videos, People *magazine and even sound movies.*

The Hoosier Poet didn't captivate the masses just because he had a way with the written word. Almost as significantly, Riley was a spellbinding entertainer, a touring performer who overcame severe stage fright. He became wealthy thanks to his crowd-pleasing storytelling and poetry readings on both sides of the Atlantic.

The slender, puckish man hailed by Mark Twain as one of the stage's best entertainers was born in Greenfield, Indiana, in 1849. His father, attorney Reuben Riley, was Greenfield's first mayor; his mother, Elizabeth, occasionally wrote poems published in a Hancock County newspaper. They named their son after James Whitcomb, one of Indiana's first governors.

Known as "Jim," young Riley was eleven when his father left to serve as a captain in the Civil War. Reuben Riley survived the conflict, but returned with injuries that affected his arm and hearing. He resumed his law practice and was disappointed that his son displayed no aptitude for the law. A lover of music, theater and art as well as the outdoors, Jim Riley was a gifted mimic though an indifferent student. His father found him a job as a Hancock County sign painter.

A sort of young drifter, Jim Riley wrote jingles and verse. Eventually he joined the staff of a newspaper in Anderson. Riley began drawing crowds to his poetry readings; he moved to Indianapolis and became "resident poet" for the Indianapolis Journal *newspaper. Riley's first book of poems,* The Old Swimmin' Hole and 'Leven More Poems, *was published n 1883. A star was born. A major national publisher based in Indianapolis, eventually known as the Bobbs-Merrill Company, would publish about ninety of his books.*

Often written in rural, Midwestern dialect, Riley's poems featured several characters that became favorites for generations, including the "Raggedy Man" and "Little Orphant Annie." Touring constantly to give recitals, Riley didn't own the house in which he lived. Instead, he was a boarder—a permanent "paying guest"—at the home of friends who lived in the Lockerbie neighborhood of Indianapolis. Meanwhile, his framed poems began adorning parlors across the country.

By the time he died in 1916, Riley had written more than a thousand poems. The "Children's Poet" was a lifelong bachelor, but after his death several friends established the Riley Hospital for Children in Indianapolis as a tribute.

It was almost like the cavalry coming to the rescue. But in this case the cavalry was a medicine wagon that rolled into Greenfield in May 1872. In need of rescue was an aimless, twenty-two-year-old sign painter named James Whitcomb Riley. His father was exasperated with the unfocused young man; Jim's adored mother had died suddenly two years earlier, and his grief was still sharp.

But the arrival of "Doc" McCrillus' traveling medicine wagon perked him up. Talking his way into a job, Riley painted signs advertising Doc's potions, lotions and other remedies. A talented mimic and storyteller, Riley also entertained the crowds that gathered at the wagon as Doc sold his "cures." In what would be nearly a lifelong way of existence, Riley became a wanderer, accompanying Doc as a sort of assistant/entertainer/painter.

He left the medicine show to paint advertisements on fences and barns across Indiana, and between jobs, he recited his poems and yarns at Hoosier churches and schools. His writing landed him a job on the *Anderson Democrat* newspaper in 1877.

Six months later he was unemployed—fired for a hoax that brought him national notoriety. Frustrated by his inability to get his work published on the East Coast, Riley created a poem he identified as a long-lost work of the legendary Edgar Allan Poe. He wanted to prove that literary critics would praise anything attributed to a famous person.

Sure enough, the "Poe poem" was published across the country by excited newspaper editors—who were outraged when Riley 'fessed up to the fraud. Disgraced, he returned to Greenfield. But he continued to entertain audiences with his poetry and stories, slowly reaping regional fame. He was touring New England as early as 1882.

The invitation that resulted in national recognition came in 1887. Beckoned to New York to perform among a gathering of literary lions, Riley dazzled the audience by reciting his works, including a poem that would become one of his most famous—"When the Frost is on the Punkin." During the two days of his performances, his audiences choked back tears, howled with glee, and were swept through about every emotion in between.

> *When the frost is on the punkin and the fodder's in the shock,*
> *And you hear the kyouck and gobble of the struttin' turkey-cock,*
> *And the clackin' of the guineys, and the cluckin' of the hens,*
> *And the rooster's hallylooyer as he tiptoes on the fence;*
> *O, it's then's the times a feller is a-feelin' at his best,*
> *With the risin' sun to greet him from a night of peaceful rest,*
> *As he leaves the house, bareheaded, and goes out to feed the stock,*
> *When the frost is on the punkin and the fodder's in the shock.*

Admirers at the New York gatherings included Bill Nye, a well-established wit and entertainer. The two began a joint tour and were signed by a booking agent about a year later. The wandering urge now had a legitimate outlet; Riley, who had toured earlier, took to the road with renewed seriousness.

Continuing his prolific output of poems, the Hoosier Poet achieved fame and stayed famous for the rest of his life. Universities such as Yale and Penn awarded him honorary degrees; so did Indiana University and Wabash College. He was invited to the White House by Mrs. Grover Cleveland. Rudyard Kipling dedicated a poem to him.

Much of Riley's appeal involved his use of dialect—unvarnished, rural American speech—and his genius at recognizing the public's craving for rural nostalgia at a time when America rapidly was becoming urban.

Elegant, witty and cultivated, Riley enjoyed dining at Indianapolis' finest restaurants. His cronies included such other legendary Hoosiers as Carl Fisher, a founder of the Indianapolis Motor Speedway, and union organizer Eugene V. Debs. But although he reaped wealth and fame, Riley struggled with depression and alcoholism. Hoosiers from Richmond and Greenfield to Terre Haute whispered about his drinking. Although many people denounced drinking as immoral, few in those days regarded alcoholism as a disease that required treatment.

Riley wrote admiringly to women, but did not marry. Often those closest to him realized he was lonely and ill at heart.

In any case, tales about Riley's drinking didn't lessen the public's affection for him. Neither did critical barbs about the "bathos" and corn of Riley's poems. He was beloved as "the people's poet," someone who celebrated village life, appreciated simple virtues and wasn't afraid of sentimentality. His recitals packed in audiences everywhere, but nowhere more than in Indiana. During a performance in Greenfield—Riley's first performance in his hometown in fifteen years—so many people crammed into the Masonic Hall that old-timers worried the historic building might collapse, particularly if audience members stamped their feet, roared and cheered as was typical at a Riley recital.

In the Lockerbie neighborhood, Riley lived with a family of Indianapolis civic leaders, kept a poodle as a pet, and bought his cigars at a general store across the street.

"He'd also buy Kis-Me chewing gum for us kids," Agnes Search Bridgford, the daughter of the store's owner, recalled in a 1998 interview when she was ninety-two. "The gum was wrapped in brightly colored tissue paper.

"Mr. Riley would buy the gum from my father, then he would drop it on the grassy knoll near Lockerbie Street and tell us children, 'That gum grows there, you know.' "

She laughed and dismissed the notion with a wave of her hand. "Of course, we knew gum didn't grow on the grass, but it tickled us to hear Mr. Riley say it. Sometimes he even dropped Lincoln pennies on the ground for us."

Although the celebrated poet maintained an active social life and a series of recitals in his final years, he became feeble and suffered a series of strokes.

"I remember noticing that curious people would rush out and gather around the home to watch Mr. Riley be helped in and out of cars," Mrs. Bridgford recalled. "As an adult, you realize how cruel that is—to stare at an older famous person just to see how infirm he is."

On the poet's sixty-sixth birthday in 1915, President Woodrow Wilson paid tribute to "the many pleasures Riley has given me, along with the rest of the great body of readers of English." Nine months later, Riley died in his sleep at the Lockerbie house. Thirty-five thousand mourners filed past his casket, which lay in state in the rotunda of the Indiana Statehouse.

Even contemporary critics concede that few American poets ever have been as celebrated as Riley. If he had done nothing else, the Hoosier introduced poetry to thousands of people who otherwise never would have read verse.

Still, it's a shame the vagabond bard never really had a contented home life of his own.

Eugene V. Debs

Eugene V. Debs

Socialist and labor leader

He ran for president five times—and received the most votes (more than nine hundred thousand in 1920) while in federal prison. In fact, Eugene V. Debs' campaign played up his plight, with buttons featuring his convict number (9653) and his face beside bars.

This was particularly unusual because he was a Socialist, a member of a party usually scorned by mainstream Americans in the post-World War I era. Most citizens equated Socialists with the Communists who had recently taken over Russia. Debs was a "radical," a man from the fringes, in an era when most Hoosiers were becoming suspicious and inward-looking.

A founder and preeminent personality in the Socialist Party in the United States and the organizer of the American Railway Union, the first industrial union in the country, Debs was born in Terre Haute in 1855. His father, a French immigrant, operated a general store and was awarded the coveted French Legion of Honor for his success in selling French merchandise to Midwesterners. Jean Daniel Debs read Voltaire and Goethe to his son and even chose his middle name, Victor, as a tribute to Victor Hugo.

Despite the elder Debs' literary interests and moderate financial success, times were tough. Eugene, one of ten children, quit school at fourteen to take a succession of railroad jobs. He was a sign painter, a job that some accounts say left him with gnarled hands because of the corrosive chemicals used in the era to make and strip paint. Debs then was promoted to a fireman for the railroad.

He first achieved fame for—and served his first prison term in connection with— his role in organizing the Pullman strike of 1894. Although his second prison term was a sentence of ten years, Debs was freed after two and a half years on Christmas Day 1921. He was freed by Warren G. Harding, who had been his opponent in that 1920 presidential race, in part because Debs by then was over sixty-five. A pacifist, he had been imprisoned under a wartime espionage law for speaking out against American involvement in World War I. Debs' health never fully recovered from the second prison term. He died at a sanitarium near Elmhurst, Illinois, in 1926.

"How can a labor leader, a champion of the toiling class, live in such a plush home?"

Eugene Victor Debs had to answer that question many times from his fellow Terre Haute residents. It's no wonder. Sporting a fireplace with cobalt blue tiles, Tiffany lamps and other French furnishings from the general store owned by Debs' father, the Victorian home cost forty-five hundred dollars to build in 1890. The average working man made six hundred dollars that year.

Debs usually defended himself by saying that his wife, Katherine, wanted a comfortable home—and deserved one because she often was alone in it while her husband crisscrossed the country with his labor organizing and Socialist Party activities. In any case, the posh home, now a museum operated by the Eugene V. Debs Foundation, was built primarily with money inherited from Katherine's aunt.

Although many didn't agree with Debs' leftist politics, Terre Haute residents generally treated him with affection. Known around the city as "a sucker for a hard-luck story," Debs was sincerely generous, often arriving home with empty pockets because he had given away all of his money to vagrants, immigrants, children or others he had encountered on the way.

A natty dresser, Debs counted among his friends such men of prominence as James Whitcomb Riley (who lauds Debs in a poem entitled "Regardin' Terry Hut"), poet Carl Sandburg, and wealthy Terre Haute businessman Herman Hulman, a neighbor whose conservative, capitalistic politics were the opposite of Debs' views. Before he founded the Socialist Party, Debs twice was elected city clerk of Terre Haute as a Democrat and served a term in the Indiana General Assembly.

Many of his ideas, radical at the time, became mainstream decades later. In an era when twelve-hour workdays and six-day workweeks were the norm, Debs advocated shorter workweeks, pension plans, workmen's compensation, sick leave and women's suffrage.

Tall, gaunt and balding by age thirty, Eugene Debs resembled his brother, Theodore, who nearly always was at his side and served as his secretary. A whiskey lover, Debs also frequently was seen with Riley, who visited so often that one bedroom in the Debs home still is known as "the Riley room."

But Debs worked as hard as he played. He founded the American Railway Union in 1893; within a year it had 150,000 members. Pullman railway car employees affiliated with the ARU; when they struck in 1894, Debs helped them. Arrested on conspiracy charges, he was jailed for six months for contempt of court—despite the efforts of one of the country's most famous defense attorneys, Clarence Darrow.

During his imprisonment in an Illinois jail, Debs completely converted to Socialism, although he probably had been moving toward it for years. Also during his imprisonment, his reputation—and legend—began to mount.

"Debs! Debs! Debs!" thousands of supporters shouted as they met him on the day he was freed. At least publicly, Debs always tried to discourage personal deification.

"If you are looking for a Moses to lead you out of this capitalist wilderness, you will stay right where you are," he said in one speech. "I would not lead you into this promised land if I could, because if I could lead you in, someone else would lead you out."

Yet he allowed himself to be nominated for President five times by his Socialist Party, and he clearly thrived on the lecture circuit, where he was a big hit.

But there was a sadness to Debs' final years—and not just because of his second prison term and his declining health. Debs frequently checked into a sanitarium in Terre Haute to rebuild his strength. In ill health, he died at Lindlahr Sanitarium near Chicago in 1926. Although always anticapitalist, Debs lived long enough to become disillusioned by the Russian revolution of 1918.

"Russia," he wrote, "has . . . actually swapped dictators . . . There is not a single one of the actual leaders of the Russian Soviet Government who is a proletarian."

Gene Stratton-Porter

Novelist, naturalist, photographer

When she was born, her parents named her Geneva Grace Stratton. During an era when many women stayed at home, the Hoosier who achieved fame as Gene Stratton-Porter was a best-selling novelist, a gifted wildlife photographer and a pioneering environmentalist before the term was coined.

She was born in 1863, the twelfth child in a Wabash County farm family. Her passion for nature was evident early. In Honing with the Birds, Stratton-Porter wrote that she nursed a wounded chicken hawk when she was a small girl.

"In one season, when under ten years of age, I located sixty nests, and I dropped food into the open beaks in every one of them," Stratton-Porter recalled in What I Have Done with Birds. "Soon the old birds became so accustomed to me, and so convinced of my good intentions, that they would alight on my head and shoulders in a last hop to reach their nests with the food they had brought. Playing with the birds was my idea of fun. Pets were my sort of dolls."

Because her mother contracted typhoid fever during Gene's childhood and never fully recovered, she was raised primarily by her father, a farmer and part-time preacher. He taught her that plants and animals were God's gifts and, as such, deserved respect. When she was eleven, the family moved to Wabash. Gene balked at the regimentation of Wabash High School, dropping out shortly before graduation.

Two years later, she visited Sylvan Lake near Rome City, a popular resort. (Later, the lakeside would become the site of Stratton-Porter's second famous Limberlost Cabin.) There she was seen from afar by Charles Dorwin Porter, a druggist from Adams County who was vacationing. He obtained her address from a third party and the couple began a correspondence. In one of Gene's letters to Charles, she denounced "confining" marriages. Still, the couple wed in 1886, but Gene's independent streak persisted.

"The fever to write had raged within Mother until it became a compelling influence and dominated her whole life," Stratton-Porter's daughter and only child, Jeannette Porter Meehan, recalled years later in Lady of the Limberlost (1928). "After I was old enough to go to school, Mother spent many secret hours with her pen."

The family settled in Geneva, where Charles operated a lucrative drugstore. Stratton-Porter called their home a "cabin"—her first Limberlost Cabin—although it was a spacious, two-story house reputed to be the most expensive in town. Less than a mile away was an uncharted wilderness, the vast, foreboding Limberlost Swamp. Its colorful birds, from cardinals and blue jays to red-tailed hawks and great owls, were a magnet to Stratton-Porter, who stomped through the marshlands, unbroken forest and murky waters. Soon her nature photographs were published in outdoor magazines. In 1901, she published her first short story, "Laddie, The Princess and the Pie."

Shortly before her fortieth birthday, the Indianapolis-based Bobbs-Merrill Company published her book The Song of the Cardinal (1903). Inspired by an incident in which Stratton-Porter discovered the corpse of a cardinal that had been shot in target practice, the plot concerns a lovesick redbird that lives near Limberlost and is stalked by a hunter.

Limberlost also was the setting for her next book, Freckles (1904), about a one-

Gene Stratton-Porter around 1920. (Below) One of Stratton-Porter's famous bird photos, taken around 1910.

Both photos from the collection of the Indiana State Museum and Historical Sites

handed orphan who protects the trees from thieves. A commercial triumph, Freckles *was followed by other best-sellers, including* A Girl of the Limberlost *(1909) and* Laddie *(1913). Although critics dismissed her writing as sentimental and idealized, Stratton-Porter's novels and nature books—the latter illustrated with her own photographs—were as popular overseas as in America.*

Her life was far from carefree, though. Stratton-Porter was outraged by the slow, steady destruction of Limberlost Swamp by lumbermen and farmers. In 1912, she bought a hundred and twenty acres on Sylvan Lake and began work on a new Limberlost Cabin, a log cabin with a library and a darkroom for her photography. She settled in "Limberlost North" about three years later. Stratton-Porter and a crew planted six, one-acre flower beds resulting in a total of three thousand plants, trees, shrubs and vines. But her fame drew gawkers to the estate, which she called Wildflower Woods, even though Stratton-Porter put up "No Admittance" signs.

Although Stratton-Porter had intended to spend the rest of her days at her second Limberlost Cabin (also known as the cabin in Wildflower Woods), the hard physical work and exposure to the outdoors took their toll. In 1918 an exhausted Stratton-Porter, fifty-four, checked herself into a clinic in New York; the next year she traveled to Southern California to recuperate in a sunny climate. Captivated by the desert, mountains and ocean, Stratton-Porter eventually settled in Los Angeles. Her husband remained in Indiana, visiting Gene periodically.

Meanwhile, Stratton-Porter began construction of a retreat on scenic, rugged Catalina Island. She also formed a movie production company. The film company and another house being built in Bel Air were underway when she was killed in 1924 in an automobile accident, her limousine colliding with a streetcar in Los Angeles.

Townsfolk in the 1890s thought her mother was a bit peculiar, but little Jeannette Porter loved her—and was determined to buy her the best Christmas gift ever.

The eight-year-old girl paid ten dollars for her mother's first camera. Beaming, Jeannette knew this would be the perfect gift. Several months earlier, *Recreation* magazine had accepted an article submitted by Geneva, Indiana, resident Gene Stratton-Porter. But the magazine and the writer were disagreeing over illustrations to accompany the piece.

"The editors who had accepted my work began to send me drawings of mounted birds, articulated with wire, stuffed with excelsior, and posed by men," Stratton-Porter recalled years later. "Those pictures repelled me. I was horrified."

Little Jeannette's gift of the camera—a four-by-five Vive—eventually solved the illustration dilemma. Stratton-Porter practiced with the camera for four years; in February of 1900, *Recreation* published her first article. Later, when Stratton-Porter became more serious about photographing wildlife and needed more sophisticated equipment, she sold some old family jewels to buy a better camera.

Selling heirlooms was exactly the kind of behavior that made her the subject of so much town gossip. Most turn-of-the-century women—particularly those who, like Gene, were the wives of prosperous businessmen—were appalled at the notion of plunging into dark, dangerous swamps and backwoods, armed with a gun for protection against dangerous snakes. Not spirited Stratton-Porter. Toting a camera and a gun, she regularly explored and photographed Limberlost Swamp, a mucky, smelly wilderness full of mosquitoes, muskrats, frogs, gnats, owls, and venomous snakes.

She described Limberlost activity in *Freckles* (1904), her first best-selling novel:

A prowling wildcat missed its catch and screamed with rage. A lost fox bayed incessantly for its mate.

The hair on the back of Freckles' neck rose like bristles, and his knees wavered under him. He could not see if the dreaded snakes were on the trail, nor, in the pandemonium, hear the rattle for which McLean had cautioned him to listen. He stood rooted to the ground in an agony of fear.

For her pioneering nature photography, Stratton-Porter primarily used glass plates—which required tremendous skill and precise timing. "I spent over a thousand dollars in equipment," she wrote in *Honing with the Birds*. "All of the money accumulated from nature articles and a few stories went to pay for four cameras, each adapted to a different brand of outdoor work, also a small wagonload of field paraphernalia . . .

"I used the kitchen sink for plate and print washing . . . my dark room was the family bath, my washing tanks the turkey and meat platters in the kitchen sink."

Shrugging off her neighbors' disapproval and ignoring rigid societal expectations for the behavior of middle-aged women, Stratton-Porter indulged her passion for wildlife with more abandon every year. The second Limberlost Cabin was a custom-designed home on Sylvan Lake near Rome City. As with her first cabin, Stratton-Porter even turned her family's living quarters into a natural observation laboratory. Jeannette described the first Limberlost Cabin this way:

Almost any place in our house you might find a glass turned down over a little patch of moth eggs on a rug to protect them; . . . a wounded bird, which was being doctored, perched almost anywhere; . . . several different size boxes containing baby caterpillars just hatched, feeding on the particular kind of leaves that they ate; . . . and newly emerged moths and butterflies flying through the house and feeding on the flowers in the conservatory.

Flowers and ferns on the estate surrounding the second Limberlost Cabin included transplanted orchids, arrowhead lilies, and rosemary.

In addition to her writing, photography and outdoor projects, Stratton-Porter became a political crusader. She was outraged in 1917 when the Indiana General Assembly passed a law that allowed for drainage of state-owned swampland in Noble and Lagrange counties. She saw the legislation as a direct threat to her beloved wetlands. As a result of a ferocious battle waged by Stratton-Porter and other Hoosiers, the legislation was repealed in a special session of the General Assembly in 1920.

Political opponents and town gossips weren't Stratton-Porter's only critics. Literary reviewers often denounced her books as sugary. Still, most of the works were wildly popular. They sold more than ten million copies during Stratton-Porter's lifetime and brought her a substantial income, extremely rare for a woman of her era.

And even her critics conceded that Stratton-Porter galvanized thousands of Americans. She inspired them to explore and appreciate the outdoors, laying the groundwork for the environmentalists of future generations.

Madam Walker

Businesswoman, self-made millionaire

Hers is one of the most remarkable success stories in American history, not just Hoosier folklore. Born to ex-slaves on a cotton plantation in Louisiana, Madam C. J. Walker started out as a poor, orphaned washerwoman and ended up probably the nation's first black woman millionaire. "I got myself a start by giving myself a start," she told the New York Times *magazine in 1917.*

Not only did Madam Walker's thriving business on the west side Indianapolis result in jobs and economic independence for thousands of African Americans; it created a revolution in black hair care.

The entrepreneur who would become internationally famous as "Madam Walker" was born Sarah Breedlove on a cotton plantation near Delta, Louisiana, in 1867. She was orphaned at age six and married at fourteen. By twenty, she was a widow with a two-year-old daughter to support.

Yet this enterprising, innovative woman didn't just reap astounding business success. She was truly a trailblazer in an era of oppressive race relations—indeed, Madam Walker was a philanthropist and a political activist. In Black Women in America, *editor Darlene Clark Hine describes a scene at the 1912 National Negro Business League convention. Even though league founder Booker T. Washington refused her request to be included on the program, Madam Walker rose on the last day of the gathering and defiantly addressed the delegates with these words, among others:*

I am a woman who came from the cotton fields of the South. I was promoted from there to the washtub. Then I was promoted to the cook kitchen, and from there I promoted myself into the business of manufacturing hair goods and preparations . . . I have built my own factory on my own ground.

Her speech was so rousing that Madam Walker was invited back the next year as a keynote speaker. By then, she was crisscrossing the country as a lecturer and business promoter; she also traveled to Jamaica, Cuba, Haiti, Costa Rica and Panama to expand the market for her products. Madam Walker hired former maids, housewives, schoolteachers, and farm workers—more than twenty-thousand in all—to fill jobs at every level of her enterprise, from factory worker to sales agent.

In 1916 Madam Walker moved to New York City, turning over the day-to-day management of the Indianapolis manufacturing operation to three staff members. She lived on the East Coast for only three years before losing a long struggle with high blood pressure. While introducing a new line of products in St. Louis in 1919, Madam Walker became ill and was rushed by private train car to New York, where she died.

Her will, which she reworked in the final weeks of her life, left thousands of dollars to black colleges, civic organizations, YMCAs, YWCAs and the Alpha Home for the Aged in Indianapolis. She also had planned the Walker Building and Walker Theatre on

Madam Walker, a major donor to the YMCA, with other Indianapolis civic leaders at the dedication of the Senate Avenue YMCA in July 1913.

Indiana Avenue in Indianapolis. Completed nine years after her death, they are listed on the National Register of Historic Places.

At her death, Madam Walker was generally considered to be the wealthiest black woman in America,

She was the first member of her family to be born free.

But life on a Louisiana cotton plantation named Grand View was hardly a breeze for little Sarah Breedlove. Her parents, Owen and Minerva Breedlove, sharecroppers at Grand View, died in 1874 when Sarah was just six. Orphaned, Sarah and her two older siblings tried to work the land, but they were too young. To make matters worse, the cotton crop failed in 1878 and a yellow fever epidemic struck. Now ten, Sarah moved with her older sister, Louvenia, across the Mississippi River to Vicksburg.

To support themselves, the girls took in laundry from white families and worked as domestics. Laundry work at the time was almost as backbreaking as sharecropping; dirty clothes were washed in large tubs and beaten with wooden sticks and washboards to pound soil out of the fabric. As author Noliwe M. Rooks notes in *Hair Raising: Beauty, Culture and African-American Women*, by the time Sarah was fourteen, she "had experienced two of the primary occupations allowed to working-class African-American women—laundress and fieldhand."

Much to Sarah's distress, Louvenia married a man whom Sarah recalled years later as "cruel and contemptuous." Partially to get away from her new brother-in-law, Sarah got married at age fourteen to a Vicksburg laborer named Moses McWilliams. In 1885 when she was seventeen, Sarah gave birth to a daughter, Lelia, who would later be known as A'Lelia Walker. The girl was just two years old when her father was killed in an accident.

What was Sarah, a twenty-year-old widow and single mother, to do?

Told there were jobs for laundresses upriver in St. Louis—and that wages were higher there than in Mississippi—Sarah headed north. For the next seventeen years, she eked out a living as a laundress and became an active member of St. Paul African Methodist Episcopal Church in St. Louis. Sarah may have worked briefly in 1904 as a sales agent of hair care products for the Poro Company, founded by Annie Turnbo Pope Malone. (Some historians insist that Malone, not Madam Walker, was the first black American woman to achieve millionaire status.)

In any case, a horrified Sarah noticed that some of her hair was falling out due to an ailment called alopecia that was common among black women of the era because of poor diet, damaging hair care treatments and stress. Sarah Breedlove decided to develop her own line of hair care products.

With a mere dollar and a half in savings in July 1905, Sarah and Lelia moved to Denver. Sarah worked briefly as a cook for a pharmacist and may have discussed her hair care formula with him. She began selling her products door-to-door and married Charles Joseph Walker, a newspaper sales agent.

Adopting his surname, she developed such hair care products as Vegetable Shampoo and a product that contained medication to combat dandruff. Although Madam Walker often is credited with inventing the "hot comb" or steel straightening comb, she probably converted metal combs and curling irons popular in France to the needs of black women. Soon Madam Walker also developed a mail-order business in Denver and a beauty parlor and training school in Pittsburgh.

Her move to Indianapolis in 1910 was calculated—and it was a masterstroke. The Hoosier capital was then the country's largest inland manufacturing center, with access to eight major railway systems. After setting up the manufacturing facility and company headquarters in Indianapolis, Madam Walker became an influential and generous civic leader in her new hometown. Responding to a national plea in 1911 to build YMCAs in black communities across the country, she gave a thousand dollars to the building fund of the Senate Avenue YMCA in Indianapolis. In the midst of all this, she had a personal disruption; Madam Walker divorced her husband, although she always retained his name.

She was sensitive to the debate about whether black women should straighten their hair to achieve white standards of beauty. Her "hot comb" technique involved heating a metal comb and running it through the hair, which temporarily straightened it. But Madam Walker stressed that her product was intended as a grooming method to condition the scalp and make hair easier to comb, not really to straighten it.

"I want the great masses of my people to take a greater pride in their personal appearance and to give their hair proper attention," she told the *Indianapolis Recorder* newspaper in 1919.

Headlines on her ads read IT MAKES SHORT HAIR LONG AND CURES DANDRUFF, and she asked newspaper writers to refrain from using the phrase "hair straightener" when discussing her product.

Her move to New York City was initiated by A'Lelia, who was convinced the company needed a base there to be successful internationally. When Madam Walker made the move in 1916, her company had twenty thousand agents in the United States, Central America and the Caribbean. She created a national organization of her agents (the Madam C. J. Walker Hair Culturists Union of America) to protect them from competitors.

Emphasizing self-sufficiency and economic independence for women, she told a convention in 1913: "The girls and women of our race must not be afraid to take hold of business endeavor and . . . wring success out of a number of business opportunities that lie at their very doors . . . I want to say to every Negro woman present: Don't sit down and wait for the opportunities to come . . . Get up and make them!"

Fittingly, after her death in 1919, she was succeeded as company president by a woman. Madam Walker's successor was A'Lelia, once the little girl for whom she had sacrificed and built so much.

Booth Tarkington

Novelist and playwright

Except for William Faulkner, he is the only novelist to have twice won the Pulitzer Prize for fiction. And Indianapolis native Booth Tarkington's captivating Penrod stories are considered among the best ever written about Midwestern boyhood.

Most of his own boyhood was spent in Indianapolis, where Newton Booth Tarkington was born in 1869.

By the time he died in 1946, Tarkington had written forty-one novels and collections of short stories and twenty-three plays, almost all of them wildly popular. His two Pulitzer Prizes were for The Magnificent Ambersons *(1918), a novel about an aristocratic family coping with social and economic upheavals in a fictional city everyone recognized as Indianapolis, and* Alice Adams *(1921), the story of a girl's futile attempts to advance in society.*

"To the world Booth Tarkington was the dean of American letters," The Indianapolis News *editorialized upon his death at his North Meridian Street house. "To Indianapolis he was the first citizen of Indiana, a distinction that probably most pleased the man who died, as he would have wished, amid the familiar scenes of home."*

No more drinking. And a new devotion to writing.

Those were the pledges Booth Tarkington made in November 1912 when he married Susannah Robinson, his second wife. Although she originally was from Dayton, Ohio, Susannah had heard stories about Tarkington's colorful reputation and party-loving past.

Newton Booth Tarkington was the son of John Stevenson Tarkington, an attorney and circuit court judge, and his wife, Elizabeth, a refined, ambitious woman descended from early settlers of New England.

Booth was bookish as a boy, but he disliked school. He loved music, drawing and putting on plays. He dreamed about being an illustrator. After Booth played hooky from Shortridge High School for nine weeks, his parents withdrew him.

Thanks to the generosity of his prominent namesake uncle, Newton Booth, the governor of California, teenage Booth was sent to one of the most prestigious boarding schools in the country: Phillips Exeter Academy in New Hampshire.

His adolescent "growing pains" proved useful years later. Tarkington undoubtedly tapped his own vivid memories of boyhood when, two years after marrying Susannah, he wrote *Penrod* (1914). Consider this account of a rowdy neighborhood fight in Tarkington's classic:

Thus began the Great Tar Fight, the origin of which proved, afterward, so difficult for parents to trace, owing to the opposing accounts of the combatants. Marjorie said Penrod began it; Penrod said Mitchy-Mitch began it . . .

Novelist Booth Tarkington was for several decades considered the most famous resident of Indianapolis. The art collection in his Tudor-style home on North Meridian Street became the talk of the town. (Left) Tarkington at the age of twenty-eight.

Mr. Schofield's version of things was that Penrod was insane. "He's a stark, raving lunatic!" the father declared, descending to the library from a before-dinner interview with the outlaw, that evening. "I'd send him to military school; but I don't believe they'd take him. Do you know why he says all that awfulness happened?"

"When Margaret and I were to scrub him," Mrs. Schofield responded wearily, "he said 'everybody' had been calling him names."

" 'Names!' " her husband snorted. " 'Little gentleman!' That's the vile epithet they called him! And because of it he wrecks the peace of six homes!"

Tarkington had models for mischievous Penrod besides himself. He also observed his three nephews, the sons of his sister, Haute Tarkington Jameson. The nephews, John, Donald, and Booth Jameson, grew up across the street from their uncle in Indianapolis.

By the time Tarkington set about to write Penrod, he was following his pledge to Susannah. Tarkington was concentrating on his talent with a discipline he had earlier lacked.

After Exeter, Booth had returned to his home state to attend Purdue University, where he courted women and studied illustration. Then he spent about two years at Princeton University; "Tark," as he was known on the Ivy League campus, immersed himself in theatrical productions (as an actor and baritone soloist) and parties.

He returned to Indianapolis determined to become a writer. But for the next five years Tarkington primarily accumulated rejection slips for his submissions, mostly melodramas and historical romances.

Finally he rewrote a manuscript he had completed shortly after leaving Princeton and gave it a new title: *The Gentleman from Indiana*. He also polished a manuscript for the book that became *Monsieur Beaucaire*.

So his forceful sister, Haute, came armed with material in 1898 when she staged a dramatic "sit in" at S. S. McClure, a New York publishing office. She refused to leave until an editor considered some of Tarkington's manuscripts. The result was the publication of *The Gentleman from Indiana* as a book in 1899 and its serialization in *McClure's* magazine.

The Gentleman from Indiana became a best-seller—and Booth Tarkington suddenly was a national celebrity. But the dashing young Hoosier lacked discipline.

Tarkington married Laurel Louisa Fletcher, the daughter of an Indianapolis banker, in 1902. He spent several years in Europe, living extravagantly and drinking heavily. His personal life began to unravel: The Tarkingtons were divorced in 1911; their only child, a daughter, suffered from schizophrenia and died at sixteen.

His marriage to Susannah—and the promise to give up alcohol—transformed Tarkington's career. He became extremely prolific and wrote a string of popular plays. Then he topped himself with his successes as a novelist.

Penrod and another collection of stories about adolescence with a slightly older protagonist, *Seventeen* (1916), not only were tremendous popular hits, they drew critical raves. Tarkington was acclaimed for his realistic depiction of adolescence and his focus on ordinary, daily experiences that shape character.

The famous novelist began dividing his time between his Indianapolis home and a mansion in the posh seaside resort of Kennebunkport, Maine, where Tarkington spent summers. He completed a trilogy of novels about social change: *The Turmoil* (1915); *The Magnificent Ambersons* (1918); and *The Midlander* (1924).

By far the most enduring of the trilogy (which Tarkington titled *Growth*) is *The Magnificent Ambersons*, a classic chronicle of the decline of an aristocratic family in Midland, a Midwestern city obviously based on Indianapolis. The Ambersons cope with the industrialization of urban life and social changes caused by, among other factors, the automobile. Here is Tarkington's description of genteel, class-conscious city life at the beginning of the novel:

> *In that town, in those days, all the women wore silk or velvet and knew all the other women who wore silk or velvet, and when there was a new purchase of sealskin, sick people were got to windows to see it go by. Trotters were out, in the winter afternoons, racing light sleighs on National Avenue and Tennessee Street; everybody recognized both the trotters and the drivers; and again knew them as well on summer evenings, when slim buggies whizzed by in renewals of snow-time rivalry . . .*

By novel's end, the Amberson fortune had been lost. The book's spoiled, headstrong protagonist, George Amberson, was struggling to adjust to a new city and a new culture.

The roaring success of *The Magnificent Ambersons* gave Tarkington lasting fame. More than twenty years after the novel's publication, legendary filmmaker Orson Welles chose it as his follow-up project to his masterpiece, *Citizen Kane*; the 1942 screen version of *Ambersons*, with Welles playing George, was nominated for four Academy Awards.

Meanwhile, Tarkington remained a national celebrity. But after *Alice Adams* in 1921, which many consider an even better novel than *Ambersons*, none of Tarkington's writing achieved the same critical success. In the 1940s, some reviewers dismissed his work as superficial, although his books continued to sell.

For several years Tarkington grappled with major health problems. In the late 1920s and early '30s, he suffered from cataracts and nearly was blind. Even then, though, he wrote—by dictating stories. After several operations, Tarkington partially regained his vision.

Almost until his death a few weeks before his seventy-seventh birthday, Tarkington was writing every day, including Sundays. The novelist more than fulfilled his pledge of discipline to his wife.

He is buried in Crown Hill Cemetery near James Whitcomb Riley.

Theodore Dreiser

Novelist

Colorful notoriety and an unstable emotional life marked the career of a Hoosier novelist acclaimed as a trailblazer of naturalism in American writing. Theodore Dreiser, the controversial author of An American Tragedy *(1925) and* Sister Carrie *(1900), forcibly moved the novel from Victorian notions of decorum and gentility to the realistic style of the twentieth century.*

Is it any wonder that, during a trip through Indianapolis in 1915, he decided not to meet celebrity poet James Whitcomb Riley, a man Dreiser said he admired "with a whole heart"? Of the poet—whose style was sentimental, his topics the joys of wholesome, rustic life—Dreiser said: "I had heard that he didn't approve of me."

Lots of folks didn't approve of Theodore Dreiser. "Hard scrabble" is an apt description for Dreiser's life right from his birth in 1871 in Terre Haute. He was the ninth of ten children (actually, thirteen—three died in infancy or childhood) in a poverty-stricken family, rowdy and boisterous. His father, a German immigrant and ardent Catholic named John Paul Dreiser, came to America with big dreams that were never realized. His mother, Sarah, was of Mennonite background and barely literate.

Despite the family's desperate circumstances—shortly before Theodore's birth, John Paul lost his job as manager of a woolen mill—the Dreisers produced two creative notables. Besides Theodore, there was his older brother Paul, who under the name Paul Dresser became the composer of popular songs such as "On the Banks of the Wabash" (chosen as Indiana's state song in 1913) and "My Gal Sal."

But success for the younger Dreiser came decades later. Theodore's turbulent youth was spent in a series of towns and cities such as Sullivan ("dirty old Sullivan," one of his sisters called it), Warsaw and Evansville as well as Terre Haute.

"There were ten (children) all told—a restless, determined, half-educated family who, had each been properly trained according to his or her capacities, I have always thought might have made a considerable stir in the world," Theodore wrote years later.

His mother, he wrote, was a "dreamy, poetic, impractical soul (who served) to the best of her ability as the captain of the family ship" after John Paul's bitter failures. "I recall clothes so old and so made over and patched that they were a joke," Dreiser wrote.

During his childhood, Theodore and his youngest siblings (charismatic, good-looking Paul had left to join traveling minstrel shows as an entertainer-songwriter) frequently were separated from one parent or the other to save money. Wherever they were, the Dreisers always prompted whispers among the neighbors. Theodore's brothers were drinkers and rabble-rousers, his sisters the town flirts. Fiery and contemptuous of the world, John Paul was fanatically passionate in his Catholicism.

"Dreiser saw one brother jailed for forgery, and another hit the road to die of dissipation," Robert Penn Warren noted in an introduction to the 1962 edition of An American Tragedy. *"He saw one sister seduced by a political big-shot, and another sister come home to give birth to an illegitimate child."*

Theodore Dreiser

Stability—at least by the family's standards—came in Warsaw, where the Dreisers settled in the 1880s. Shy, studious Theodore liked school, but he was distraught over the ridicule his family endured. Not yet sixteen in the summer of 1887, he announced he was leaving home for Chicago, which seemed a promised land.

Chicago of the late 1880s was a city of narrow, brooding streets, dimly lit by gas lamps. It was a city of extremes—dangerous immigrant enclaves along with the elegant new neighborhoods of industrialists who were building their fortunes on the backs of the poor. In this city, Theodore Dreiser's dreams came crashing down. The teenager from small-town Indiana scrambled to survive in the biggest city in the Midwest. Dreiser envied the wealthy with their posh hotels, servants, private clubs and dazzling nightlife.

Theodore could only watch and yearn. To support himself, he toiled as a stove cleaner and dishwasher. His fate seemed bleak—almost Dickensian—until one of his teachers from Warsaw, Mildred Fielding, became principal of a Chicago high school and re-encountered Theodore. She offered to send him to Indiana University in the fall of 1889.

He was elated, but the joy didn't last. Intimidated by well-dressed and comfortable classmates in Bloomington, Theodore dropped out after his freshman year and returned to Chicago. That was the end of his formal education.

Newly fueled by ambition, he managed to get a job as a journalist. He was intrigued by the profession because some reporters got to interview the rich and famous. Ultimately he worked for newspapers in Chicago, St. Louis, Pittsburgh, and finally New York. As he hoped, the work brought him into contact with the prosperous people of the "Gilded Age."

But it also exposed him to miseries, though of a slightly different sort than he had endured in small-town Indiana—crowded tenements, street violence and filth. And as a reporter, he could never leave behind the truths of the other side of the tracks—the dark side of the Industrial Revolution in the city. Even the rich and famous had their private woes, he noticed.

His mind filled with the brutal details of what he'd seen—and inspired by the scandalous life of one of his sisters, Emma—Dreiser sat down and wrote *Sister Carrie*. Like Emma, the fictional Carrie moves to Chicago, discards her virtue and enjoys affairs with various men, some married. (His real sister, Emma, had an affair with an architect.) The plot was considered outrageous in 1900 primarily because Carrie feels no guilt over her behavior and is never punished. Although she finds herself alone at the conclusion of the novel, Dreiser implies that this fate awaits most people.

The story of *Sister Carrie*'s publication has become one of the legends of American literature. The manuscript was accepted for publication by Doubleday Page & Co. Then company president Frank Doubleday returned from a European vacation and immediately expressed outrage at *Sister Carrie*. Many suspect Doubleday's wife was horrified by the book and asked him to squelch it. In any case, Doubleday printed only a thousand copies and never promoted it; fewer than five hundred copies were sold.

Devastated by the turn of events—and distraught over personal problems, including the tribulations of several of his brothers and sisters—Dreiser was driven to a nervous breakdown and thought about killing himself.

He rallied and kept his faith in *Sister Carrie*. At age thirty-five, Dreiser found a new publisher for the novel. Its second publication in 1907 was a respectable success; today *Sister Carrie* is acclaimed as a brilliant indictment of the American dream and a perceptive depiction of urban agony, although critics fault Dreiser's style as frequently clumsy and verbose.

The same criticisms are made of Dreiser's most famous novel, *An American Tragedy* (1925). He based the plot on a sensational murder scandal in 1906, the Gillette-Brown case. A young man named Chester Gillette drowned his pregnant sweetheart, Grace Brown, in Big Moose Lake in upstate New York.

In *An American Tragedy*, a young opportunist named Clyde Griffiths, lusting after wealth, elegance and respectability, kills a woman during his climb to the top:

> *How different it all seemed from the world to which so recently he had been accustomed . . . So many imposing wrought-iron fences, flower-bordered walks, grouped trees and bushes, expensive and handsome automobiles either beneath porte-coch'eres within or speeding along the broad thoroughfare without . . .*
>
> *The beauty! The ease! What member of his own immediate family had ever even dreamed that his uncle lived thus! The grandeur! And his own parents so wretched—so poor, preaching on the streets of Kansas City and no doubt Denver . . . A little disgusted and depressed he turned to retrace his steps, for all at once he felt himself very much of a nobody . . .*
>
> *Clyde flushed, since obviously this was a notice to him that his social position here was decidedly below . . . that of these girls . . . Clyde, left quite to himself for the moment, was thinking what an easy, delightful world this must be—this local society. For here they were without a care, apparently, between any of them. All their talk was of houses being built, horses they were riding, friends they had met, places they were going to, things they were going to do.*

An American Tragedy became a Broadway hit, then served as the basis for two Hollywood movies, including the classic *A Place in the Sun* (1950) starring Elizabeth Taylor, Montgomery Clift, and Shelley Winters as the pathetic victim.

Like his protagonist, Dreiser was not destined for much happiness—despite his eventual literary successes. He was alienated from his home state for many years. And Dreiser had few close friends for most of his life. Arrogant and haunted by his troubled youth, he often was very unpleasant company.

Near the end of his life, he moved from New York to California. Dreiser died of a heart attack in 1945 in Hollywood.

Carl Fisher

Speedway founder

Born half blind in Greensburg, Indiana, in 1874, he almost always wore thick glasses.

Despite his weak eyesight, daredevil Carl Graham Fisher became a stunt bicyclist, drove one of the first cars in Indiana and helped start a racetrack that brought international fame to Indianapolis. A visionary and a genius at showmanship, Fisher not only launched the Indianapolis 500, he turned a Florida mangrove swamp into the resort of Miami Beach.

He began his roller coaster career as a twelve-year-old grocery clerk and peaked as a tycoon with estates in Indianapolis and Miami Beach. Yet when Carl Fisher died in 1939, he was a pauper.

It was inconceivable. A five-car garage? Most Hoosiers didn't even own a car—one car—in the 1910s. Yet the lavish estate of Carl Fisher on the west side of Indianapolis included indoor tennis courts (with a special box seat reserved for his celebrity pal, poet James Whitcomb Riley), a greenhouse and, yes, a five-car garage.

Well, what would you expect of Fisher, a flamboyant entrepreneur fascinated since boyhood with land, vehicles and the boundless possibilities of both?

Fisher was the young chap who thrilled downtown Indianapolis by stringing a tightrope between the upper floors of the city's two tallest office buildings and pedaling across on his stunt bicycle, defying death.

He was the dreamer who wanted to start a world-famous racetrack. Along with A. C. Newby, owner of the Newby Oval bicycle track, headlight and battery manufacturer James Allison and businessman Frank Wheeler, Fisher helped create the Indianapolis Motor Speedway in 1909 as a testing area.

He was even a participant in the first race—a hot-air balloon contest in which an exuberant Fisher piloted an entry titled "Indiana." Two years later, in 1911, Fisher's ultimate vision became reality: the first Indianapolis 500, which has thrilled millions of spectators every year since.

The automobile wasn't invented when Fisher was born in 1874, one of at least three children in a Greensburg family. When the Fishers were left fatherless, Carl quit school at about age twelve. He became a grocery clerk, then a vendor on passenger trains, selling candy, peanuts, tobacco and magazines. Amazingly, he was able to save the sum of six hundred dollars.

With that, Carl as a seventeen-year-old was able to open a bicycle repair shop in Indianapolis; his brothers worked with him there. Charismatic and fearless, he began daredevil stunts—including the tightrope ride above downtown—to promote the shop. Business boomed. Fisher even joined a team of professional racing cyclists.

Then came the automobile; Fisher was one of the first aboard.

He owned one of the first cars in Indiana and opened an auto showroom about 1902.

Indianapolis Motor Speedway

Carl Fisher

Fisher sold and serviced Wintons; he also sold Premiers, which were manufactured in Indianapolis. He helped start the Hoosier Motor Club and was an organizer of the Lincoln Highway Association, which marked the first transcontinental road suitable for automobiles.

His fortune came not just from the auto showroom, but from Prest-O-Lite Storage Battery Company, which he started with Allison and inventor P. C. (Fred) Avery. Prest-O-Lite perfected a system to light automobile headlamps.

Because the manufacturing facilities were prone to explosions, Fisher and his partners established a plant far west of downtown. The plant was near the new Indianapolis Motor Speedway that Fisher and Allison had built with Arthur Newby and Frank Wheeler.

Also nearby was Fisher's estate, Blossom Heath. The hostess there was Fisher's first wife, Jane. She was just fifteen in 1909 when she saw the celebrated entrepreneur at a dance. (Jane had noticed him from afar earlier as Fisher, in one of his promotional stunts, floated above Meridian Street in a car attached to a balloon.) Soon thereafter, her family's house caught fire—and the first person she could think of to call for help was wealthy problem-solver Carl Fisher.

"I'll be right over, little honey," Fisher told her, according to folklore. The couple married later that year, although he was more than twice her age.

They began spending most of their time in Florida after Fisher, always driven to top himself, announced he intended to turn a piece of swampland into "the most beautiful little city in the world." As Miami Beach blossomed, the Fishers moved into a mansion at the seaside resort.

Famous humorist Will Rogers quipped: "Had there been no Carl Fisher, Florida would be known today as just the turpentine state . . . He rehearsed the mosquitoes till they wouldn't bite you until after you bought."

Itching to top himself again, Fisher turned to New York and the development of a summer resort on Long Island. But the ravages of nature destroyed his fortunes: A hurricane in 1926 devastated Miami Beach.

Unfortunately, Fisher had used his Florida property as security to finance the Long Island project. Miami Beach was rebuilt, but Fisher had to back out of his New York project and suffered a huge loss.

He and Jane were divorced amicably in 1926. Although Fisher rebounded and married Ohio native Margaret Collier, the Wall Street crash of 1929 aggravated his financial situation. He was "nearly penniless," according to several accounts, when he died ten years later in Miami.

Major Taylor with his wife, Daisy, and daughter, Sydney, in a family portrait in 1907.

Major Taylor

Bicycle racer

One of the very first black athletes to become internationally famous was a Hoosier, but he had to leave his home state— and eventually his country—to achieve great success. Along the way, world champion bicycle racer Major Taylor confronted racial prejudice, vindictive competitors, self-serving promoters and the eventual under-appreciation of his sport in his homeland.

He was named Marshall W. Taylor at his birth on the outskirts of Indianapolis in 1878. His poverty-stricken family lived in rural Marion County; Taylor's father, a Civil War veteran, was a coachman for a wealthy Indianapolis family.

The "Major" nickname probably came at thirteen, when Marshall was working at an Indianapolis bicycle shop. He performed trick rides on sidewalks while wearing a military cap and a uniform with large brass buttons and braid—apparel associated with U.S. Army majors.

A man of principle—throughout his life, Taylor refused to compete on Sundays because of a promise to his mother "to lead an upright Christian life"—the legendary Hoosier bicycle racer had a turbulent adulthood with stunning successes and nearly unendurable miseries.

The handsome, wiry racer known as "The Ebony Streak" became an American and world champion, met the kings and queens of Europe and enjoyed fabulous, albeit fleeting, wealth and fame. He also came close to a nervous breakdown and coped with death threats, a painful divorce and financial disasters. When he died in near obscurity in 1932, Taylor was buried in an unmarked pauper's grave.

Crowds of excited Hoosiers lined Massachusetts Avenue in Indianapolis to watch a heavily promoted bicycle race. But one aspect of the event in June 1895 hadn't been publicized: the participation of a sixteen-year-old black competitor.

The secret bicycle racer was impulsive, energetic Marshall W. "Major" Taylor. He was entered in the "scratch" position, meaning he would start at the very back of the pack. The road race was to take the athletes from downtown Indianapolis northeast seventy-five miles to the small town of Matthews.

Despite the teenager's secret entry into the race, his supporters had faith in him, and they included some prominent Hoosiers. Major Taylor's primary backer was Indianapolis businessman Louis Munger, thirty-two, a former bicycle racing star and ex-world record holder. Munger, a bicycle manufacturer, had hired young Major Taylor as a company messenger and his personal valet.

He had reason to have faith in his protege. When Major Taylor was just thirteen, he had defeated a top amateur field in a ten-mile road race. Then he set unofficial records at the Capital City velodrome in Indianapolis.

Munger's faith was rewarded. Even though some of the riders in the Indianapolis-to-Matthews race shouted racial slurs at Major Taylor—and torrents of rain began to fall—he pulled in front of the other competitors.

Taylor kept pedaling even though the heavy rain turned the dirt roads into mud and ooze. Drenched and exhausted, he rode into Matthews alone. Not only did Taylor win the grueling race, he was the only one in the field to even finish The teenager "proved himself a wonder," according to *The Indianapolis Sentinel* newspaper.

But some of the attention directed at the talented teenager was far from worshipful: His triumphs prompted death threats. And officials at Indianapolis bicycle tracks resented the fact that a black man held the records at their facilities. Soon bicycle tracks in Indianapolis were restricted to whites only.

Unable to compete in his home state and seeking greater opportunities with Munger, Taylor left Indiana in 1896, just one year after his triumph in the race to Matthews. He went with Munger to Worcester, Massachusetts, where the bicycle manufacturer had decided to relocate his business.

In leaving Indianapolis, Major Taylor wasn't simply escaping painful episodes involving racial prejudice. His time there was also the source of some warm boyhood memories. Because his father, Gilbert, had worked as a coachman in Indianapolis for the prominent Southard family, young Marshall reaped benefits rare for a black youngster.

He was a playmate of Daniel Southard, the family's son who was about Marshall's age. Their close friendship meant young Taylor shared lessons with his companion from a private tutor, as well as clothes, toys and sports that Daniel enjoyed.

Once he moved to the East Coast, Major Taylor began achieving national, then international, fame. But he never was free from bigotry—not even as he was setting world bicycle racing records in seven different distances.

In some cities on the racing circuit, Taylor had to scramble to find places to eat and sleep. Gangs of white riders often worked together to try to force him to wreck or box him in. He even changed his racing strategy to compensate for that. In his early races, Taylor was known for staying off the lead and zooming to victory with a "gunpowder" finish. When he noticed other racers were ganging up on him, he simply tried to take and maintain a lead all the way through every race.

Bicycle racing boomed in America between 1890 and 1910, becoming as popular as baseball and boxing. But the enthusiasm for the sport fell off rather abruptly. In Europe, however, bicycle racers always earned more prize money, and enthusiasm for the sport never diminished.

In 1899, after winning the world sprint championship, Taylor had turned down a ten-thousand-dollar offer to race in Europe because the competitions were to be on a Sunday. But two years later he toured Europe with the promise there would be no Sunday racing; "The Ebony Streak" became hugely popular, particularly in France.

Taylor and his wife, Daisy, and their daughter, Sydney, met royalty, stayed in elite hotels, traveled first-class on the era's greatest ocean liners and dined at exclusive restaurants. His barnstorming, sixteen-city tour in 1901 ended with forty-two victories in fifty-seven races, including a seventy-five-hundred dollar victory at the world championship in Paris. A world tour in 1902 also was a triumph.

But the Hoosier athlete was becoming exhausted. He considered retirement as early as 1902, but an offer of five thousand dollars plus all expenses (and no Sunday racing) to compete in Australia was too tempting to turn down. Although Taylor netted vast winnings and competed in Australia the following year as well, he encountered vicious tactics from white competitors there, just as he had in America. Frustrated and weary, he returned to Massachusetts and nearly suffered a nervous breakdown.

A lawsuit followed from European promoters, who alleged contract violations. He toured Australia, stopped racing, then went back to Paris in 1909, but competed poorly and retired from the sport a year later. Never a good investor of his winnings—and hampered by opportunistic or inept advisers—Taylor became nearly destitute.

With the car craze in America, competitive bicycling lost its public allure. Taylor's records were forgotten. Desperate, he wrote his autobiography, *The Fastest Bicycle Rider in the World*, in 1928, but it was a financial disaster. Left penniless and divorced by Daisy, Taylor moved to a YMCA in Chicago. He died in 1932 in the charity ward of Cook County Hospital.

Although he was buried in an unmarked pauper's grave, Taylor got recognition sixteen years later from a man who never forgot his heroics—Frank Scwhinn of the Schwinn Bicycle Company. During a belated memorial service at a Chicago cemetery attended by many of the country's outstanding black athletes, Schwinn provided a bronze tablet that bears Taylor's image and this inscription:

> *World champion bicycle racer who came up the hard way without hatred in his heart. An honest, courageous and God-fearing, clean-living gentlemanly athlete. A credit to his race who always gave out his best. Gone but not forgotten.*

In 1982, as bicycle racing began a resurgence, Taylor was honored in his hometown. One of the country's best racetracks was built in Indianapolis. Its name—the Major Taylor Velodrome.

D. C. Stephenson

D. C. Stephenson

Ku Klux Klan leader

"I am the law in Indiana." Repugnant and incredible as it now seems, the Grand Dragon of the Ku Klux Klan—a native Texan named David Curtis Stephenson—was able to make that boast during the 1920s. Under his flamboyant leadership, the Klan claimed a membership of about a quarter of a million in Indiana, took credit for electing a Republican governor and blatantly manipulated an Indianapolis mayor.

Born in Houston, Texas, in 1891, Stephenson spent much of his youth in Oklahoma. He briefly served in the Army during World War I, then drifted to Evansville in 1920. After an unsuccessful run for Congress as a Democrat, he settled in Indianapolis in 1922.

The downfall of Stephenson was just as spectacular as his rise. In 1925, less than a year after the election of Klan-supported Governor Ed Jackson, Stephenson was arrested for his role in the death of an Indianapolis woman, a state employee he had brutally raped.

He was found guilty of second-degree murder and sentenced to life in prison. While imprisoned, he leaked details to newspapers about his role in Hoosier politics, ruining the political careers of Jackson, Indianapolis Mayor John Duvall and others.

After thirty-one years at the Indiana State Prison in Michigan City—apparently the longest imprisonment ever in the state for second-degree murder—he was released in 1956. Stephenson left Indiana in 1962. Years later, it was revealed he had moved to Jonesboro, Tennessee; that's where he died in 1966.

George Oberholtzer was filled with anger and outrage at his ominously powerful neighbor, a political leader who lived in magnificent style in Irvington on the east side of Indianapolis.

In April 1925, postal clerk Oberholtzer swore out a warrant for the arrest of charismatic D. C. Stephenson in connection with the rape of his twenty-eight-year-old daughter, Madge, an office manager for the Indiana Department of Public Instruction. The initial warrant charged Stephenson with kidnapping and assault; when Madge died twelve days later, the charge became murder.

The arrest—and Stephenson's eventual conviction after a sensational trial in Noblesville—ended the reign of perhaps the most unlikely man ever to control Indiana's political machine. Among other things, Stephenson was, as his biographer M. William Lutholtz put it, a chronic liar—someone who "told so many lies so often that it is difficult to know the truth" about his life.

Stephenson falsely claimed to have thrived in various professions, including that of attorney, before becoming grand dragon of the Ku Klux Klan in Indiana and overseeing Klan operations in twenty-two other Northern states. Actually, he was the son of a poor sharecropper and only had achieved an eighth-grade education. A second lieutenant who served in Iowa and Minnesota during the waning days of World War I, Stephenson worked as a typesetter, a grocer and a traveling salesman.

By the time he showed up in Indiana in 1920, he had already abandoned a wife and daughter in Oklahoma. He arrived to find a rejuvenated KKK seeking members in Northern states. A postwar backlash against foreigners and Catholics nurtured its growth, as did the "Red Scare," the panicked response to the Communists' seizure of power in Eastern Europe.

The same year Stephenson arrived in the Hoosier state, the Klan began its first recruiting drive north of the Mason-Dixon Line. Shrewd and aggressive, Stephenson, a coal salesman by trade, became one of the Klan's best recruiters.

After moving to Indianapolis, Stephenson helped fellow Klansman Hiram Evans unseat the imperial wizard, William Simmons. As a reward, Stephenson was named grand dragon. An eloquent, persuasive speaker, he was in charge when the Klan recruited 30 percent of Indiana's white, native-born male adults as members. Stephenson became wealthy thanks to commissions on new memberships and the sale of Klan sheets and hoods.

In July 1923, Stephenson arranged for Kokomo to be the site of the largest Klan conclave (called a "Konclave") ever held in the United States. After thousands of members assembled, Stephenson arrived in a business suit and delivered a speech about how the government had strayed from the founding fathers' intentions.

The next year, he threw his considerable support in the governor's race behind Ed Jackson, a former secretary of state. "Steve," as Stephenson's cronies called him, also convinced Indianapolis Mayor John Duvall and other officials, including the Marion County sheriff, to sign pledges saying that they only would make appointments acceptable to Stephenson. He hid some of the pledges, along with other documents that incriminated public officials, in black boxes.

At the time of his arrest in the Oberholtzer case, Stephenson was hatching a plan to have himself appointed to the U.S. Senate as a replacement for ailing Senator Sam Ralston. He even was dreaming of being president of the United States.

It all unraveled with Madge Oberholtzer's deathbed statement. She described how she had met Stephenson at the governor's inaugural banquet at the Indianapolis Athletic Club. As a former teacher, she was recruited to help Stephenson in another of his schemes—to write a book on nutrition, then make it required reading in Hoosier schools.

But Miss Oberholtzer vanished for several days in March 1925. When a Stephenson aide finally returned her to her parents' Irvington home, she was gravely ill. She died from the effects of mercury bichloride poison, which she had taken following a brutal rape on a train ride to Chicago. She said she swallowed the poison in a Hammond hotel room. She may have been planning to commit suicide or perhaps just intended to scare Stephenson.

In response, a grief-stricken George Oberholtzer swore out the arrest warrant and declared, "I am going through with this uphill fight for the sake of humanity—for the sake of other fathers and their daughters." Stephenson eventually was convicted by a white, all-male jury primarily made up of Hamilton County farmers.

After Stephenson's dramatic downfall, the Klan lost its grip on Indiana politicians and average Hoosiers. The group's membership and influence rapidly declined. In 1928 *The Indianapolis Times* newspaper won a Pulitzer Prize for "meritorious public service" for its investigation and exposure of the Klan in Indiana. Most Hoosiers were ashamed they had let the state fall into the hands of hooded thugs.

Cole Porter

Composer, lyricist

You're the top!
You're the Colosseum
You're the top!
You're the Louvre Museum.
You're a melody from a symphony by Strauss,
You're a Bendel bonnet,
A Shakespeare sonnet,
You're Mickey Mouse.
You're the Nile,
You're the Tow'r of Pisa,
You're the smile
On the Mona Lisa.
I'm a worthless check, a total wreck, a flop,
But if, baby, I'm the bottom
You're the top!

A Hoosier wrote those lyrics—and for a long time, he WAS the top. Cole Porter composed the music and lyrics for dozens of songs that have become standards of American popular music.

This legendary man born in Peru, Indiana, went on to personify international chic and became the toast of Broadway for nearly forty years beginning in the 1920s. His was a world of penthouses, chiffon, chandeliers, limousines and tuxedos—right out of a Fred Astaire and Ginger Rogers movie, for which Porter wrote many of the scores.

Bob Hope called Cole Porter a genius. Few would disagree. Yet this Hoosier born to luxury, who achieved further riches, fame and worldwide acclaim, also lived with tremendous pain. Fortunately for romantics and music lovers, his private suffering didn't diminish his capacity to create tunes that burst with pure joy.

PERU, Indiana—He was born here in 1891 and returned to his family's Miami County mansion, Westleigh, several times every year for holidays and to visit his mother.

But legendary composer-lyricist Cole Porter, the creator of such enduring show tunes as "What is this Thing Called Love?," "Begin the Beguine," and "In the Still of the Night," lived much of his life in glamorous places including New York, Paris, Venice, and the French Riviera.

"He inherited money, married money, and made money," Porter's cousin, James Cole, said in 1991 during an interview at Westleigh.

The Cole fortune was begun in the mid-1800s by Hoosier entrepreneur J. O. Cole, Porter's grandfather. Cole, who settled in Indiana about twenty-five years after the Hoosier

Courtesy of the Miami County Historical Society Inc.

Cole Porter

state entered the Union, made his wealth initially from a brewery in Peru and from selling supplies to miners heading to California for the Gold Rush. He also became a lumber and coal tycoon.

"He was the kingpin, the patriarch," James Cole recalled of his great-grandfather, who died in 1927. "He seemed like a giant to me, although he was not a big man. He was very regal, very opinionated."

Legend has it that J. O. Cole disapproved of the musical inclinations of his talented grandson, who was playing the piano and violin before his sixth birthday. J. O. was determined that the boy become a lawyer. However, J. O.'s daughter, Kate Cole Porter, doted on her son, and she encouraged Cole's interest in music, insisting that he practice every day. Cole was her third child, but the only one to survive infancy.

Cole's father, Sam, was a druggist of average means. So the future toast of Broadway was born in a frame home in Peru that now is an apartment house marked by a plaque. Later, Kate moved her family to Westleigh and its nine-hundred-acre estate.

In 1902, when Porter was only eleven, his mother arranged for the publication of one of his compositions, "The Bobolink Waltz." Kate is said to have lied about the composer's age when she showed the waltz to a Chicago publisher, shaving off two years to make Cole seem even more of a prodigy. Confusion about Cole Porter's age persisted for the rest of his life; to this day many reference books incorrectly give 1893 as the year of his birth.

A few years later, when he was about thirteen, Cole left Peru to attend Worcester Academy, an elite boarding school in Massachusetts. He never really lived in Indiana after that. Following prep school, Cole enrolled in Yale University, where he put on shows and wrote his first hit song—the Ivy League school's famous football fight song, "Yale Bulldog," which is sung on campus to this day.

To please his grandfather, Cole then entered Harvard Law School. During his second term, he switched his studies to his real love, music. According to some accounts, J. O. Cole threatened to disown his grandson, but was talked out of it by Kate.

"She was the ramrod in the family—a delightful, refined, prim woman," James Cole recalled.

With his musical education from Harvard, Cole sought work in New York. He wrote the score for a musical comedy, *See America First*, in 1916. The musical was a flop, running only fifteen performances. The composer was devastated.

With the dawn of World War I, mystery surrounded Porter's life. After he became famous, he perpetuated the idea that he had served briefly in the French Foreign Legion during that time, but biographers and historians have disputed this claim.

In any case, Porter landed in Paris, where he met socialite Linda Lee Thomas, a wealthy divorcee from Louisville, Kentucky. Although she was more than ten years older than Porter, Linda often was described as the most beautiful woman of her era. The two married in 1919.

Thanks to Linda's high-society connections, the Porters became avid partygoers, cruise lovers, and fashion plates. Ever dashing, Porter always had a carnation in his lapel. It's said he sometimes went through three a day so the flower always would be fresh. The Porters hobnobbed with the legendary "Paris in the '20s" crowd that included Picasso, Hemingway, and F. Scott Fitzgerald.

Porter kept composing, but enjoyed only modest success. The transplanted Hoosier was regarded primarily as a dilettante until 1928, when he was asked to write the score for *Paris*, a musical comedy. One of its songs, "Let's Do It, Let's Fall in Love," became a huge hit. The next year, 1929, Porter topped himself twice with two smash shows: *Fifty Million Frenchmen* and *Wake Up and Dream*, with songs that included "What Is This Thing Called Love?"

Then came Porter's remarkable string of triumphs on Broadway: *The Gay Divorcee* in 1932, featuring Fred Astaire and the song, "Night and Day," which swept the country as a sensation; *Anything Goes* (1934), with Ethel Merman and a whole show full of hit songs including "You're the Top," the title tune, and "Blow, Gabriel, Blow"; and *Jubilee* in 1935, which Porter wrote on a 'round-the-world cruise with playwright Moss Hart. *Jubilee* featured one of Porter's greatest hits ever, "Begin the Beguine."

But tragedy suddenly entered the famous composer's seemingly charmed life. At age forty-six in 1937, Porter was thrown from a horse, which then fell on top of him, crushing his legs. Doctors later concluded that his legs should have been amputated immediately, but Porter's wife and mother argued against it.

So the frail musician endured about thirty-five operations and remained in constant pain. A meticulous man and natty dresser, Porter felt humiliated by having to use braces, canes or a wheelchair. Sometimes his valet had to carry him from room to room, a situation that acutely embarrassed the sophisticated composer.

For a while, he threw himself into his music. In the last part of the thirties, Porter alternated his work between New York and Hollywood, with the goal of opening one Broadway show and scoring one hit movie every year. The films included *Rosalie* in which Nelson Eddy sings "In the Still of the Night."

> *In the still of the night,*
> *As I gaze from my window,*
> *At the moon in its flight,*
> *My thoughts all stray to you.*
> *In the still of the night,*
> *While the world is in slumber,*
> *Oh, the times without number,*
> *Darling when I say to you,*
> *Do you love me as I love you?*

In the late 1940s and '50s, Porter enjoyed another spurt of Broadway hits: *Kiss Me Kate*, *Can-Can*, and *Silk Stockings*. But during this period, he was devastated by the deaths of his mother and, two years later, his wife.

In 1958, Porter finally relented and allowed surgeons to amputate his right leg. He plunged into despair afterward and never wrote another song.

"He became a recluse in the later stages," his cousin said. "After the amputation, there was no more music. Someone asked him why. You know how he put it? He said, 'I can't reach the pedals.' " James Cole paused and sighed. "I also remember him talking about the pain in his toes. He was complaining about what we now call phantom pains."

But Cole Porter's cousin has joyous memories, too. For much of the composer's life, he was a ham. James Cole remembers his famous cousin singing and accompanying himself on the piano.

"His voice was not that bad," James Cole said. "We have records of him singing. Oh, how he loved to entertain."

Cole Porter died in 1964. He is buried in Peru.

The Cole Family and Westleigh

For decades, the keeper of the Cole Porter flame was the legendary composer's cousin, James Cole. At the composer's request, James moved into Westleigh, the family mansion near Peru in Miami County, upon the death of Cole Porter's mother, Kate, in 1952. When Cole Porter died twelve years later, James Cole's family inherited the bulk of the composer's estate.

A gray-haired, bespectacled attorney who declined to reveal his age, James Cole was besieged with requests to share anecdotes about Porter during galas in 1991 that marked the centennial of the composer's birth. There were star-studded Cole Porter tributes in London, and at Carnegie Hall in New York and the Circle Theatre in Indianapolis.

Film crews from TV shows such as CBS' *Sunday Morning with Charles Kuralt* and PBS' *American Masters* interviewed James Cole at Westleigh, where he was managing the nine-hundred-acre estate. James also oversaw Cole family properties that include large tracts of timberland in West Virginia.

Seated on the spacious front porch of Westleigh, James Cole talked about his family and his home. Built over a three-year period beginning in 1910, the origins of the mansion's name are a mystery, according to Cole.

"All the wood came from the family sawmill in Cincinnati," he noted. "The lumber for the house was hand-picked and knot-free. Westleigh was built like a fortress." After eight decades, the woodwork still gleams.

The mansion's artifacts include period furniture in the composer's bedroom. The room looks almost exactly as it did when the internationally famous composer, who was known for his flair and sophistication, visited between stays at his luxurious homes in New York, Paris, Venice, and the French Riviera.

"Cole usually came here with an entourage, a group of friends that included [actor] Monty Woolley—they were classmates at Yale, you know—and [Secretary of State] Dean Acheson," Cole recalled. "Cole was a wonderful host, but more of a listener than a talker. When he did speak, though, he always was clever and witty."

James Cole, the famous composer's cousin, at Westleigh in 1991.

Courtesy of *The Indianapolis Star/News*

Wendell Willkie

Wendell Willkie

Presidential candidate

"We want Willkie! We want Willkie! We want Willkie!"

That chant exploded from the galleries at a Philadelphia convention hall in June of 1940. Boisterous delegates would not be silenced at the Republican National Convention, which was searching for someone to run for the White House against the formidable Franklin D. Roosevelt.

The delegates' choice after six ballots seemed the most unlikely candidate in the land. "The miracle of modern politics," analysts called the upset nomination of Wendell Willkie.

Indeed, no other major party presidential nominee has had Willkie's dark horse background. "Political maverick" understates it. The native of Elwood, Indiana, had never held elective office—not even county clerk. Until a few years before the GOP convention, Willkie had been a lifelong Democrat. He had a late start in seeking the nomination, capturing it in just forty-eight days. He was opposed by several of his party's bigwigs, and his campaign was organized mostly by amateurs. "Like Topsy, it 'just growed,' " Willkie said of his candidacy.

Yet this dark horse raced at full gallop. Colorful and fearless, Willkie waged one of the most raucous presidential campaigns of the twentieth century. "There had never been anything like it," Time magazine said of the whirlwind crusade once the dust had settled.

A ruddy-faced, beefy, self-made man who had become one of America's top utility executives, Willkie stumped across the country at the most vigorous possible pace. For more than seven weeks, he made as many as fifteen speeches a day until his voice became so hoarse it was a croak.

"Boos don't hurt me," he told hecklers. "All I ask is a square shake."

Willkie's speech in his hometown on a sweltering Saturday afternoon in August 1940 drew a crowd estimated at 215,000, making it one of the largest political gatherings in Indiana history. Undaunted by 102-degree heat, Willkie spoke ninety minutes at Callaway Park in Elwood. By the time he wound down, 360 people needed to be treated for heat-related disorders.

Willkie, who was quotable and blunt, told the press he hoped the Democrats would nominate FDR in what would be an unprecedented move for a third term. "I want to meet the champ," Willkie said, smiling.

Although his campaign—he called it "a crusade to save democracy"—was unsuccessful and he never controlled a political machine, Willkie wielded significant influence in America for the next four years.

"I'd rather be right than president," he said at one point. Before his untimely death of a heart attack at age fifty-two in 1944, he had even become a best-selling author of the book, One World, *and, of all things, the personal representative of President Roosevelt (his former arch-rival) to the Allied nations of Europe.*

How did the boy born in Elwood in 1892 rise to such prominence? His path to power and fame was unusual—like the Hoosier himself.

Quirks of fate in Wendell Willkie's life begin with his name. And his pioneering streak can be traced to his parents.

Both were attorneys in Elwood. His mother, Henrietta Trisch Willkie, was the first woman admitted to the Indiana bar. His father, Herman, was a prosperous lawyer and land-owner in Elwood, a booming manufacturing town in the 1890s.

They named their son, who was born in 1892, Lewis Wendell Willkie. The switch to "Wendell" came by accident years later: In 1917, Willkie enlisted in the Army as the country entered World War I. Because of a clerical error, his first and middle names were transposed on military records. When he pointed out the mistake, though, Willkie was advised to ignore it. "By the time we get the records corrected through all of the red tape of Washington, D.C., the war will be over," he was told. Uncharacteristically for a man who constantly challenged authority, Willkie accepted the error—permanently. He probably complied because he never cared for the name Lewis.

By the time he became a twenty-five-year-old Army private, Willkie already had led a scrappy, adventurous life. A hard worker like his parents, he was one of six children in the ambitious, literature-loving Willkie family. According to legend, Herman kept more than six thousand books in the house and made a habit of waking his children in the mornings by shouting quotations from the classics. Lewis—or Wendell—attended an eight-room Elwood schoolhouse and spent a summer at Culver Military Academy in northern Indiana.

The family's upper-middle-class lifestyle—and the fortunes of Elwood—collapsed with the exhaustion of natural gas wells after the turn of the century. To earn money, Lewis worked for a junk dealer (he removed nails from the trash), drove a bakery wagon, toiled as a short-order cook, and became a barker at a tent hotel.

Willkie enrolled at Indiana University, where he acquired a reputation as an orator and as a campus radical of sorts. He often raged against fraternities, although he eventually joined one.

After enlisting in the Army, Willkie asked a librarian from Rushville to marry him. Her name was Edith Wilk.

"Edith, I'd like to change that Wilk to Willkie," he claimed to have told her.

Her hometown would become his haven. Known as "Rushville's favorite son-in-law," Willkie even conducted his rollicking presidential campaign in 1940 from a Rushville hotel. He owned about fifteen hundred acres of Rush County land—five farms near Rushville.

Despite his depiction in the 1940 campaign as "an Indiana crackerbox" by the media (and to some extent by Willkie himself), Willkie was urbane. After serving in France during World War I, he settled in Akron, Ohio, and carved out a brilliant career as an attorney during the 1920s. The president of Commonwealth and Southern, a giant utility holding company, told his executives: "Do not let this young man get away from us."

Summoned to New York in 1929, he became an attorney for the utility—and within four years was named president. So at just forty-one he was heading one of America's largest corporations with assets of more than one billion dollars.

Fearless as ever, Willkie tangled with FDR's administration. The spectacular feud concerned the government's new Tennessee Valley Authority, which, as Willkie saw it, was competing with his electric company's holdings in Tennessee. But labeling Willkie as just anti-FDR is simplistic.

"I won't be dropped into a mold," he often said. "I want to be a free spirit."

An internationalist and an ardent champion of civil rights, Willkie took liberal positions on many social issues. He pulled together some of his ideas for America in "We The People," an article for *Fortune* magazine that had a tremendous impact. It helped galvanize the "We Want Willkie!" whirlwind crusade for the GOP presidential nomination.

During the 1940 campaign, Willkie made a show of turning down the support of religious and social leaders whom he considered bigots. "I don't have to be president of the United States," he said, "but I do have to live with myself."

Among the symbols depicted on his grave in Rushville is a crusader's sword.

Several of composer Hoagy Carmichael's early songs were inspired by Hoosiers whom he encountered. "Rocking Chair" (1929) was inspired by an elderly black Bloomington woman known for her homemade beer. Louis Armstrong made it a hit.

Hoagy Carmichael

Composer

If songs which become international standards make a composer immortal, then Hoagy Carmichael lives around the world wherever there is a gathering of jazz aficionados or lovers of music with a dreamy, almost surreal quality. "Stardust," "Georgia on My Mind," "Up A Lazy River," "The Lamplighter's Serenade," "Lazy Bones," "The Nearness of You"—Carmichael composed them all, along with about forty-five other hits.

Hoagy also was a singer, radio and TV personality and an actor sometimes dubbed "Hollywood's original piano man." He portrayed a piano-playing character in classic movies such as To Have and Have Not *(1944) and* The Best Years of Our Lives *(1946). As a composer, he won an Academy Award for "In the Cool, Cool, Cool of the Evening," a tune in the 1951 Bing Crosby film* Here Comes the Groom. *The enduring image of Carmichael for most moviegoers comes during* Canyon Passage *(1946) when thin-faced Hoagy dons a top hat, rides a mule and warbles his tune "Old Buttermilk Sky."*

Married twice and the father of two sons (Hoagland Bix and Randy), Carmichael died in Rancho Mirage, California, in 1981.

The 1910s was an era of racial segregation in Indianapolis, and most of the ragtime performers were black. And yet, this particular teenager often seen hanging around ragtime piano players was white. Young Hoagland Howard Carmichael, who had been born in Bloomington in 1899, was drawn to ragtime and jazz.

The music was magnetic. And the Hoosier ragtime piano players and other performers didn't mind answering questions form the skinny kid with the funny first name. They could tell that young Hoagy clearly adored their music. On an informal basis, many of the black jazz musicians taught him technique.

Hoagy, whose family alternated between homes in Bloomington and Indianapolis, was particularly fascinated by Reggie DuValle, a ragtime piano player in Indianapolis. DuValle showed "the kid" how to improvise on the keyboard. He taught Hoagy complex rhythms and the stress of the afterbeat.

Ever since Hoagy could remember, he had been captivated by music and show business. He adored his mother, a terrific pianist who taught her son to play. (Other than the instruction from her, he never took formal lessons.) Hoagy also would tag along with his mom to movie theaters where she worked as an accompanist for silent films.

Inspired by the Indianapolis ragtime musicians, Hoagy even formed a jazz band while in his twenties. "It was disjointed music, unorganized, but full of screaming notes and a solid rhythm," he recalled years later. At Indiana University, Hoagy formed a band called The Collegians.

Even though Hoagy was studying law at IU, his passion was music. Usually he could be found at a Greek-owned candy and malt store just off campus called The Book Nook. The shop had a piano in the back room, and Hoagy began composing tunes on it, including "Washboard Blues," "Riverboat Shuffle" and "Rockin' Chair."

In the early 1920s Hoagy attended a party at the Friars Club in Chicago and heard legendary cornetist Bix Beiderbecke perform. Hoagy brought Bix and the Wolverines to I.U. for spring dances in 1924 at the Kappa Sigma fraternity house, and reveled in the sounds of "Tiger Rag" and other jazz compositions. Hoagy began a "Bix cult" and brought the Wolverines back to campus ten weekends in a row.

Hoagy yearned to be a musician like his idols, but he thought it was a pipe dream and assumed a sensible career as a lawyer would be his fate. He worked as an attorney in New York City, Indianapolis, and Bloomington and headed to West Palm Beach, Florida, in 1926. He thought with the land boom in southern Florida there would be plenty of work for a good lawyer.

"There probably was, too—only I wasn't a good lawyer," Hoagy recalled later in life. "A note to me was something that belonged on a musical staff."

Eventually he surrendered to the demands of his talent and tried to carve out a songwriting career in Hollywood, then along Tin Pan Alley in New York. He wasn't wildly successful in either place. Hoagy kept returning to the town that always would be his fist love, Bloomington.

Then came magic in the form of "Stardust." Hoagy had written the music and early versions of the lyrics in the mid to late 1920s, years before it became a hit. As would be the case with many of his songs, Hoagy came up with the titles, themes, or lyrics that were rewritten or polished by others.

In the case of "Stardust," the lyrics were written by Mitchell Parish. In other cases, Hoagy composed the music and completely relinquished the words to a lyricist, often his friend Johnny Mercer.

Although Hoagy initially had composed "Stardust" with an up-tempo pace, the tune became a hit in 1930 when orchestras recorded it in a slow, dreamy style. In less than ten years, "Stardust" sold one million copies and brought Hoagy lifelong fame.

Show business became his world. He wrote the scores for dozens of movies and for Broadway shows such as *Walk With Music* (1940) starring Kitty Carlisle. In 1944, the wife of film director Howard Hawks hinted that Hoagy would be perfect for the part of "Cricket," a piano player in *To Have and Have Not*. Another career was born.

Even though Hoagy's movie roles usually were small, his scenes sometimes packed a wallop. In *The Best Years of Our Lives* (1946), the classic movie about readjustment to post-World War II life, Hoagy's character teaches a double-amputee played by Harold Russell (a real-life veteran who had lost his hands) to play "Chopsticks" with his hooks.

Hoagy told the story of his life in two autobiographies, *The Stardust Road* (1946) and *Sometimes I Wonder* (1965). With the passion he previously had reserved for show business, he took up golf. Eventually, "Georgia On My Mind" became the state song of Georgia and is continually revived by performers ranging from Ray Charles and Willie Nelson to Michael Bolton.

And in 1971, Hoagy Carmichael—along with Duke Ellington and eight other greats—was elected to the Songwriters Hall of Fame.

John Dillinger

Outlaw

The man and the era are inseparable.

The Mooresville farm boy who would become one of the most notorious, colorful criminals in American history terrorized—and captivated—the public during the Depression. It was an era when millions of struggling Americans despised banks but also lived in fear of machine-gun-toting gangsters who cruised city streets, ready to rob banks.

Elusive, glamorous and cocky, John Dillinger made a quick fortune during the Depression and inspired dozens of copycat bandits, including Ma Barker and "Pretty Boy" Floyd. Dillinger started out as a petty hoodlum and ended up as Public Enemy Number One on the Federal government's most-wanted list. He cut a swath through the Midwest with a series of bank robberies and spectacular jailbreaks. Improbably enough, some people almost regarded him as a folk hero—a crook, but not a really bad man.

He was a bank robber and a gangster, not a hero of any sort. His crimes frightened so many Hoosiers—it's said locksmiths across the state made a fortune from panicked homeowners—that the Indiana National Guard wanted to use tanks, airplanes and poison gas to stop or kill him. The Indiana chapter of the American Legion offered to arm thirty thousand members to patrol the state and assist in his capture. The U.S. Justice Department organized a squad in Chicago under agent Melvin Purvis to stop Midwestern crime sprees.

The gangster's brief, flamboyant career ended in July of 1934 at the entrance to a dark alley near the Biograph Theatre, a Chicago moviehouse. Dillinger, just thirty-one, was gunned down by federal agents or police officers from East Chicago, Indiana, following his betrayal by a legendary "Lady in Red."

His notoriety was such that more than a thousand people flocked to the Biograph despite 101-degree heat when they heard about Dillinger's violent death. Some dipped handkerchiefs or even their clothes into his blood so they would have souvenirs. The grotesque aspects continued the next day as thousands of gawkers lined up in the basement of the Cook County Morgue to view his body displayed on a slab.

Born in 1903 in Indianapolis, the future "public menace" lost his mother when he was three years old. His father, a kindly, moralistic grocer known as "Honest John" Dillinger, remarried. Young "Johnnie" quit school by the time he was sixteen. After his sixteenth birthday, the family moved to a sixty-acre farm near Mooresville. Admired for his prowess on local baseball teams, Johnnie Dillinger seemed destined for the rustic life.

But he was restless. Johnnie began talking to his teenage buddies about his idol, wild West gunslinger Jesse James.

At his family's Mooresville farm, Johnnie Dillinger honed his marksmanship. With his dog, he disappeared for hours into the nearby woods to shoot at rodents and crows. He was a restless teen.

Johnnie periodically lived in Indianapolis as well as Mooresville, picking up jobs in ma-

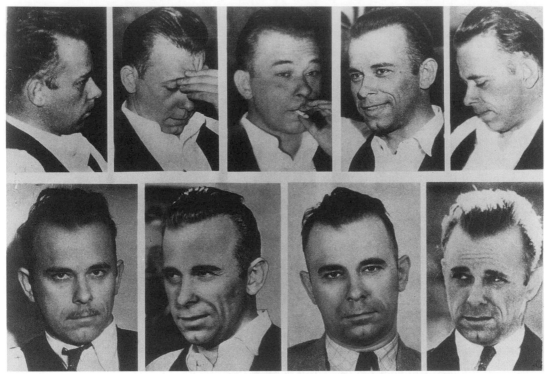

(Above) Many faces of John Dillinger: This bulletin with "nine characteristic closeups" was distributed shortly after Dillinger's armed escape from the Crown Point, Indiana, jail. (Below) This was the U.S. Department of Justice's "Wanted" poster for John Dillinger in 1934, when federal agents declared him "Public Enemy Number One."

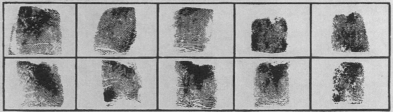

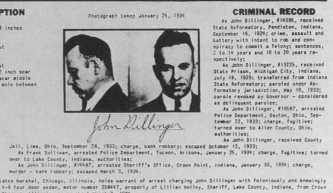

chine shops and a varnish factory. A youthful carouser, he joined the Navy and was assigned to a battleship. But Dillinger resented the Navy's discipline and deserted in 1924 after only six months' service.

After being dishonorably discharged, John Dillinger returned to Mooresville. Soon he met and married a sixteen-year-old Martinsville girl named Beryl. Neither had a solid job. They alternated living with their sets of parents; John killed time by hanging around a Mooresville pool hall.

Young Dillinger enjoyed drinking moonshine liquor with Ed Singleton, a charismatic ex-convict. During one tipsy get-together, the two hatched a plan. Dillinger sat on the back steps of a church one September night in 1924; Singleton either joined him on the steps or was waiting in a getaway car, according to various accounts.

In any case, the two watched an elderly grocer close his store. Dillinger and Singleton suspected he might be carrying his weekly receipts. Armed with a revolver, Dillinger rushed the grocer, announced it was a stickup and beat him with an iron bolt.

But their victim fought back and grabbed the revolver. It discharged, wounding the elderly grocer, according to some accounts. Singleton sped away in a car, leaving a half-drunk Dillinger to flee on foot. Both men were picked up by authorities.

Singleton, who was savvy about the justice system, hired an Indianapolis lawyer and pleaded innocent. Although a jury found him guilty on a lesser charge, Singleton served only two years in prison.

The Dillingers took a different approach. Assured that young John probably would get a light sentence if he pleaded guilty, "Honest John" didn't hire an attorney and convinced his son to confess. A stern judge promptly handed John the maximum sentence—two to fourteen years for conspiracy to commit a felony and another ten to twenty for assault with intent to rob.

For decades afterward, Dillinger's supporters expressed outrage at the inequity in the sentences of the two would-be stickup men. Reflecting on Dillinger years later, Indiana Governor Paul McNutt denounced the "obvious injustice" of the punishments and said: "This made a criminal out of Dillinger."

In any case, John Dillinger's life from then on was linked to crime, the underworld and prisons.

At the Indiana State Reformatory in Pendleton, he was an outstanding shortstop on the baseball team. But there were devastating setbacks. In 1929 Beryl divorced him. Turned down for parole about the same time, Dillinger asked to be transferred to the Indiana State Prison in Michigan City. According to legend, he made the unusual request because the state prison had a better baseball team. He spent four years in Michigan City until a parole in 1933.

The nine years behind bars had embittered the former farm boy. He also had been "schooled" in crime by other inmates.

After his release, Dillinger began a series of bloody sprees that, in a mere fourteen months, elevated him to the head of a marauding gang. In little more than a year, he went from virtual anonymity to the nation's Number One outlaw, the most notorious bank robber since Jesse and Frank James.

With two companions he held up a bank in Daleville, Indiana. Soon after, he hit banks in Montpelier, Indiana, and Bluffton, Ohio. Next came a daring crime. Using machine guns and bulletproof vests, the Dillinger gang held up a bank in Indianapolis not far from state police headquarters.

Through all this, Dillinger remembered his pals at the Indiana State Prison. Before his parole, he devised plans to "hatch" ten of them in what would become one of the most stunning prison breaks in American history.

One night in September of 1933, Dillinger tossed a package of pistols and cartridges over the prison walls. The bundle was picked up the next morning in the prison yard and turned in to the guards, so Dillinger had to try again. This time he successfully smuggled the guns in by putting them in a box of thread and shipping it to the prison's shirt factory, where his inmate cronies found the weapons.

Later that month the gang seized the factory's superintendents as hostages. Concealing the weapons under stacks of shirts they were carrying, the prisoners forced the officials to accompany them outside while guards watched unawares.

By then, Dillinger was jailed in Ohio. He had been captured while visiting the sister of one of the convicts, a divorcee with whom he was infatuated. No sooner was Dillinger jailed than his escaped buddies from Michigan City showed up to free him—killing the Lima, Ohio, sheriff in the process.

Bank robberies across the Midwest followed. Years later lawyers and others involved with the outlaw claimed that some of the robberies were prearranged by the banks themselves. The banks, they charged, wanted to create or conceal losses. The claim seems patently ridiculous today.

The robberies riveted the nation and terrified Hoosiers. In East Chicago, a policeman was slain when he attempted to block Dillinger and his gang as they fled.

Captured again, Dillinger was taken to an "escape-proof" jail in Crown Point. Exuding nonchalance, the outlaw posed for photos with the Lake County prosecutor, who even tossed his arm around the gangster's shoulders in a picture published across the country. (The memory of it later ruined the prosecutor's career.)

Soon Dillinger escaped. For decades, legend had it that he carved a wooden "gun" in his cell and bluffed his way out by convincing guards that the weapon, stained with shoe polish, was a genuine revolver.

As a fugitive, Dillinger shot his way out of a trap at a Wisconsin resort known as "Little Bohemia." The brazen outlaw even returned to Mooresville at least once for a party with relatives and friends during what newspapers called "the country's greatest manhunt."

Apparently he sensed the law would never think of looking for him in his small Indiana hometown. Authorities did look for him in Mooresville, but missed him somehow.

They eventually found "Public Enemy Number One" in Chicago. At the Biograph, the story of a bloody man came to a bloody end.

The Final Days of John Dillinger

Early 1934—In hiding in the Chicago area, Hoosier gangster John Dillinger dyes his brown hair black. He grows a mustache and dons eyeglasses occasionally.

May 27 or 28, 1934—Dillinger has his face altered by a German plastic surgeon with a criminal past. The outlaw nearly dies during the secret operation because of the crude anesthetic, overadministered.

Late May or early June—The same surgeon scars Dillinger's fingerprints with acid to prevent identification. (Ironically, his distorted fingerprints became a unique, conclusive piece of identification for his bullet-ridden corpse.) The scarring procedure is intensely painful, but Dillinger is stoic, merely wincing.

June—A Chicago couple meet a man who calls himself "Jimmy Lawrence." They double date with "Jimmy" and his girlfriend. They notice scars on his face, but don't ask about them out of respect for his feelings.

June 30—Merchants National Bank in South Bend is robbed of $29,890. Dillinger and his gang are armed with machine guns. It's his final crime.

Mid-July—Federal agent Melvin Purvis and his anti-Dillinger squad close in on their quarry. They are tipped off to his plans to attend a movie by Anna Sage, a native Romanian and former brothel keeper in East Chicago. She was about to be deported as an undesirable alien.

July 22, 8: 30 P.M.—Purvis and his agents watch as a threesome buy tickets at the Biograph Theatre to *Manhattan Melodrama*, a film starring Clark Gable and Myrna Loy. The threesome are Dillinger, his girlfriend and her landlady, Anna Sage, "The Lady in Red." (According to most accounts, she actually wore an orange skirt.) The agents decide to hold off until the movie is over to trap Dillinger. As Dillinger and his companions enjoy the movie, the agents, clad in suits, wait in 101-degree heat outside the theater. "It was the longest two hours of my life I ever spent," Purvis tells reporters later.

July 22, 10: 35 P.M.—Dillinger and the two women emerge from the Biograph. They start walking down the street when Dillinger notices his pursuers. Hoping to escape, he runs toward an alley. Purvis and his men close in. As Dillinger reaches for his gun, he is shot four times and falls face down, dead.

Jessamyn West

Jessamyn West

Author

Her family moved from her home state shortly before her seventh birthday, but novelist Jessamyn West once wrote, "I have two 'old countries'—England and southern Indiana. I spoke their language and loved them both."

The writer with the intriguing name set much of her fiction in Indiana, including two of her best-known works, The Friendly Persuasion *(1945) and* The Massacre at Fall Creek *(1975), both based on historical or family incidents.*

Born in rural Jennings County in 1902, West was a second cousin of Richard Nixon through her great-uncle, Frank Milhous. After the Wests moved to Southern California, she occasionally baby-sat "cousin Richard." She was educated at Whittier College like her famous relative—although, unlike him, West considered herself a progressive Democrat. She also studied at Oxford University in England. West was married to H. M. McPherson, a school superintendent. After an illustrious writing career, she died following a stroke in 1984. Life involved hard lessons to fulfill a career that elevated her to the ranks of America's foremost writers.

She was feeling sick—and illness couldn't have come at a worse time.

It was August 1931, shortly after Jessamyn West's twenty-ninth birthday. More significantly, she was about to take her oral examinations for a doctorate in English literature.

Having spent a summer studying at Oxford University in England—a rarity for an American woman in 1929—she wanted to obtain a Ph.D. from the University of California at Berkeley. First, though, Jessamyn hoped to triumph in her "orals."

But on that awful day she collapsed and began to hemorrhage from her lungs. Then came devastating news: Medical specialists announced West was tubercular—and in the advanced stages of the dreaded disease. In 1931, about 95 percent of the victims of advanced tuberculosis were dead within five years.

She was sent to a tuberculosis sanitarium near Los Angeles. Because of her deteriorating condition, she was placed in a terminal ward. The routine was deadening. The food was bland. And, she recalled later, the staff seemed unable—or unwilling—to exert any effort to convince patients to cling to life. Jessamyn West lived at the sanitarium two years.

Finally, staff members pronounced West "incurable." They advised her mother to "take her home and let her die amongst her loved ones."

Grace Milhous West complied with only the first part; this steadfast woman, descended from proud, prosperous Indiana Quakers, was not about to watch her daughter go to an early grave.

For several months, Grace cared for a bedfast Jessamyn. To strengthen her, Grace fed her constantly; Grace's "remedies" included a seemingly repulsive potion of orange juice and raw eggs.

To amuse her daughter, Grace brought Jessamyn quirky or entertaining gifts. To divert her attention from her illness, Grace told Jessamyn stories. They were tales about Grace's ancestors in Indiana, beginning during the Civil War and continuing through the turn of the century.

"Since I had no life of my own, past or future, in which to live, she gave me her own life . . . as a Quaker girl on a farm in southern Indiana," Jessamyn said years later.

Probably without realizing it, Grace also gave her daughter the best possible gift: inspiration that resulted in a career as a famous storyteller. Her mother's tales prompted West to write a series of gently humorous sketches about a Quaker farm couple, Jess and Eliza Birdwell, and their brood.

These eventually became the short stories published as *The Friendly Persuasion* (1945), an instant critical and popular success. It was followed by a sequel—or "companion," as West called it—titled *Except for Me and Thee*, whose beginning passage reveals the lyrical description, family affection and love of humanity which distinguish her writing:

> *Jess and Eliza Birdwell stood in the snowy twilight outside their own parlor window and gazed back inside like children at a peep show. The window, which was a farmhouse bay, was framed with lace curtains stiff and white as frost tracery. A lighted tree stood in the window, and around the tree was gathered a group of young people.*
>
> *Little Elspeth, the grandchild, a Quaker like the rest of them, and as untaught as they in dancing, was dancing; a tiptoe step to touch a branch, then quickly back to her mother, as if she needed to offset the magic of the Christmas tree by the touch of something known and familiar.*

Because she was bedfast when she started her career as an author, West wrote in longhand in a reclining position for the rest of her life—even though she recovered from tuberculosis and lived fifty more years. Her works include poetry, screenplays, memoirs, several novels and short stories.

About a decade after *The Friendly Persuasion* first appeared in print, it became a Hollywood movie. The film starred Gary Cooper as a dignified Hoosier Quaker and Anthony Perkins as his sensitive son who struggles with his conscience about whether to take up arms against the Confederacy.

Throughout the rest of her life, West mined Indiana for material. *The Massacre at Fall Creek* (1975) was based on a little-known but precedent-setting incident in a Hoosier frontier town near Pendleton. In 1824, nine Seneca Indians, including three women and four children, were slaughtered. The white assassins were convicted and executed, a result that marked a turning point in white-Indian relations on the frontier.

Newsweek magazine called the book "honorable" and "affecting"—words many people had been using for years to describe Jessamyn West. Inspiration and love had saved her life, and she passed those qualities along in her writing

Hoosiers in Hollywood

Carole Lombard

"You'll never know how much I've missed you all," one of the world's most glamorous women told a crowd of twelve thousand nearly worshipful Hoosiers on a cold January day in 1942. "I've always wanted to come back for a good visit, and now I'm here."

Hollywood star Carole Lombard, a Fort Wayne native married to the man who was almost every American woman's fantasy, was on a two-day visit to Indianapolis to sell World War II bonds. She set a sales record, in fact, accounting for sales of more than $2 million—no shock, considering the fact that, at one point in the 1930s, Lombard was Hollywood's highest-paid actress.

But her heartfelt swing through the Midwest (she had traveled to her beloved Fort Wayne before the rally in Indianapolis) ended tragically. The airplane Lombard boarded to return to southern California—and to her husband, movie star Clark Gable—crashed in Nevada, horrifying millions of fans around the world. Even five decades later, *Entertainment Weekly* magazine called the thirty-three-year-old actress' death "one of the damndest shames in movie history."

The leading lady of screwball comedies such as *My Man Godfrey* (1936) and *Nothing Sacred* (1937) was born Jane Alice Peters in Fort Wayne in 1908. She lived in a house near the St. Mary's River, often fishing and swimming there.

"I was a complete tomboy," Lombard told an interviewer years later. "My brothers were my best friends I ever had, and whatever they did, I did—sometimes a little rougher and always to the dismay of my mother."

Lombard shouldn't be remembered just for her untimely death, though. Her talent had an impact on movie lovers from the early 1930s on. Exuding an endless capacity for fun, she appeared with William Powell (who became her first husband) in *Man of the World* (1931) and John Barrymore in the classic *Twentieth Century* (1934).

"Such was the giddy glamour of Lombard that she could do a pratfall in an evening gown or look stunning with an ice pack on her head," noted *Entertainment Weekly*.

After her final war bond rally, she told interviewers, "Some of my happiest memories of my family revolve around Indiana and Fort Wayne. So many times I find myself wanting to just come back and walk around, meet the people I knew years ago and relax. However, I've created a life for myself that seems at times void of the little things . . .

"I will be back, and when I return it will be with words of victory and peace."

Irene Dunne

She earned five Academy Award nominations, achieving fame as an actress, singer and comedienne in the 1930s and '40s—and Irene Dunne made her professional singing debut in Indianapolis. The future movie star spent much of her youth in Madison, Indiana; her singing debut came while attending the former Indianapolis Conservatory of Music about 1918.

A gracious, winsome actress who starred with such leading men as Cary Grant and

Charles Boyer, Dunne was born in Louisville, Kentucky, probably in 1898. As a child, she moved with her mother to Madison after the death of her father, a steam vessel supervisor.

After she graduated from high school in Madison, a local civic group boosted her career by giving her a scholarship to the music conservatory in Indianapolis. While she took lessons, she sang at local churches and lived in the Woodruff Place neighborhood.

Following graduation from the conservatory, Dunne moved to Chicago, then New York, all the while dreaming of a career with the Metropolitan Opera. Instead, she landed the lead in a road company of *Show Boat* and arrived in Hollywood in 1930. Her first Oscar nomination came the next year for *Cimarron*, a western.

Although she starred in musicals such as *Roberta* in 1935 and the 1936 screen version of *Show Boat*, Dunne was extremely versatile. She became known as a bright comedienne in movies such as *The Awful Truth* (1937); Dunne also handled dramas with skill, including *Penny Serenade* (1941). Perhaps her most famous role was as a beloved Norwegian immigrant in *I Remember Mama* (1948).

Throughout her stellar career, Dunne told interviewers that she considered herself a Hoosier. She retired in the 1950s and died in 1990.

Steve McQueen

His childhood and adolescent years in the Indianapolis area were far from serene—and they certainly did not offer a sneak preview of success. But Steve McQueen went on to become one of Hollywood's biggest box office stars of the 1960s and '70s.

Known for his reckless behavior off-screen—and his portrayals of rugged characters on it—McQueen starred in about two dozen major motion pictures, including *The Great Escape* (1963), *The Sand Pebbles* (1966), *Bullit* (1968) and *The Towering Inferno* (1974).

"My life was screwed up before I was born," McQueen said after he had achieved fame.

He was referring to family turbulence before his birth as Terrence Steven McQueen in Beech Grove in 1930. According to biographer Marshall Terrill, McQueen's mother, Jullian, was a teenage runaway and an alcoholic by the time her son was born. McQueen's father, a stunt pilot for a flying circus, abandoned his family when Steve was six months old.

Without a steady job, Jullian moved with Steve back and forth between Indianapolis and Missouri, where her parents lived. Finally, when Steve was not quite four, Jullian left him with her mother in Slater, Missouri. During the Depression, Steve and his grandmother lived on an uncle's nearby farm. Eventually he returned to Indianapolis with his mother and her new husband.

McQueen found his way into acting in the 1950s. He began appearing in television dramas; his big break came by playing a bounty hunter in the TV series *Wanted: Dead or Alive* (1958–1961). Movie successes followed, including *The Magnificent Seven* (1960), *Hell is for Heroes* (1962), *The Cincinnati Kid* (1965) and *The Thomas Crown Affair* (1968).

His battle with cancer—and use of unorthodox treatments to combat the disease—were making headlines when he died in Mexico in 1980.

Will Hays

The phrase "the Hays Office" was heard constantly in Hollywood for more than forty years—and the general public knew the reference so well that it was often tossed off without explanation by film characters.

The Hays Office was a regulatory agency the movie industry set up to police itself after

Fort Wayne native Carole Lombard appeared at a War Bonds rally in Indianapolis in 1942 with Movie Czar Will Hays (second from right). Lombard, along with her mother, was killed in a plane crash while returning to Hollywood after this rally.

Irene Dunne

Steve McQueen

sensational drug and sex scandals involving Hollywood stars in the 1920s. Churches, civic groups and parent organizations across the country were pressuring their state legislatures to censor movies; that would have made national distribution of Hollywood films impossible.

Hence the formation of the Motion Picture Producers and Distributors of America in 1922. Hollywood studio heads recruited a respected Hoosier, Will Hays, to head it up—and "the Hays Office" became the slang phrase for the industry's self-censorship arm.

In 1930 the Hays Code was officially adopted; by the mid-1930s, "the production code," as it became known, strictly regulated profanity and depictions of sexual activity in movies. The Hays Office was responsible for reading scripts, screening finished movies and giving films its seal of approval. Without the seal, a movie would not be shown at studio-owned theaters.

"Good taste is good business," Will Hays said at one point, summarizing his approach.

According to Hollywood lore, the Hays Code's enforcers demanded that, if a married couple were shown in bed, someone's foot had to remain on the floor. The Hays Code remained in place until 1966, although provisions were significantly relaxed over the decades.

It's no surprise Hays was chosen to lead the cleanup campaign. He was a prominent, conservative politician and an active Presbyterian. To accept the job, Hays, a Republican, resigned as U.S. Postmaster General under President Warren G. Harding.

William Harrison Hays was born in 1879 in the southern Indiana town of Sullivan. He graduated from Wabash College, became an attorney and quickly rose through the ranks of state and national GOP politics. As Republican national chairman in 1918, he helped reunite a badly divided GOP; he managed Harding's presidential campaign in 1920.

Hays took the job in Hollywood only on the condition that he not be a figurehead, but exert real power. He insisted that he be like the commissioner of baseball, which had begun to regulate itself a few years earlier in the wake of the 1919 "Black Sox" scandal. Because sportswriters called the baseball commissioner "the baseball czar," Hays became known as "the movie czar."

Hays' power reached far beyond movies' content. He was involved with labor relations, public relations and dealings with foreign governments. According to a biography by his son, Will Hays Jr., the "movie czar" once even faced down Italian dictator Benito Mussolini in a dispute over Italy's refusal to pay money owed to American producers.

Hays stepped down as "movie czar" in 1943, although the production code remained for twenty-three more years. He died in Sullivan in 1954. His son went on to be a Crawfordsville mayor, attorney, Hollywood screenwriter and scriptwriter for television.

Red Skelton

Radio, TV, movies, vaudeville, the circus—the Vincennes-born comedian with the distinctive name labored in almost every aspect of show business except opera.

As the only redhead in a family of four brothers, Richard Bernard Skelton was almost certain to get his nickname shortly after his birth in 1911. His father, Joseph Skelton, a clown with Hagenbeck and Wallace Circus, died two months before Red's birth. Plunged into poverty, all of the Skelton brothers went to work at an early age. They shuttled between relatives in Vincennes and Mansfield, Ohio.

In his autobiography *I'll Tell All* (1941), Skelton wrote that he prompted his first laughs with an unintended pratfall: When he was ten, Red was performing in a medicine show and tumbled off the stage, smashing several bottles of potions. The audience howled, and Red, who wasn't hurt, never stopped going for belly laughs. Skelton left school after the seventh grade, toured with traveling medicine shows across Indiana and then performed on show-boats that traveled the Ohio and Missouri rivers.

Next came burlesque shows and jobs as a circus clown. Skelton became a hit on the vaudeville circuit in the 1930s with a doughnut-dunking pantomime. (He repeated the routine many times in movies and TV shows years later.) Mickey Rooney loved the bit and suggested that MGM include Skelton in the movie *Having A Wonderful Time* (1938).

More movies followed, along with his own radio show. Playing the character of "Junior," a mean little kid, Skelton introduced an expression that became a national catch phrase in the early 1940s: "I dood it." (One of his starring movies, a 1943 comedy with Eleanor Powell, even had the phrase as its title.) His comedy style—goofy but endearing and heartfelt—became a huge success on television; the Hoosier enjoyed a twenty-year run with *The Red Skelton Show* (1951-71).

His comic characters included Clem Kadiddlehopper, a confused bumpkin, and Freddie the Freeloader, a hobo who never spoke. Skelton's closing line on his shows was always the same: "God bless." Since his program's cancellation, Skelton generally kept a low profile until his death in September 1997.

Herb Shriner

"I came to Indiana as soon as I heard about it."

So joked an Ohio-born comedian who became famous on television in the 1950s as "the Hoosier Humorist." Herb Shriner, born in Toledo in 1918, moved as a toddler to the Fort Wayne area, where his mother worked as a department store detective.

Sometimes compared to Will Rogers, folksy, easygoing Shriner punctuated his rustic banter—which often included quips about Hoosiers—with tunes on his harmonica. His heyday was on radio and TV variety shows from the late 1940s through the '50s. A sample of his gentle, low-key style: "Hoosiers are congenitally inquisitive. That means nosy, in a nice sort of way."

In 1953 Shriner became the father of twin sons who entered show business. They are Wil and Kin, named for Hoosier cartoonist Kin Hubbard. In a 1988 interview, Wil said that, upon his birth, his dad looked at the nearly identical babies and wisecracked, "Am I supposed to have a choice?"

After Shriner's success on TV, Herb and his children (who also included a daughter named Indiana) often spent their summers at a lakeside cottage in Angola, Indiana. The blissful family life ended tragically when Herb Shriner and his wife were killed in an auto accident in 1970.

The twins and their sister went to live with a grandmother. Like his father, Wil Shriner became a comedian; during the 1980s, he was the host of a syndicated TV talk show. His twin, Kin, is a soap opera actor best known for his role on the long-running TV show *General Hospital*.

Dean Jagger

The bald, distinguished-looking actor had only a few leading parts in movies, the primary one the title role in *Brigham Young—Frontiersman* (1940).

Instead, Dean Jagger of rural, northeastern Indiana was known as a top character actor for more than forty years, winning the Academy Award in 1949 for his performance as a compassionate Air Force commander in *Twelve O'Clock High*. On television, Jagger por-

Comedian Red Skelton and his wife, Georgia, and children, Richard and Valentina.

Dean Jagger

Herb Shriner and his harmonica-playing family in 1956. (Left to right) Wil, Herb, his wife, Pixie, Indiana, and Kin.

trayed the kindly principal on the series *Mr. Novak* (1963–65). Whatever the role, he always radiated integrity.

Dean Jagger was born near Lima, Ohio, in 1903.

"Dean and his parents moved to Indiana when he was three or four years old," recalled his cousin Kenny Jagger, an Indianapolis organist. "He always thought of himself as a Hoosier. Our relatives had an onion farm. Dean hated that kind of work, though."

Dean Jagger grew up on the farm near the tiny town of Collins; it is close to Larwell in the northeastern corner of the state. He attended Larwell High School and took elocution lessons. Then Jagger enrolled at Wabash College and eventually started teaching eighth-graders at an Indiana school.

But he gave in to his desire to act during the 1920s, moved to Chicago and toured on the Chautauqua circuit. In the late 1920s and early '30s, Jagger appeared in a few movies.

"He could ride a horse with ease," Kenny Jagger said. "Dean would shuttle between New York and Hollywood, making cowboy movies at Republic Studios because of his skill on a horse."

Primarily, though, Jagger was known as a Broadway star through the 1930s, appearing in the classic stage production of *Tobacco Road* (1933). Hollywood beckoned him back with *Brigham Young*, a film biography of the Mormon leader. Dozens of A-quality movies followed, including classics such as *White Christmas* (1954) with Bing Crosby and *Elmer Gantry* (1961) with Burt Lancaster.

Dean Jagger died in 1991.

Phil Harris

Some generations knew him as Jack Benny's radio sidekick and as the husband of glamorous movie musical star Alice Faye. Other generations knew him as the voice of "Baloo the Bear" in the movie *The Jungle Book* (1967).

Some recall that Phil Harris' biggest claim to fame was as a popular bandleader for more than fifty years. Whatever his claim to fame, he maintained his ties to Linton, a small town in western Indiana. For years—up to and including his ninetieth birthday in 1994—he presided over a celebrity golf tournament and variety show in Linton. The Phil Harris Festival raised thousands of dollars for college scholarships for Hoosiers.

"I love Indiana, and I love the race," Harris, then eighty-eight, said during an interview in 1992 at the Indianapolis 500, another event in his home state that he never missed. "I'm feeling OK, but what the heck can you expect when you are eighty-eight? I'm happy just to be around."

Harris was around a long time, passing away in 1995 at ninety-one. Up until the final year of his life, he regaled interviewers with tales about his annual trips to Alaska for salmon fishing and his taste for Jack Daniels.

Born in 1904, Harris lived in Linton until he was twelve. Then his family moved to Nashville, Tennessee. He always considered himself a Hoosier, though—even after achieving success as a nightclub bandleader, comic singer and occasional movie personality. Harris appeared in more than a dozen Hollywood films, often playing himself ("brash, illiterate me," as he put it). Those films included *Man About Town* (1939), *The Glenn Miller Story* (1954), *The High and the Mighty* (1954) and *Anything Goes* (1956).

In addition to leading the band on Jack Benny's top-rated radio show beginning in 1936, Harris played a comic character on the program. He also co-starred with Faye, whom he married in 1941, on a popular radio show from 1946–54.

Clifton Webb

Suave and sinister, Webb created one of the most memorable screen villains of the 1940s in the suspense classic *Laura* (1944). It was one of three performances for which Clifton Webb received an Oscar nomination. The others were in *The Razor's Edge* (1946), and *Sitting Pretty* (1948), a comedy in which he played a self-centered, put-upon baby sitter.

That performance led to a popular series of "Mr. Belvedere" comedies in which Webb was typecast as a finicky, sharp-tongued character. Before his Hollywood career, Webb was a dancer, opera singer and a star of Broadway 1930s musical comedies and revues such as *Three's a Crowd* and *As Thousands Cheer*.

His Hoosier connection: Webb was born in Indianapolis, probably in 1891. His real name was Webb Parmalee Hollenbeck.

He was only a young child when his stage-struck mother took him to New York City and arranged for his stage debut. They never returned to Indiana to live. After enjoying a long Broadway and Hollywood career, which had even included a few silent movies, Webb died in 1966.

Marjorie Main

To millions of moviegoers, she was "Ma Kettle," the eccentric, cornpone mother in a series of hillbilly movie comedies of the late 1940s and '50s.

Marjorie Main was born in rural Shelby County in 1890. Her name at birth was Marybelle Tomlinson. She changed her name because her father, a minister, objected to acting. From 1905 to 1906, she attended Franklin College and was a charter member of what became Delta Delta Delta sorority there. After a year at Franklin, Marjorie transferred to a dramatics school in Lexington, Kentucky.

She traveled across the country for several years in vaudeville and stock companies. Her big break came when she portrayed the anguished mother of a gangster in the classic stage (1935) and screen (1937) versions of *Dead End*. In a riveting scene in the movie, Main slaps the face of her son (Humphrey Bogart) and cries, "Ya dirty yellow dog!"

Her "Ma Kettle" character first appeared in the movie *The Egg and I* (1947). She was nominated for an Academy Award for that performance; Main repeated the "Ma Kettle" role in the popular film series with Percy Kilbride as Pa Kettle. Her last movie was *The Kettles on Old MacDonald's Farm* (1957). She died in 1975.

Frances Farmer

Frances Farmer's story was one of Hollywood's most harrowing real-life plots.

Her hometown was Seattle, where she was born in 1913. Outspoken and high-strung, Farmer flirted with Communism and quarreled with her domineering mother. Farmer made her screen debut in the mid-1930s and won critical raves for her roles in *Come and Get It* (1936), *Rhythm on the Range* (1936), and other movies. Unpopular with studio executives, Farmer left Hollywood for the New York stage and reaped more laurels for her performance in the Group Theater production of *Golden Boy* (1937).

After a few more films, though, there were dark times. Drinking problems, fights with studios, nightmarish publicity, and mental illness halted her career. Forced institutionalizations cost her eight years in the 1940s; in her autobiography, Farmer revealed that she

(Clockwise from top left) Phil Harris, Marjorie Main, Clifton Webb, and Frances Farmer. (Photofest)

was raped by orderlies at a mental institution. She was living in obscurity in Eureka, California, when she was discovered by a promoter who became her third husband.

That's when she became a Hoosier. Her new husband brought the ex-Hollywood star to Indianapolis for a summer stock production in 1958. Although they eventually divorced, Farmer spent the rest of her life in Indiana. An executive for NBC-TV's affiliate in Indianapolis asked Farmer to be the hostess of the station's afternoon movie show. She accepted, and *Frances Farmer Presents* was broadcast daily for six years. She was fired in 1964, rehired, then fired again.

During her Indiana years, Farmer played in several roles in productions at Purdue University and local dinner theaters. She died in 1970.

Her turbulent life became the basis of a movie in 1982 (Jessica Lange was nominated for an Academy Award for playing Farmer) and a TV-movie. Farmer's haunting autobiography, published posthumously, was titled *Will There Really Be A Morning?*

Karl Malden

Gary, Indiana, is his hometown, not either of the two cities Karl Malden has been associated with in television and movies—San Francisco and New Orleans. Malden was the star of the popular TV crime series *The Streets of San Francisco* (1972–77) and, long before that, won an Oscar for his role in the 1951 movie version of *A Streetcar Named Desire*, set in New Orleans. He also played in the legendary Broadway production of *Streetcar* in 1947 with Marlon Brando.

"Does this look like the face of a leading man?" bulbous-nosed, raspy-voiced Malden once was quoted as saying, "I came out of the steel mills of Indiana and had to work like crazy to be successful as an actor."

The son of Serbian immigrants, he was born Mladen Sekulovich in 1912 in Chicago, but grew up across the state line in Gary. His father, a mill worker, had been a performer in Europe; he believed children of immigrants could learn about their culture through music and theater, so young Karl starred in school plays. He began working at U.S. Steel's open hearth after graduating from Emerson High School.

Finally, he had enough of the rigorous mill life. Malden studied at a drama school in Chicago and launched a New York stage career in the 1930s. In *Streetcar*, the Tennessee Williams classic, he portrayed "Mitch," a gentle friend of Brando's brutish character. He followed it up by appearing with Brando in another of the most famous movies of the 1950s, *On the Waterfront* (1954); Malden was nominated for an Academy Award for his role as a sensitive Catholic priest, although this time he didn't win.

In *The Streets of San Francisco*, he portrayed a grizzled, veteran police officer paired with a brash young inspector. Malden won an Emmy Award in 1985 for his role in a TV-movie, *Fatal Vision*.

Anne Baxter

She was the granddaughter of one of the world's most famous architects. When she was born in Michigan City, Indiana, in 1923, Anne Baxter's illustrious grandfather, Frank Lloyd Wright, was living and designing not far away, in the Chicago neighborhood of Oak Park. Anne's mother, Catherine, was Wright's daughter; Anne's father, Kenneth Baxter, was an executive for the Seagram's Distillers Company.

The Baxters didn't live in Michigan City very long. When Anne was a child, the family

Actress and TV personality Betsy Palmer (left) was a stenographer in East Chicago when an aptitude test revealed she had a flair for the performing arts.

Anne Baxter and Karl Malden

moved to New York City's suburbs. By age ten, Anne had announced her intention to be an actress; she made her Broadway debut as a teenager in a murder mystery, *Seen But Not Heard* in 1936.

After that, it was a lifetime of show business for the husky-voiced, versatile actress with an appealing personality. Her first significant film role was in an innovative movie based on a novel by a fellow Hoosier—*The Magnificent Ambersons* (1942), Orson Welles' screen version of Booth Tarkington's classic.

Anne Baxter was one of Hollywood's busiest actresses during the 1940s and '50s, winning an Academy Award in 1946 as Best Supporting Actress for her role as an alcoholic, hysterical widow in *The Razor's Edge*. In 1950, she played the title role in a movie many film buffs consider one of the best ever made, *All About Eve*. Baxter had leading roles in dozens of other movies, including the part of the Egyptian princess Nefertari in *The Ten Commandments* (1956).

She was still active in TV, movies and theater when she died in 1985.

Betsy Palmer

The longtime panelist on one of television's most durable game shows, *I've Got a Secret*, has a secret of her own: She was born Patricia Betsy Hrunek ("It's pronounced like a sneeze," she once said) in 1926 near East Chicago.

Although she primarily became known as a TV personality, blond Betsy Palmer also starred in several major motion pictures during the 1950s—*Mister Roberts* (1955) with Henry Fonda and Jack Lemmon and *Queen Bee* with Joan Crawford among them—and played leading roles on the stage. On Broadway, she appeared in *Cactus Flower* and a revival of *South Pacific* in the 1960s.

Originally a stenographer in East Chicago, Palmer enrolled as a drama major at DePaul University in Chicago during the late 1940s.

Then came dozens of roles in live, New York-based television of the 1950s. Several times Palmer was cast opposite a Hoosier destined for even greater stardom than hers—James Dean. The two became fast friends.

Her sunny disposition helped Palmer win jobs on *Secret* (she was a panelist from 1957 to 1967) and, for about a year in the late 1950s, as the co-host on *The Today Show*, NBC-TV's long-running morning news program. In 1980, Betsy Palmer played against her perky image by portraying an ax murderess in a horror film that went on to become a teen cult favorite, *Friday the 13th*.

James Dean

Movie star

His eternal image—in the red windbreaker, white T-shirt and blue jeans—adorns posters from Munich to Melbourne.

The James Dean phenomenon has made the Grant County town of Fairmount (population three thousand) known around the world, particularly every September 30, the anniversary of James Dean's tragic death in a California car crash in 1955.

Born in Marion in 1931 and just twenty-four at the time of the fatal accident, the future American icon was a 1949 graduate of Fairmount High School. His early years were spent in California, but he returned to Indiana at age nine following his mother's death from cancer. He grew up under the care of his aunt and uncle, Marcus and Ortense Winslow, on a family farm near Fairmount.

After high school, Dean returned to Southern California and landed bit parts in movies and TV productions, then moved to New York for Broadway roles and appearances on live television in the "golden age" of TV. Less than two years before his death, he came back to California to star in three movies: East of Eden *(1954),* Rebel Without a Cause *(1955), and* Giant, *released posthumously in 1956.*

The interviews with Fairmount residents and Dean enthusiasts were conducted in 1985. Adeline Nall, Dean's drama teacher at Fairmount High School and one of a succession of maternal figures in his life, died eleven years later.

FAIRMOUNT, Indiana—There was the James Dean of the flickering screen—a lonely, misunderstood "teenager" who stammered, slouched and winced his way into hundreds of hurt hearts.

"I was in a shell all my life, and it was Jimmy who pulled me out," said Greg Larbes, thirty-eight, a polio victim, Cincinnati resident and editor of the James Dean Fan Club's national monthly newsletter.

There was the Jim Dean of the Fairmount farm—a bespectacled boy who rode motor-cycles, collected rocks, and pulled pranks.

"It's unbelievable," said Hugh Caughell, seventy-eight, a retired biology teacher from the old Fairmount High School. "Here's a normal kid I had in school, a normal kid I had in 4-H who becomes . . . well, he becomes JAMES DEAN!"

There was the Jimmy Dean of high school speech contests and the basketball court—a motherless youth with spectacular oratorical skills, a competitive streak and a sensitive, soulful side.

"He had a spiritual quality, of course," recalled Adeline Brookshire Nall, seventy-nine, his high school drama teacher. "Jim told me once that he wanted to be a minister. And he would have been a good one, believe you me."

James Dean had small parts in Sailor Beware *(1951) and* Has Anybody Seen My Gal? *(1952) before landing the lead role in* East of Eden *(1954), the movie that made him a star. His last movie role was in* Giant *(1956).*

There was the James Dean of the Hollywood scandal sheets—the thrill-seeking loner who insulted film moguls, indulged in wild mood swings and varoomed around Tinseltown in snazzy sports cars.

A miniature replica of his last sports car—a silver Porsche, mangled in exactly the manner of the original after his fatal crash—sits under glass in the Fairmount Historical Museum.

At the other end of town, a poster in Lewis' Restaurant shows four faces of the actor: James Dean smirking, James Dean giggling, James Dean with a pained pout and James Dean with his head tossed back, laughing at the world.

"There was more than one Jimmy Dean," commented a Fairmount resident. "You could say there were four or five."

A conservative crowd estimate, no doubt.

The enigmatic actor's burial place in the town cemetery has prompted pilgrimages for thousands and become a legend in itself; his tombstone has been hauled from the ground and stolen three times.

"We just had twenty-six students from Seiwa, Japan," said Ann Warr, president of the museum. "They came here from across the water just for Jimmy Dean."

The actor with the worldwide following had major roles in just three movies, two Broadway plays, a Pepsi commercial and several dozen New York television productions.

But his impact was such that sociologists have called him the first student protester, even the "first teenager."

Some residents of Fairmount are quick to point out that James Dean is not the town's only hold on fame. Cartoonist Jim Davis, creator of Garfield the cat, and CBS-TV correspondent Phil Jones also grew up here.

At the historical museum, which houses memorabilia ranging from the cowboy boots Dean wore in *Giant* (1955) to yearbooks and movie stills, James Dean postcards, drinking glasses, T-shirts and posters share shelf space with Garfield artifacts.

But feelings about Dean remain by far the most intense, with barely concealed rivalries about who should be rightful "keepers of the flame." Longtime residents confide that some of their neighbors—who frequently are quoted about their "memories" of the teenage Dean—never knew him.

No such doubts exist about the credibility of Mrs. Nall, who taught Dean for six years in classes ranging from Spanish to speech. She gave him a D in the former (where he frequently nodded off) and an A in the latter, where he honed the oratorical style that made him 1949's state champion.

"Part of his secret, part of his success, was that anything he wanted to do, he did well," Mrs. Nall recalled. "He surely had the ability to concentrate."

The sitting room of Mrs. Nall's rural Marion home is a monument to her former student, with glossy photographs, artists' sketches, busts and letters displayed on counter tops, her piano and all four walls.

"I loved him," she said. "He changed my life."

Mrs. Nall met Dean when he was a seventh-grader sent to her for coaching in a speech contest. He lost the event and initially blamed his failure on the teacher.

"Frankly, he couldn't take criticism," she said. "My feelings were hurt—both Jim and I were awfully sensitive people—and finally Marcus (his uncle) came to school and told me, 'Don't let it bother you. He is very critical. He's that way at home.' "

But with a shake of her white-haired head and theatrical sweeps of her hands, Mrs. Nall dismissed most of the talk of Dean's haunting loneliness.

"No one mistreated him in town, and Ortense (his aunt) is as close to an angel as you'll find," she emphasized. "He wasn't a heartbreaker with girls, but everyone liked him."

She concedes there might be some truth to what biographers have called a "mother complex" in her favorite student. "I know Mrs. Dean adored that kid. Her death was a terrible blow to him."

For many, the most vivid memories of the young Dean are of his hustling performance on the basketball squad. About five-eight at his full adult height, Dean was among the shortest players, particularly during his sophomore year.

"He always gave 110 percent—and then some," said Harry Warr, a retired insurance company manager and a member of Fairmount High's class of 1935.

"He'd get on that putt-putt cycle of his, and you'd know he was coming. But other than that, he was a regular boy here."

To legions of others, however, Dean is anything but a "regular boy." And after thirty years, the hero worship shows no signs of diminishing.

"It's just as strong now, if not stronger, than it's ever been," said Bill Lewis, forty-four, an Anderson resident and president of the James Dean Fan Club. "I don't like to think of us as a cult. We don't go up there and worship a dead body. We remember him because he meant something special to us."

What would have happened to James Dean had he survived?

Humphrey Bogart, who knew him slightly, always claimed the Hoosier actor would not have been able to surmount his initial publicity—that Dean was the right hero in the right era who died the right kind of death at the right age.

But millions of movie fans worldwide disagree. So do thousands of aspiring actors. As movie star Martin Sheen once put it, "When I was in acting school, there was a saying, 'If Marlon Brando changed the way people acted, then James Dean changed the way people lived.' He was simply a genius."

Although no one will ever know the directions Dean's career would have taken, there is one certainty: His influence on generations of teenagers—and on actors—has been monumental.

Legends of Our Own Day

Herman B Wells has been a presence at Indiana University for about eighty years. He's been everything on the Bloomington campus from a student to president and chancellor.

Herman B Wells

Indiana University president and chancellor

"Mr. IU," Hoosiers nicknamed him. And who deserved the nickname more than Herman B Wells?

For nearly eighty years—to six generations who spent time on the Bloomington campus of Indiana University—his was the preeminent personality. In the Roaring Twenties, Herman B Wells was your charismatic classmate. In the thirties, he was your professor. For a quarter century from the late thirties to the early sixties, he was your university president. For the next thirty-five years, he was your chancellor.

But the length of his clout wasn't the most remarkable thing about him. The remarkable thing was how Wells used his clout—whether standing up to segregationist merchants or narrow-minded state legislators, helping shape international economic policies or pushing for the development of a music school that would win worldwide acclaim.

Wells was born in 1902 in Jamestown, Indiana, then a "rural village" of six hundred people. The son of Granville and Anna Bernice Wells was, from birth, Herman B: His mother's family tradition dictated that middle names begin with B, but his parents could not agree on a choice—so the "B" stood alone.

Until he was nine, Wells lived in a house without electricity or plumbing. During his sophomore year of high school, the family moved to Lebanon. He was interviewed on the IU campus in 1988.

The legend fell down.

The setting was a sidewalk in West Berlin. The octogenarian was among a group strolling to an opera performance.

"Subsequently, a hospital determined he had broken his collarbone," noted Frank Banta, a retired Indiana University professor of German.

"But before any of us knew that, he charged on, sat through three hours of what I will diplomatically tell you was not a very well-performed opera, and only *then* asked to be taken to the hospital.

"He must have been in tremendous pain. Yet he apparently felt causing any commotion would have been disruptive."

Ach-yes. Commotion.

In some ways, indefatigable Herman B Wells has been causing a stir for nearly seventy years, clear back to his days as a merrymaking undergraduate. Observers say he tooled around IU's Bloomington campus with a raccoon coat, an open touring car and an oh-what-a-wonderful-morning spirit.

It was a campus of not yet three thousand when Wells showed up as a teenager in 1921, back in an era when the college president was transported to his Maxwell Hall office in a horse and buggy. Seventy-five years later, with Wells as chancellor, there were more than thirty thousand students on the Bloomington campus.

Yet Herman B—no period, please—Wells started out underestimated, as the nation's youngest state university president and a man pegged as an intellectual featherweight. He was expected to be a caretaker president—certainly not a serious contender for the job that became his for a term most sources say won't be equaled.

That term began with inauguration in 1938, the year Orson Welles terrified the nation on Halloween, and concluded in 1962 during a Camelot autumn of the Kennedy administration.

Along the way, he became known as a colossus of higher education.

"You're talking about Indiana University personified when you talk about Herman B Wells," stressed Cliff Travis (class of '51), the university's counsel for twenty years. "Describing him that way doesn't take away anything from anyone else. It's just the unvarnished truth.

"Top academic leaders still call on him for advice, just the way you would call on your family doctor."

In *Profiles of Excellence*, a collection of essays about Hoosier legends, author Martin L. McAuliffe Jr. argues that Wells' thumbprints on the state are just as significant as his mark on IU.

"No man," McAuliffe contends, "did more to widen the horizons of Indiana . . . than Herman Wells."

But if he started out underestimated, some say the eighty-six-year-old university chancellor has become that way again. Partly, that's the result of time's passage, and it's partly due to Wells himself, who is modest to an almost exasperating extreme.

Yet many credit Wells—a former economics professor whose reputation as a businessman ballooned during the early 1930s as a supervisor with the State Department of Financial Institutions—with drafting legislation that reformed Indiana's banking laws for decades.

Waving aside all questions concerning his own triumphs, the man who titled his autobiography *Being Lucky* responded with "You'll have to talk to someone else about that" or "My role has been greatly exaggerated." But others say his stature with the Indiana Legislature was instrumental in protecting academic freedom at Indiana.

"I came here from Ohio State," noted Donald Gray, an IU professor of English since 1956. "There were groups there imitating what Joe McCarthy (an arch-conservative U.S. senator blamed for stifling research) was doing in Washington.

"That didn't happen here, and I'll tell you why. It was because of the presence Herman Wells had with the legislature and the fact that he was willing to stand up for unfettered intellectual inquiry."

Noting that Wells remained unwavering in his support of zoologist Alfred Kinsey, whose sex research created a blizzard of controversy in the 1950s, Banta said:

"It's amazing that this research could have occurred in a conservative state like Indiana during that kind of era. Believe me, it could not have occurred without Herman B Wells."

Wells said simply, "Either you have academic freedom or you don't. There is no compromise. Without it, you don't have a university. You have a trade school."

A Boone County native, Wells was the only child of two teachers—although his mother, later the official IU hostess during the Wells presidency, ended her formal education with the eighth grade.

In *Being Lucky*, Wells marvels at her character (Anna Bernice Harting Wells went from a sheltered life as a small-town housewife to a woman presented to the queen of England) and credits her for the glow of his own public persona.

"The personal popularity I seemed to acquire dated from this period (when she became hostess) and was altogether due to her guidance in involving me in the life of the university community."

Claude Rich, eighty-one, a former IU Alumni Association secretary and a distant cousin who has known Wells more than seventy years, said the chancellor's most trying period did not spring from any flap during his long college presidency—but rather from adjusting to his mother's death in 1973. "It took him a long, long time to get over that," Rich said.

Wells' father, whose imposing portrait dominated one wall of his office, started out as a farmer, teacher and principal but later became a banker in Lebanon.

A vivid memory from Wells' boyhood involved his father standing up to the Ku Klux Klan—despite the radical group's threat to start whispers about the bank's solvency during an era in which "bank rumors" often resulted in catastrophe.

Several sources detected a pattern in the younger Wells' career as university president. When Wells took command, segregated tables for blacks existed at the IU Commons, the popular student dining spot in the Union Building. Quietly but firmly, Wells ordered the "Reserved" signs removed.

Restaurant owners balked, fearing they would have to blend black and white patrons as well. Students issued demands for integrated service elsewhere. Wells was invited to a secret meeting with merchants.

"There I was informed that, unless we persuaded the students and their faculty supporters to remove their demands for service, the restaurant owners were prepared to close all downtown restaurants (to people affiliated with IU)," Wells writes in *Being Lucky*.

Sources said the university president called their bluff. He told them to do as they pleased. The university would simply expand the Commons to accommodate the boom in business that would result. End of tumult.

Similarly, when Wells became president an informal understanding prevailed among Big Ten basketball coaches that they would not recruit black players. (Young black men also were exempt from compulsory ROTC service on the pretext, perpetuated by university physicians, that they all had flat feet.)

With typical stealth, Wells plotted strategy with black alumni and asked IU's coach to recruit Bill Garrett, an outstanding high school player. The color ban broken, other coaches scrambled for the top talent.

"Herman Wells not only turned out to be an exceptionally fine businessman, able to see the material needs, but he became a leader and an outstanding academician," said Dwight Peterson, ninety-one, a member of the board of trustees that named Wells president.

"Under his guidance, not only the business school flourished—of course, you would expect that with his background—but also the School of Music. My heavens, the music school's national reputation had its origin right in Herman Wells' imagination."

Hearing that comment, Wells demurred, stressing that credit for the music school's success belongs to Wilfred C. Bain, the school's longtime dean. Others praised Bain, but they said Wells' protestation missed the point—that the university president was a masterful recruiter and visionary.

"He always took great care," Banta said. "He chose outstanding faculty, gave people support when they needed it and otherwise kept out of their way . . .

"There is universal respect and love for him by those of us who worked with him and under him. Believe me, in this case love is not too strong a word."

Reverend Theodore Hesburgh in his office at the University of Notre Dame in 1987, the year he retired after thirty-five years as president of the university. At the time, he had the longest tenure of active presidents of American universities.

Reverend Theodore M. Hesburgh

University of Notre Dame president

"Father Ted," some call him. Born in 1917 in Syracuse, NY., Rev. Theodore M. Hesburgh was interviewed on the University of Notre Dame campus in 1987, shortly before stepping down as president.

He served in that capacity for thirty-five distinguished and influential years; at the time of his retirement, his was the longest tenure among current presidents of American institutions of higher learning. Since his retirement, "Father Ted" has been Notre Dame's president emeritus.

He still is listed in the "Guinness Book of World Records" as the recipient of the most honorary degrees—at latest count, 131. Hesburgh also has written two books: God, Country, and Notre Dame *(1990), his autobiography; and* Travels with Ned and Ted *(1992), a chronicle of his journeys with executive vice president emeritus, Reverend Edmund "Ned" Joyce.*

SOUTH BEND, Indiana—She was scared, she was overwhelmed, she was just about to cry.

Her daughter, Molly, was going off to college, to the University of Notre Dame with 9,676 students. There they were, mother and daughter, two frightened faces in the frenzy of a freshman orientation rally.

Then the father figure spoke.

His voice—charismatic and commanding, but warmed by an Irish lilt—filled the basketball arena.

Suddenly, Judy Mahoney felt soothed.

"I was way, way up in the bleacher seats, but he was able to touch me," said the forty-six-year-old library assistant. "You know what? He gave me a family feeling."

Caught unprepared, she was witnessing Reverend Theodore Martin Hesburgh at his captivating best.

He is the priest who has toiled thirty-five years at a job he claims he never wanted.

He was a chaplain for undergraduates who, upon assuming the Notre Dame presidency at age thirty-five, confided to fellow clergymen, "I want to be remembered as the student's president."

Yet he is an administrator blasted by some for a blizzard of off-campus activity that distances him from Notre Dame's young men and women.

He is the confidant to popes and presidents and icons of pop culture, the man to whom advice-giver Ann Landers fled for comfort during her divorce.

He is the human rights activist who bounced Herbert Hoover from the *Guinness Book of World Records* as the recipient of the most honorary degrees from the world's colleges and universities.

He is the educator who turned down offers from Lyndon B. Johnson to be the first administrator of NASA, from Richard Nixon to head the poverty program and from Jimmy Carter to fill the top government spot for Latin American affairs.

He is the social reformer who was fired by Nixon from his job as chairman of the U.S. Commission on Civil Rights—and who, during the Vietnam conflict, scolded some federal administration hawks as "mental midgets."

"His image among the students here is larger than life," said Robert Vacca, a Notre Dame professor of classics. "They don't see him much of the time, so that just adds to the mystique."

A campus quip that has remained popular for two decades:

"What's the difference between God and Father Hesburgh? God is everywhere. Father Hesburgh is everywhere but Notre Dame."

Fodder for detractors comes from newspaper accounts of his travels to 130 countries, his intervention in hotspots such as El Salvador, his celebrating Mass among penguins on the South Pole. (That was in the early 1960s, when Hesburgh, a science buff, joined a twenty-four-man expedition to Antarctica.)

Some students, who claim their only glimpse of the gray eminence has been as he motors through campus en route to a jet, point to the statue of a biblical character near Sorin Hall, the oldest dormitory on campus.

The stone Moses raises his hand skyward—and has been nicknamed "There Goes Hesburgh."

Such barbs still sting, even as Hesburgh prepares to turn seventy in May and make his exodus from the top administrative slot. He has chalked up the longest tenure of active presidents of American universities.

"When I am on campus, I work double shifts," maintains Hesburgh, whose Irish good looks ("matinee idol quality," *People* magazine once gushed) somehow make him appear simultaneously rugged and distinguished. "They are getting their money's worth out of me."

"He is here until 4 in the morning sometimes," confirmed S. L. Montague, fifty-four, a janitor in Notre Dame's gold-domed administration building.

"It never fails, though. He always has the time to talk to me, to ask me how my work is going and how I feel. He is the type of guy you could go to with a problem."

Right up there with all the other legends about Reverend Hesburgh (and legends, academic and athletic, are the soul of Notre Dame) is his infinite capacity for compassion.

"I was returning from a banquet with him once and we stopped at a gas pump," said Mike Switek, a Notre Dame senior and student body president.

"Father Hesburgh knew the Hispanic attendant, spoke to him in Spanish, boosted his spirits and encouraged him to enroll in continuing-education classes on campus. He talked to that man the same way he would talk to a vice president."

At the other extreme:

"We were just at a forum in Scottsdale [Arizona] attended by CEOs of the Fortune 500 companies," said Rev. Edward A. "Monk" Malloy, who will replace Hesburgh as president. "I was astounded. All these powerful people—the heads of Ford, GM, Kodak, General Electric, you name it—came up to him seeking ethical advice or telling him what his help has meant to their lives.

"These are men under stress who often have difficulty relating on an emotional level. But they were comfortable with Father Hesburgh. No matter who you are, he speaks your language."

Why does he seek out suffering?

"I have been disappointed in what has been written about him," said his brother, James Hesburgh, a California businessman. "No one points out where his compassion came from.

"In my opinion, it originated in our home life, in our mother and father and their values during the Depression. They expected us to do volunteer work. That may be trendy now, but it was not trendy then."

The son of an Irishwoman (maiden name: Murphy) and the German-American branch manager of a plate glass company, Theodore Hesburgh grew up in Syracuse, New York. He recalls arriving home from Catholic school and encountering a neighbor weeping in the arms of his mother.

"I shrugged and went in the kitchen to get a peanut butter sandwich," he said. "Later I asked what the fuss was about.

"My mother said, 'She's leaving the neighborhood.' I asked why. 'She's Jewish,' my mother said. 'So what?' I asked.

" 'This neighborhood has a ridiculous attitude that you can't live here if you are Jewish,' my mother told me. I said, 'Mother, you don't believe that. Why are you different?'

"She said, 'Because I grew up in the Bronx with Jewish families to the right, to the left, above us and below us. The Irish and the Jews had to get along to survive.' "

Another time, a Syracuse neighbor gave young Hesburgh a nickel. His mother commanded him to save the coin.

One of Hesburgh's three sisters, however, convinced him to spend it. Theodore fibbed to his parents about his intentions.

Later, the devastation on his mother's face—more than the punishment (to bed without dinner)—made him vow "never again."

The bright, dark-eyed boy undertook the role of Jesus Christ in a high school passion play and grew up determined to be a priest. Beyond that, he wanted to become a missionary—considered the ultimate in hardship and self-sacrifice.

What many now call the "Hesburgh era" began in 1952. The university was known primarily for football triumphs and repressive rules that earned the school a popular reputation as the "Catholic West Point."

Hesburgh slashed student rules by four-fifths, shifted power from church leaders to a lay board in 1967 (making Notre Dame the first Catholic university to do so) and supervised the conversion to a co-ed campus in 1972.

His oratorical skills and appetite for the banquet circuit helped boost an endowment that was a meager $10 million at the beginning of his presidency. Today it often tops the $380 million mark.

Detractors accused the ambitious priest of forcing Notre Dame to ape Princeton, unquestionably Hesburgh's secular model in academia. Supporters consider him beyond such sniping.

"We are more sure of ourselves now," said Richard Conklin, Notre Dame's assistant vice president of university relations. "We can be a model of our own.

"In terms of a beacon of learning, Father Hesburgh's vision has been to re-create the medieval Catholic university."

To do that, Hesburgh stresses tomes rather than touchdowns, constantly attempting to stretch the university beyond its "football factory" association with Knute Rockne, the legendary coach and best-known faculty member—before "Father Ted."

In 1962, when *Time* magazine put Hesburgh on its cover (even then calling him "the most influential figure in the reshaping of Catholic higher education"), the publication could not resist a jab. The theology department, *Time* said, "is regarded by all students and most faculty as the worst department on campus." Faculty members now consider the theology department among the finest—not just at Notre Dame, but in the entire nation.

Asked what he regards as his life's low point, Hesburgh instantly pointed to the student unrest of the late 1960s. The priest-president made international headlines in 1969 with a missive to Notre Dame students that became known as the "fifteen-minute letter."

He warned demonstrators tempted to violence that they would have fifteen minutes to ponder their actions and desist. After that, he would call the cops.

"Everything was improvisation," he says now. "One week, one university president was fired for calling the police—while another was fired for *not* calling the police. You had to trust your instincts."

Several sources suggest that Notre Dame's current students, along with their counterparts across the country, share a "Wall Street mentality": go to a prestige grad school, get a plum job and exhaust your efforts on a profitable career.

Hesburgh bristles at such judgments.

To the silver-haired social activist, the strife-torn 1980s and '90s are no time for complacency. To the religious leader who disdains both rock music and nuclear weapons, the 1980s and '90s are no time for disposable values.

And he rejects any implication that the students under his charge might cherish less altruistic ideals.

"I was at 11 o'clock mass last Sunday night and the services were jam-packed," he said. "Teenagers were in the aisles. Students were shoved up against the chapel walls.

"The best young people I know today are giving something back. They work with retarded children. They tutor. They work in soup kitchens."

The five-foot-ten-inch university president has hopped from his chair and is pleading with his listener to accept the best interpretation.

How high and noble he sets his expectations, faculty sources commented later.

But that, they explained, is what fathers are for.

Kurt Vonnegut, Jr.
Novelist

The 1940 graduate of Shortridge High School who went on to become one of the world's most influential contemporary writers has endured enough agony in his personal life to fill half a dozen novels. Born in Indianapolis in 1922, Kurt Vonnegut persevered through everything from a stint as a prisoner of war in Germany during World War II (he witnessed the destruction of Dresden during a bombing raid) to the mental illness of loved ones.

Descended from a prominent German American family—in the 1890s Vonnegut's grandfather, an architect, designed the Athenaeum, a centerpiece of ethnic cultural life in downtown Indianapolis—Kurt Vonnegut initially was known as a science fiction writer and a cult favorite on college campuses.

But he achieved broad, international critical and popular acclaim with such novels and collections of short stories as Cat's Cradle *(1963),* Welcome to the Monkey House *(1968), and* Slaughterhouse-Five *(1969), most written with distinctive, satiric humor and many with antiwar themes and traumatized protagonists. As early as 1969,* The Washington Post *was praising Vonnegut as "America's leading novelist of the whimsical, a constant spoofer of excess and champion of ordinary folks." His numerous honors include the Guggenheim Fellowship (1968–69) and the Literary Award from the National Institute of Arts and Letters in 1970.*

His older brother Bernard, a distinguished scientist about whom Vonnegut spoke with fondness during an interview in 1991, died in 1997 at age eighty-two.

At least one of Kurt Vonnegut, Jr.'s personal agonies eventually was resolved. After talking candidly about an upcoming divorce in the following '91 interview, Vonnegut reconciled with his second wife, Jill Krementz.

You expect him to be a curmudgeon.

"He's puckish, but prickly," said his friend, George Plimpton, the writer-amateur athlete.

Plimpton, the author of *Paper Lion*, owns a weekend cottage on Long Island next to Kurt Vonnegut, Jr.'s eighteenth-century house. "He charges through the hedges every once in a while, smoking a cigarette and armed with wry remarks about the world."

Not only that, Vonnegut is in the midst of what he calls a "debilitating divorce" from photographer-writer Jill Krementz.

And on national TV last week, he blasted Geraldo Rivera, his former son-in-law, as a "scumbag." Rivera, the controversial TV personality, reveals in a new autobiography that he enjoyed frequent flings while married to Vonnegut's daughter Edie.

To top it off, Vonnegut recently broke his back while horseback riding near his home. Assured the injury was merely muscle strain, the Indianapolis native went ahead with an overseas trip to Palermo last month, where he was awarded Italy's highest literary prize.

Kurt Vonnegut, Jr.

"The pain turned out to be excruciating," he reported.

Isn't all that enough to make a man surly?

Even under tranquil circumstances, Vonnegut is known for his dark humor, pessimism and sharp edge. His novels and short stories about human folly and cruelty have been required reading for decades in literature classes from Harvard University to the University of Washington.

Without a scheduled interview appointment, you work up the courage to call.

You expect the sixty-eight-year-old author to bark—at best.

Instead, what you get is a polite, patient man who speaks in soft, even tones. The author of *Cat's Cradle* (1963) and *Slaughterhouse-Five* (1969) is generous with his time and eager to talk about his roots.

"Indianapolis made me what I am today," Vonnegut said. "The city was a terrific influence. Of course, my parents and most of my relatives were well-educated people, so their houses were full of books and music. I could not have done better for myself.

"I represent a strong liberal strain Indiana ought to be proud of, a strain of people who took an interest in the lives and rights of the working stiffs."

The fourth-generation German American and grandfather also spoke with pride about his relatives. He referred several times to his admiration for his older brother Bernard, an atmospheric scientist and college professor in Albany, New York.

"He is easily as distinguished as I am," the critically acclaimed author said. "He probably knows more about tornadoes than anyone else on Earth."

Vonnegut was similarly effusive when talking about his son Mark, a pediatrician in Massachusetts. The younger Vonnegut wrote *The Eden Express* (1975), an account of how he started a hippie commune in the Canadian wilderness—and of his subsequent schizophrenic breakdown and commitment to mental hospitals.

"Mark recently won an honor higher than the Nobel Prize," Vonnegut said. He described an award given to his son by fellow health care workers and nurses.

Denying reports he was irritated by the revelations in *The Eden Express*, Vonnegut said, "That's a very important book and has helped a lot of people. I was just pained, as any father would be, by the struggles he went through."

Mark and his sisters Edie and Nanette, both accomplished artists, are Vonnegut's children from his first marriage to Indianapolis native Jane Marie Cox.

Vonnegut also has an eight-year-old daughter, Lily, from his marriage to Krementz. Currently, Vonnegut, whose new collection of essays, speeches and recollections is called *Fates Worse Than Death*, lives alone.

Make that almost alone.

"I have a snow-white cat with one blue eye and one yellow eye," he reported. "The cat adopted *me*. It started yowling outside. I let it in, and we have been together ever since."

His rapport with horses has not been so satisfying. When Vonnegut learned he would be returning to his hometown for a visit, he got the itch to saddle up.

"I figured I used to enjoy this in Indianapolis, so why not enjoy it now? We had relatives in the Oaklandon area, so I would ride their horses when we visited.

"This time I had an accident. I was told it was muscle strain, so I went to Palermo—*in agony*! Turns out I had broken my back. But I'll be all right by the time I get to Indianapolis."

Vonnegut's father, also named Kurt, was an architect and hardware store owner. The author of *Welcome to the Monkey House* (1968) objected to descriptions of the elder Kurt and of his mother, Edith, as leftists.

"They were middle-class people. My dad was a Democrat and my mother a Republican. To have been a leftist in the thirties would have implied membership in something like the Socialist or Communist parties. My parents never were.

"In any case, what is a leftist in the United States now is nothing but what a Democrat was back then. We have no 'left' left in this country."

Saying he believes a nuclear accident is inevitable, Vonnegut offered this view of contemporary society: "We're living like drunks now, like reformed alcoholics, just day-to-day . . . The system promotes to the top people who don't care about the planet."

Ironically, Vonnegut once was a public relations man. After his stint as a police reporter with the Chicago City News Service in the mid-1940s, he worked for General Electric for three years.

Asked to describe his current writing routine, Vonnegut said: "I'm sixty-eight years old now, soon to be sixty-nine, so I am four years beyond conventional retirement age. I'm slowing. Most people my age have about four good, productive working hours in them daily."

He paused and laughed. "That's even true with doctors my age, which scares me. Anyway, my observation is you can teach your body to spend those four hours (at work) any time around the clock—but you are limited to four hours. I choose to work from 7 or 8 A.M. until noon."

His friends include fellow writers like Plimpton, John Updike, Tom Wolfe, and Joseph Heller.

How often do they get together?

"I could call any of them up at any time," Vonnegut replied. "But what we do calls for isolation and concentration. All writers are loners, really. We have no real business associates. We have no organizations. In fact, we really don't have jobs."

Reflecting on his life-style, Vonnegut added, "A lot of writers are alone at the end of their lives. Hemingway was alone at the end. Certainly our greatest playwright, Tennessee Williams, was quite alone."

Talk of the theater reminded the literary icon that he wants to take in a popular satirical movie. Suddenly, his mood shifted. He sounded vital and enthusiastic.

"I can't wait to see *Hot Shots*." Referring to the producers of the movie, an irreverent version of *Top Gun*, he said, "I love what those guys do." Vonnegut enjoyed a long, loud laugh.

"Their bad taste is wonderful."

Ara Parseghian

Football coach

Some lives are roller coaster rides, with exhilarating highs and sudden, nightmarish lows. Ara Parseghian, one of the legendary football coaches at the University of Notre Dame (from 1964 to 1975), has had such a life.

All but worshipped for restoring the Fighting Irish to gridiron glory, Parseghian hasn't exactly had a joy ride in his personal life.

Among the challenges that have confronted Parseghian: a daughter who was diagnosed with multiple sclerosis and three grandchildren who inherited a rare, untreatable disorder that's almost always fatal.

Born in 1923 in Akron, Ohio, Ara Parseghian was interviewed in 1995 at his office near the Notre Dame campus.

> *There will be*
> *Only one of you*
> *For all time.*
> *Fearlessly*
> *Be yourself.*

SOUTH BEND, Indiana—A black, framed poster with that message—and several other posters that encourage a fighting spirit—adorn an outer office.

Around the corner, a legendary former coach is working the phones.

"Regis is holding for you," whispers Karen Emerick, a secretary. She is referring to TV talk show host Regis Philbin.

Dateline NBC has called. *People* magazine has just published a profile. And a *20/20* segment is scheduled for broadcast in a few weeks.

The flurry of attention involves a seventy-two-year-old grandfather who, during his pro football career with the Cleveland Browns, was nicknamed "Hardnose."

He is managing not to cry.

"I couldn't talk about this for an entire month," Ara Parseghian concedes. "It just stunned me.

"You know how devastating this has been? I would get in my car and break down. I couldn't believe this was happening."

"This" is a startling development concerning Parseghian's three youngest grandchildren. They are afflicted with a rare, inherited disease that's almost always fatal before victims reach the age of fifteen.

Parseghian made his mark, of course, as the head football coach at the University of Notre Dame. In 1966 and 1973, he lead the Fighting Irish to national championships. With

University of Notre Dame football coach Ara Parseghian in his office in South Bend in 1995.

a 95–17–4 record, he is second only to Knute Rockne as the coach with the most wins in Notre Dame history.

Until fall 1994, Parseghian had never heard of Niemann-Pick Disease Type C. It's so rare that only about five hundred American children have it.

Among them are Michael, Marcia, and Christa Parseghian.

There is no cure. Children are afflicted only if they inherit an abnormal, recessive gene from both parents. A victim of Niemann-Pick is unable to metabolize a type of cholesterol. Fatty acids accumulate in the liver, spleen and brain.

"We're in a race against time," Parseghian explains. "As in most situations in my life, I won't accept this without a fight. We must find a cure."

Michael, who is eight years old, is showing severe symptoms.

"He says to me, 'G-r-a-n-d-p-a, h-o-w a-r-e y-o-u?' " Parseghian says, dropping his booming baritone to a slow, slurred whisper.

Michael has been falling down at school. His handwriting, according to Ara Parseghian, is "atrocious." But his spirits are up.

"There is a blind boy in Michael's class," Parseghian says. "They are each other's helpers. Michael has become the other boy's 'eyes.' And the blind boy tries to catch Michael when he stumbles."

Michael's sister, Marcia, six, used to be the star of her ballet, gymnastics and karate classes. She's no longer the best, her grandfather reports. Symptoms of Niemann-Pick include poor coordination and the inability to put words together for smooth speech.

Christa, four, isn't displaying symptoms yet.

None of the three have been told they suffer from a fatal disorder. But some of the consequences have been shared with their brother, eleven-year-old Ara. An exceptional athlete and a top student, young Ara is the only sibling not afflicted.

The four children live in Tucson, Arizona, where their father, Michael Parseghian, is an orthopedic surgeon. Michael's wife, Cindy, quit a career as a cable TV and real estate company administrator to help handle the crisis.

Michael and Cindy Parseghian met as Notre Dame students.

In addition to pre-med studies, Michael played football on one of his father's final teams before Ara Parseghian retired in 1975. After that, Ara kept busy as a public speaker, an ABC-TV football commentator and as a board member of a South Bend insurance company.

Ara and his wife, Katie, began spending more time at a vacation home in Marco Island, Florida. During the 1990s, they have lived in South Bend for six months and at their Marco Island condo for the other six.

A veteran of four hip operations and knee surgery, Ara is scheduled for a long-postponed knee-replacement operation soon. His problems began with a hip injury that ended his career as a halfback with the Cleveland Browns in 1949.

"I wobble when I walk," Parseghian explains. He shrugs off other questions about his health.

The "Hardnose" nickname, according to *Sports Illustrated* accounts, came about because of his "dauntlessness." Parseghian would play through pain.

In some ways, he still does.

"He was in semi-retirement and now, at a time in life when he should be able to relax, he's busier than ever," said Emerick, his secretary. "He's a man on a mission."

The mission: Find a cure for Niemann-Pick. The retired coach and his family members have founded the Ara Parseghian Medical Research Foundation, a nonprofit, volunteer organization that funds research for the disorder.

In less than six months, the foundation has raised more than one million dollars—in part thanks to Ara Parseghian's pleas to Notre Dame alumni around the world. His goal is to generate another million in six more months.

The Parseghians have been confronted with challenges for years.

Ara's daughter Karan, forty-five, was diagnosed with multiple sclerosis as a teenager. She's been in a wheelchair for seventeen years. The mother of two sons, she lives in Akron, Ohio. His other daughter, Kristen, forty-three, lives in Granger, Indiana, and is the mother of three daughters.

"You can't dwell on 'whys,' " Parseghian says. "I admit that I do think about the staggering odds against Niemann-Pick happening. The chances of two people who carry (an abnormal) Chromosome 18 meeting, falling in love and marrying . . .

"But the foundation gives me a goal. Even my sports background helps. You learn in competition that you get emotionally knocked down, but you get right back up."

About 1993, Michael and Cindy became perplexed about their younger son. He was small and had muscle-control and balance problems.

"Since his brother Ara is so athletic, the contrast with Michael was pronounced," Parseghian recalls.

Pediatricians couldn't identify a cause. They concluded that Michael was, in his grandfather's words, "just a late bloomer, a boy who was going to develop slowly."

But the symptoms persisted. Then came the Niemann-Pick diagnosis in September 1994. That meant Michael and Cindy Parseghian's other children needed to be checked. The result: Marcia's diagnosis. Then Christa's.

The children are on low-cholesterol diets. They also take medications to slow the progress of the disease.

Meanwhile, their grandfather receives constant advice.

"A woman called this morning with herbal tea recipes," he says. "As a doctor, Michael's medical and scientific contacts are providential. We're determined to win this one."

He manages a rueful smile. The legendary coach is giving himself a pep talk.

After a valiant struggle, Michael Parseghian died from Niemann-Pick Type C disease in 1997, a few days before his tenth birthday.

Richard Lugar

U.S. senator and presidential candidate

Statesman, Rhodes Scholar, Eagle Scout. Foreign policy expert, businessman from the heartland, high school valedictorian. A family-farm owner who understands urban problems as a former mayor.

Indianapolis native Richard Lugar personifies just about everything the American public says it wants in a leader. Yet Lugar's presidential campaign in 1996 fizzled. And even though his name is almost always among a select few mentioned every four years as a likely vice presidential pick, the silver-haired senator has been passed over several times.

Some say it's because the straight-arrow, intellectual Hoosier politician lacks charisma—an accusation lobbed against Lugar for so long that he laughed about it during an interview in his office near Capitol Hill in 1996. Earlier that year, Lugar's crusade for the Republican presidential nomination ended in disappointment after a flurry of initial excitement.

"I campaigned positively," Lugar said during a rare break in his jammed schedule. He had just appeared on a Sunday morning TV news show to analyze a crisis in the Balkans. For nearly fifteen years, Lugar has been virtually "on call" to talk about—and help fellow lawmakers cope with—foreign policy crises from the Philippines to Saudi Arabia to Latin America.

"Running for President is a remarkable experience," Lugar continued. "I certainly don't regret it. My only frustrations concern the amount of money and advance planning it takes to build an effective campaign organization."

Since his days at Shortridge High School, this leader was pegged for high achievement—maybe even the presidency. His list of achievements during the past two decades is the longest such list in the state.

The long list of achievements almost didn't happen.

Not his years as chairman of the U.S. Senate Foreign Relations Committee. Not his high-profile stint as mayor of Indianapolis, when Dick Lugar initiated a bold, consolidated form of city-county government. Not his record-setting four terms as a U.S. senator from Indiana, an accomplishment achieved by no other Hoosier.

Dick Lugar inherited the job of helping run Thomas L. Green & Company, a family business which manufactures baking equipment and other food machinery. It had been founded by Lugar's maternal grandfather, Thomas Green, a savvy entrepreneur with only five years of schooling who began by making cookie cutters. Green's daughter, Bertha, was Lugar's mother.

He also inherited a six-hundred-acre corn, soybean and wheat farm in southwestern Marion County. And Dick Lugar and his wife had four young sons.

So young Dick (born in 1932) had a full plate of business and family obligations by the early and mid-1960s.

Senator Richard Lugar

Yes, he had been marked as a "comer" for years—and had been captivated by politics even longer. Lugar still is able to recall every dramatic detail of his first exposure to politicians, including his awe as an eight-year-old in a crowd near the English Hotel on Monument Circle.

From the balcony of the hotel in 1940, Hoosier presidential candidate Wendell Willkie was delivering a rousing campaign speech. Squeezing his way through the throng, small, wiry Dick was able to stand just below the stirring orator.

So began his love of politics, followed by his string of achievements. At Denison University in Ohio, Lugar was Phi Beta Kappa. He shared the class presidency with Charlene Smeltzer, who became his wife in 1956. And Lugar was the first Denison student chosen to be a Rhodes Scholar.

He capped all of this off by serving as an intelligence officer in the U.S. Navy in the late 1950s. Lugar would regularly get up at 2:30 A.M., memorize overnight intelligence reports from around the world and then brief Cabinet members, naval officers and congressmen.

But as Lugar tells it, his civic and political interests eventually gave way to the all-consuming demands of his farm, his factory and his growing family.

Then came a visit in 1964 by some Indianapolis residents with a cause, some concerns—and a plea.

"Citizens on the Westside came to our factory," Lugar recalls. "They said, 'Nobody on the school board is looking out for the Westside. We want you to run.'

"I said, 'I'm flattered, but why me?'

"'They said, 'You're too young and you're inexperienced, but you are the only person we have around.' "

Lugar accepted the invitation and won a seat on the school board, a seat from which he pushed Indianapolis Public Schools to accept federal aid and helped pioneer a local school lunch program.

Despite opposition from entrenched interests, he won many admirers, including Irving Leibowitz, an influential columnist for *The Indianapolis Times* newspaper. Leibowitz was so impressed by Lugar's visionary approach to complicated problems that the columnist asked in print, "Wouldn't it be a great thing if Dick Lugar were mayor?"

And soon he was. As mayor, Lugar convinced the Indiana General Assembly to pass a revolutionary, metropolitan form of government for Indianapolis and Marion County known as "Unigov."

A unique blend of agencies and functions, Unigov was implemented in 1970; it consolidated city and county functions with notable exceptions such as the schools and law enforcement agencies. And in one swoop, the Hoosier capital went from being the nation's twenty-sixth-largest city to its twelfth-largest.

As of the architect of Unigov, the man *Newsweek* magazine called "the Hoosier hotshot" soon launched other initiatives for his hometown, often derided as "Naptown" or "India-no-place." No more. Lugar pushed for the construction of Market Square Arena and supported other urban measures that began to transform the city's downtown—and its image.

As the only Republican mayor of a large American city in 1970, Lugar began drawing attention from several quarters and eventually was elected president of the National League of Cities.

He served as mayor until 1975, when he unsuccessfully challenged Birch Bayh for the U.S. Senate. Lugar bounced back from that loss to win election to the Senate the next year, defeating Vance Hartke, a three-term incumbent.

Then he began carving out a reputation on Capitol Hill as not only an expert on agricultural matters—a natural for Lugar, given his background—but on foreign relations.

He became chairman of the powerful Foreign Relations Committee in 1985. The next year Lugar won the admiration of Democrats and Republicans alike when he was selected as President Ronald Reagan's observer of elections in the Philippines.

The Asian nation had long been controlled by the corrupt Ferdinand Marcos regime. Lugar encouraged the country's move to democracy by recognizing Corazon Aquino as the legitimate winner of the election.

Also that year, Lugar won bipartisan support by leading the successful effort to overturn Reagan's veto of economic sanctions against South Africa.

In 1988 Lugar oversaw the Senate's ratification of a historic treaty with the Soviet Union. The treaty reduced the number of nuclear weapons in both the communist country and the United States for the first time.

Before and during the Persian Gulf War in 1991, Lugar helped drum up public support for American military action through speeches and highly publicized policy statements.

Despite his hectic schedule, Lugar retains diverse interests. Spiritual matters never seem far from his mind. As a boy, he was a Sunday school regular at Central Avenue United Methodist Church. As an adult, he has remained an active Methodist and is a frequent lay minister at churches across Indiana.

He also was a physical fitness advocate—specifically, a jogger—decades before it became trendy. In a different type of running—campaigns for political office—Lugar made Indiana history in 1994. He won a fourth consecutive term in the U.S. Senate, the first time any Hoosier had done that.

Lugar also enjoys an image as a family man. Dick and Charlene Lugar are the parents of four adult sons: Mark, Robert, John and David.

Given their dad's political interest from an early age—and his long string of ballot box triumphs, beginning with student government—has he encouraged the next generation of Lugars to run for office?

"Frankly, I've discouraged them," Lugar replies, smiling.

"I tell my sons they should make sure their careers, marriages and families are solid before they undertake political life. Politicians with integrity need to have the right set of priorities."

Dan Wakefield

Author, screenwriter, journalist

Who would have guessed? The author of the best-seller Going All The Way *(1970), a rollicking novel about the sexual escapades of two returning GIs in a repressed Indianapolis of the 1950s, goes on to become an internationally acclaimed expert, lecturer and workshop leader on spirituality, creativity and miracles.*

And the Indianapolis expatriate (after some initial Hoosier hostility to Going All The Way*) becomes a beloved figure in his hometown, which rolls out the red carpet for him during filming of the movie version in 1996. Not only did Dan Wakefield write the screenplay for the film, he served as the creator and screenwriter of the critically praised "James At 15" TV series during the 1970s.*

Born in Indianapolis in 1932, Wakefield graduated from Columbia University and was a Nieman Fellow at Harvard University. He called upon his New York City experiences—and his days (and nights) at the epicenter of the city's pulsating literary and jazz scenes—for New York in the '50s *(1992), a vivid account of the era.*

A prolific free-lance writer for publications from The Nation *and* The Atlantic Monthly *to* Gentleman's Quarterly *and* The New York Times *(Sunday) Magazine, Wakefield carved out a second career as the leader of spiritual workshops. This alternative career began after dramatic transformations in his life and the success of his books on the topic:* Creating from the Spirit *(1996), dedicated to several Hoosiers, including teachers and librarians;* Expect a Miracle *(1995) and* The Story of Your Life: Writing a Spiritual Autobiography *(1990).*

After being based in Boston and New York several years, Wakefield lives in Miami Beach and teaches at Florida International University. The author, his high school classmates and other Hoosier friends were interviewed in 1988.

> *The Lord is my shepherd.*
> *I shall not want . . .*

Like a Greek chorus, only in a healing rather than haughty manner, the Twenty-third Psalm periodically has taken center stage in Dan Wakefield's life.

So have prayers.

They have returned during bouts with alcohol abuse, atheism, drug use, physical decline, and Freudian psychoanalysis. They even were there during teenage sorrows that ranged from rejection by Broad Ripple High School's football team to acne to a tension-filled relationship with—as well as between—his parents.

Wakefield's adolescence in Indianapolis during the late 1940s also was full of warmth, ecstasy and laughs—whether from sex education class at Shortridge High School or initiation rituals at a Boy Scout camp.

Today there is far more ecstasy than sorrow, and at the age of fifty-five Dan Wakefield is described as serene and radiant by those who know him.

(Left) Dan Wakefield at a gathering of Shortridge High School classmates in 1985.

(Below) Wakefield (second row, fourth from left) and future U.S. Senator Richard Lugar (top row, third from left) and other future Indianapolis movers and shakers as Key Club members at Shortridge.

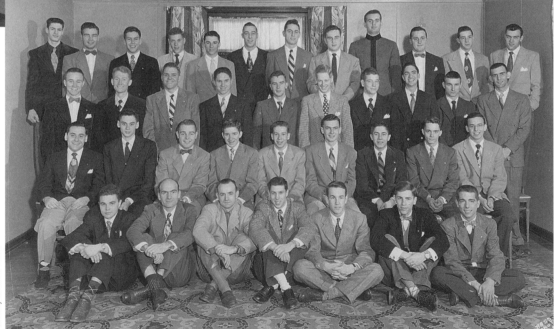

He leadeth me beside still waters.
He restoreth my soul . . .

"Sure, I still have frustrations," says the author of *Returning: A Spiritual Journey*, an autobiography published by Doubleday that's drawing national attention because of its devastating frankness.

"Frustrations never end in your life. What changes is your response to them."

Delving into Wakefield's days in Indianapolis and his wildly changing relationship with the city, the book began as a *New York Times* (Sunday) *Magazine* article. Titled "Returning to Church" and documenting the spiritual awakening of both average Americans and the author, the article drew more mail than anything Wakefield has written.

That includes his five nonfiction books and five novels that range from *Going All the Way*, notorious in Indianapolis after its 1970 publication because of its local setting, and *Starting Over*, a poignant account of a divorced man's life that became a Burt Reynolds movie.

More mail, that is, until a subsequent article recounting Wakefield's nightmarish interlude with Freudian psychoanalysis, a period when he shuttled daily between his decaying East Harlem apartment and a couch in a posh Park Avenue office.

Those episodes—just more adventures in a life that even has included work as a shepherd in the Holy Land—also are detailed in *Returning*. The book opens with the sentence: "One balmy spring morning in Hollywood, a month or so before my forty-eighth birthday, I woke up screaming . . ."

He leadeth me in paths of righteousness
For his name's sake.

The only child of a pharmacist and a housewife who lived in Broad Ripple, Wakefield attended Sunday school. In *Returning*, he includes a tender description of his teacher, an enlightened woman who emphasized that Christ loved all people and decorated her classroom with a painting of Jesus holding black, white, brown and yellow children.

"This was Indianapolis in the 1930s, which only the decade before had been a stronghold for the Ku Klux Klan," Wakefield writes.

"In fact, my father used to speak in hushed tones of how the Klan met in the church across from his drugstore and came in afterward for Cokes and ice cream."

Sports-crazed (his goal then was to coach Notre Dame football), Wakefield writes that he regarded belief in God as "part of being a good American, appropriate and even necessary for a Cub Scout working his way up to being a Boy Scout."

Prayer, along with periodic, sudden repetitions of the Twenty-third Psalm, became part of his life. The habits continued even during his heady "God-is-dead" phase as a Columbia student and later, when his days became a blur of bourbon, psychoanalysis, hostility, wine and, eventually, drugs.

Even though I walk through the valley of the shadow of
   death
I shall fear no evil
For thou art with me . . .

Wakefield traces his spiritual awakening to an impromptu visit to a Boston parish house about eight years ago. But he is quick to distance himself from the religious right.

"Falwell, Robertson, the Bakkers and those movements have been overreported," the soft-voiced journalist says. "What about the huge majority of people who just go to church on Sunday? Maybe I should call them the Quiet Majority or the Unreported Majority.

"There is hardly anything written about regular church experience. Everything is either the Moral Majority or the fringe, Shirley MacLaine, out-of-body experiences . . .

"I feel uneasy with the 'born again' phrase. It sounds so dramatic. I like to describe myself as 'turning,' which is a more gradual, continual process. 'Born again' implies that, zap, all is fine. What I talk about is a constant journey, like walking along a road."

He has gathered statistics indicating there are now more than 142 million churchgoing Americans, with a gain of 750,000 in just one year during the 1980s.

Why?

"One factor is the change in attitude about psychology," he says. "People once felt it was the answer to everything, superseding religion. There is now a widespread sense that psychology is not the whole answer, that it does not provide a *meaning* to life."

In *Returning*, Wakefield blames part of his earlier frustration with religion on the "conformist Christianity" popular in the 1950s, with—in his words—Jesus exalted as the Man in the Gray Flannel Suit. Such religious interpretations, he argues, were both superficial and offensive—but objecting to them was considered subversive.

Thy rod and Thy staff
They comfort me

Classmates and friends describe Wakefield as popular during his days at Shortridge, to which he transferred after being cut from Broad Ripple's football team.

The disappointment particularly stung, he recalls in *Returning*, because during that period at Broad Ripple all boys who desired could suit up. Wakefield was among the most inept, eliminated only because of a shortage in uniforms.

That prompted the switch to Shortridge, which the author describe as "an arch-rival high school with a reputation for catering to rich kids and being 'social' or 'snobby.' "

At Shortridge he experienced popularity and success—which included selection over classmate Richard Lugar, now a U.S. senator, to deliver the commencement speech—but Wakefield writes at length in *Returning* about his experience with acne.

The skin condition so preoccupied him that Wakefield's distressed parents took him to the Mayo Clinic in Minnesota. The abrupt approach of a physician there—"You will be scarred for life," he told the fifteen-year-old—proved shattering.

Thou preparest a table before me
In the presence of my enemies.

Repressed sexuality and Freudian psychoanalysis loomed over Wakefield's young adult years. His struggles with both are discussed in *Returning* in vivid, highly personal detail.

"It's important to share the dark side," Wakefield explains. "My feeling is that I'm honoring the subject—spiritual experience—by speaking honestly. If you are going to write about this topic, the most important there is, you have to do it all out and treat it seriously."

That does not, however, exclude humor.

The accounts of sexual repression and analysis frequently veer toward high comedy, such as his formal "sex education" at Shortridge—which consisted of one day. Separated from the girls, Wakefield and his buddies were shown photos of human skin disfigured by disease.

The account of his daily, years-long sessions with Freudian psychoanalysts while living in New York—"the analysis seemed like a black hole that continued to grow larger"—includes pointed descriptions of the analysts. Regardless of the horrors, emotions and shocking revolutions that Wakefield shared, the deliberately detached analyst responded with only, "Yes, go on."

"I don't mean to denounce psychiatry in general, just Freudian psychoanalysis," Wakefield explains. "You have no real relationship with the analyst. He does not even participate, he gives no human responses."

Kirkus Reviews has described *Returning* as "a terrifying ride to hell and back . . . Certain to boil the blood of Freudians and warm the hearts of most everyone else."

Several of Wakefield's Indianapolis friends say they lost contact with him during his psychoanalysis and the phase that followed. Others, however, say they witnessed disturbing episodes during his periodic visits to the Midwest.

Those visits have become much more frequent, coinciding with Wakefield's overhauled perception of his hometown. During the interview, his voice softened when he spoke of Indianapolis. In 1985, he returned to his hometown after staying away for several years.

> *Thou anointest my head with oil*
> *My cup overflows*
> *Surely goodness and mercy shall follow me*
> *All the days of my life*
> *And I shall dwell in the House of the Lord*
> *Forever.*

Because of some local hostility that followed publication of the fictional *Going All The Way* (various reviewers called it an account of the "oversexed in Indianapolis"), Wakefield now wishes he had set the novel in Cleveland.

"But placing it in Indianapolis gave the book an emotional center," he adds. "I care about Indianapolis. I really don't care about Cleveland."

Any other regrets? Anything else he would do differently?

"I don't think in those terms," Wakefield replies.

The point, he explains, is that all of it—from the Boy Scouts and the acne to the alcoholism and the exhilarating renewal of his spirit—has brought him to where he is now.

As a girl, singer-actress Florence Henderson used to visit the monastery at St. Meinrad, Indiana, and listened to the monks sing Gregorian chants. Their singing inspired her.

Florence Henderson

Actress-singer

Born on Valentine's Day in 1934, Florence Henderson began life as the youngest of ten children of poverty-stricken sharecroppers in Dale, Indiana, during the Depression.

She went on to become a Broadway, nightclub, TV and film star with a career that has ranged from musical comedies to her unshakable image as the "perfect suburban mom" in the ABC-TV series The Brady Bunch. *Along the way, she overcame problems that included a severe hearing loss.*

Henderson was interviewed in 1994 during one of her frequent visits to Indiana. During the 1980s and '90s, she became a perennial part of the pageantry at the Indianapolis 500-Mile Race. She sings The Star Spangled Banner *or* America *during opening ceremonies and keeps in close touch with the state of her birth.*

Here's the story of a lovely lady.

But stop right there. You may know the rest of *The Brady Bunch* theme song—but there may be a lot you don't know about Florence Henderson.

She grew up in grinding poverty during the Depression in southern Indiana.

The daughter of a tobacco sharecropper and the youngest of ten children, Henderson worked in the fields as a child (her task was to pick worms off the tobacco leaves) and sometimes went hungry and shoeless.

Her Christmas gift one year was her school reader. The Hendersons couldn't afford anything else.

"Music was my salvation," Henderson, a native of Dale, Indiana, recalled during an interview in her home state. Henderson, sixty, planned to visit some of her six surviving siblings at family gatherings in southern Indiana and Kentucky.

"I used to go to the corner store as a little girl, sit on the counter and sing my heart out for coins." Henderson paused and winked. "I guess I'm still singing for my supper."

The singer-actress met her husband, John Kappas, a hypnotherapist, when she sought treatment to overcome stage fright and the fear of flying.

The couple live on an eighty-seven-foot motor yacht called *Big Flo III* which is docked off Marina Del Rey, California.

Smiling at her husband and patting his shoulder, Henderson explained, "John is of Greek descent, so the love for the sea is in his genes—plus, he used to be in the Navy.

"He asked me, 'Florence, how would you like living on a boat?' Going from a big house in Beverly Hills to a boat would be an adjustment, I thought.

"But you know what? There's a healing, calming influence about the water. I don't think I could live on land again."

With her husband's help, Henderson has become a certified hypnotherapist, a healing technique that combines hypnosis with traditional counseling. She does volunteer work with cancer patients and others suffering from terminal illnesses.

Another little-known fact: Before she took on her most famous role (Henderson played Carol Brady on the classic sitcom from 1969–74, then in innumerable variety show specials and reunion movies), she suffered "terrifying" hearing loss.

As Henderson explains it, the possibility of deafness was especially frightening because she was primarily known as a musical star during the 1950s and '60s.

"Every once in a while during a performance, I wouldn't hear an instrument, or I wouldn't hear my introduction," she said.

Her problems eventually were diagnosed as the result of a genetic disorder called otosclerosis. Some of her siblings also have suffered hearing trouble. Surgery eventually restored her hearing in both ears.

Henderson has appeared as a guest star on a score of TV series. They include *Dave's World*, on which she has a recurring role as the mother-in-law of star Harry Anderson; *Burkes' Law*; and *The Mommies* (she popped up in an episode with fellow "perfect moms" June Lockhart and Barbara Billingsley). She has also been on David Letterman's and Conan O'Brien's talks shows, and *Roseanne*.

Referring to *Roseanne*, she said, "Believe it or not, the basic premise of that show is the same as *The Brady Bunch*—the family sticks together."

But she was turned off by the cameo role initially proposed for her in *The Brady Bunch* movie filming in California. (Shelley Long, a Fort Wayne native, portrays Carol Brady of the 1990s.)

The cameo for Henderson, who is known for her warmth and upbeat disposition, would have cast her against type as a truck driver with a cigarette pack rolled up in her sleeve. Henderson said she rejected the offer for two reasons: The script wasn't funny, and the premise seemed demeaning. She eventually accepted a cameo when the ending of the movie was rewritten, featuring a surprise appearance by her as the new brood's grandmother.

How do you get from Indiana tobacco field to Broadway and Hollywood?

Henderson started singing at home in southern Indiana. "My family has always been my biggest boosters, and I am theirs," she said. She also sang during religious services at her Catholic school and church.

At the parochial school, the girls were required to wear uniforms. Because of her family's poverty, little Florence often showed up in "ragtag" versions. She made up stories about "accidents" to explain the tattered condition of her clothes.

"The nuns knew my family situation," she said. "But they never invaded my privacy or hurt my pride, for which I'm extremely grateful."

Informed of her singing talent, family friends financed her move to New York. She studied at the American Academy of Dramatic Arts and made her Broadway debut in 1952 in *Wish You Were Here*. After legendary composer Richard Rodgers caught a glimpse of her in that show, he cast Henderson in a road production of *Oklahoma!*

"She is the real thing, right out of a butter churn somewhere," wrote Walter Kerr in *The New York Herald-Tribune*, summing up the general opinion about Henderson. She became a star thanks to rave reviews for *Fanny*, a 1954 Broadway musical in which Henderson played the title role.

One aspect of her career that may startle younger fans: She preceded Barbara Walters on *The Today Show*. Henderson was a regular with Dave Garroway on the NBC-TV morning news program in 1959–60.

"It was the only time in the show's history that it was taped," Henderson recalled. "We taped the afternoon before, then the live news segments were inserted the next morning.

"When Hugh Downs took over as host after Dave left, he asked me to join him. But they were going back to being a live, early-morning show. I loved music, I loved theater and I didn't want those kind of hours."

She also was pregnant during her *Today* stint—a fact that she never mentioned on the air. "They put me behind potted plants, desks, anything."

Henderson has four children from her first marriage to theatrical producer Ira Bernstein. Her eldest daughter, Barbara, is an actress. Her sons Joseph and Robert are musicians, and her youngest daughter, Elizabeth, recently made Henderson a grandmother for the second time.

"My kids used to say, 'Why don't you ever shout at them?' " Henderson joked, referring to their *Brady Bunch* counterparts. "Actually, they got some pleasure out of the show because they were about the same age as the *Brady* kids and became good friends with them."

As she described their friendships, the "eternal mom" beamed.

Courtesy of *The Indianapolis Star/News*

Indianapolis businessman Aldo Andretti, Mario's identical twin, in his office. Behind him is a photo of the racing Andrettis (left to right): Jeff, John, Michael, and Mario.

Mario Andretti

Courtesy of *The Indianapolis Star/News*

The Andretti Family

Mario, Aldo, Michael, John, and Jeff—
Race car drivers

If a single name is synonymous around the world with the Indianapolis 500, high speeds and racing charisma, it is "Andretti." The racing dynasty began in a little town in northern Italy in 1940. Alvise "Gigi" Andretti and his wife, Rina, became the parents of two boys, identical twin brothers. They were:

- **Mario**, *who became a superstar of racing.*

- **And Aldo**, *the twin whom even Mario has conceded was the more skillful driver. "It's hard for me to say, but Aldo was better," Mario writes in* Andretti, *his autobiography. But Aldo ultimately chose a safer path, launching a highly successful business career as the owner of an Indianapolis automotive company.*

The handsome, dynamic twins have produced three race-driving sons. Second-generation Andretti racers are:

- **Michael and Jeff**, *Mario's sons. Michael has been a standout on the Indy Car and Formula One circuits since the 1980s. Jeff, who won "Rookie of the Year" honors at the Indianapolis 500 in 1991, has recovered from devastating injuries suffered in a crash at the Indianapolis Motor Speedway in 1992.*

- **John**, *Aldo's son. A witty, personable graduate of Ritter High School in Indianapolis, John is one of the most popular of the second generation of racing Andrettis. He finished an impressive eighth in his rookie 500-Mile Race in 1988. In May 1994, John drew international attention when he made racing history—competing in the 500 in the morning, then hopping aboard a helicopter at the Speedway which took him to a private jet that flew to North Carolina, where John raced in the late afternoon in the NASCAR Coca-Cola 600 stock car race.*

Drive in two famous races on the same day? Few other than an Andretti would attempt it. When the dust settled in 1991 at the Indy 500, there was a historic first: Four relatives finished in the top fifteen at the Speedway. Michael Andretti was second, barely losing to winner Rick Mears; his cousin, John, finished fifth; Mario was seventh, and Jeff captured "Rookie of the Year" honors by finishing fifteenth.

Mario has lived most of his adult life in Pennsylvania. So have his sons, Michael and Jeff. But they deserve to be considered honorary Hoosiers as a result of their impact on the state's best-known sporting event—and their presence for so many Mays in Indianapolis, which they have called "our second home."

Hoosier "citizenship" unquestionably belongs to Aldo and his son, John, who settled in the Indianapolis area in the mid-1960s. Since John pulled off the two-races-in-one-

day feat in 1994, he has concentrated on his NASCAR career and lives for part of the year in North Carolina.

But the heart—and glamour—of the Andretti family is linked to Indianapolis. It's a link that was forged at the Speedway by the frequent presence of Mario, an Indy 500 crowd favorite, and his longtime business partner, movie star Paul Newman. Mario has added to the mystique through his appearances in movies made here such as the 1969 film Winning, *starring Newman and Joanne Woodward.*

A family secret involving Mario and Aldo: There's a fascinating "flaw" in the official photo of front-row qualifiers for the 1969 Indianapolis 500, which Mario won. The "Mario" in the photo is actually Aldo. One twin posed as the other.

"I didn't want to do it," Aldo recalled. "Mario talked me into it. He said, 'No one will notice the difference.' "

The reason for the ruse: Mario had endured a fiery crash a few days before the photo session. "He was uninjured except for burns on his upper lip and elsewhere on his face," Aldo said. "Mario didn't want to be photographed like that. So I did the favor and had my picture taken."

As the years passed and racing enthusiasts have learned the secret, the photo has become a collector's item.

Aldo Andretti was interviewed in 1994. John was interviewed in 1991 and just before his historic "double race" in 1994.

The identical twins shared everything—first in Italy, where they were born in 1940, and then in their new homeland, America.

John Andretti gets a hug from his mother, Corky, in 1988 at the Indianapolis Motor Speedway.

Courtesy of *The Indianapolis Star/News*

"Mario and I had one toy truck we took turns playing with," Aldo Andretti recalled. "Then we had a bike we shared. When we began racing, there was one car between the two of us. I would race it one week. Mario would get it the next."

But one thing wasn't divided equally: fame. Mario Andretti became world famous as a race driver and is a legendary figure at the Indianapolis Motor Speedway, the subject of countless tributes during his "Farewell, Mario" retirement tour in 1994.

Aldo Andretti has been the twin in the shadow. In addition to being identified as "Mario's brother," Aldo in recent years has been known as "John's father." That's because his son, John, born in 1963, launched an impressive career as a race driver in 1987.

And Aldo? The survivor of two near-fatal accidents, he was considered a hot prospect for a brilliant racing career when, at age thirty, he left the sport—and the spotlight.

For a few years, Aldo Andretti conceded, he wondered whether his choice to become a Hoosier entrepreneur would be satisfying, and he agonized over "what ifs." But those feelings—like his racing—are history, he said.

The unheralded Andretti, a Brownsburg, Indiana, resident, expressed contentment with life as a husband, father of five and grandfather—not to mention as the owner of a thriving Indianapolis business. His firm, Aldo Andretti Machine and Engineering Co., provides parts for medical supply and automotive companies.

"In my thirties, I had reservations," Aldo said, managing a rueful grin. "I thought, 'Gosh, I missed out on a lot.' But now Mario (has closed) a chapter on a brilliant, illustrious career. I still have a lot I can accomplish in the business world . . . Sure, I envied his success, but always in a good sense. I thought, 'I can be just as successful in another way.' "

John Andretti, thirty-one, said, "Racing lost much more by him giving it up than he lost by leaving. There's no question he would have been one of the greatest drivers . . . My biggest wish is that my dad could be racing with me. I think I got cheated."

In any case, John's itinerary on May 29, 1994 was one of the most stressful in sports—and that's not even considering the speeds he drove. He became the first driver to compete in the 500 Mile Race (11 A.M. starting time), then travel to Charlotte, North Carolina, to participate in a stock car race, the NASCAR Coca-Cola 600, at 5 P.M.

Analysts worried about his stamina, diet and conditioning, particularly the loss of fluid a driver endures in one grueling race, much less two. But John, unfazed, pulled off the double feat, explaining, "If you have two important things in life, and you must chose between one or are able to do both with some special maneuvering, there's no question as to what I prefer."

The source of his adventurous spirit is no mystery. His father and uncle have been risk takers from the word "go."

Mario and Aldo Andretti were born Feb. 28, 1940, in northern Italy near the Austrian border. After World War II, the area became part of Yugoslavia. Today it is governed by Croatia. Their father, Alvise "Gigi" Andretti, now eighty-five, and mother Rina, eighty, were prosperous wine exporters. They owned several thousand acres of farmland that had been in the family for three generations.

Beginning with their toy truck, Mario and Aldo developed a fascination with vehicles. Despite their father's objections, the twins nurtured an interest in racing. Their passion may have gone unnoticed because Alvise Andretti had larger concerns.

During World War II, Nazi soldiers commandeered a hotel in Italy owned by Mario's and Aldo's grandparents.

"At this time, there were also lists, kind of like hit lists," Mario writes in *Andretti*, his autobiography. "My father was always afraid because for no reason, even if you weren't involved in politics or anything like that, they would nab you . . . Later, my dad told me he had thirty hand grenades hidden in his bedroom."

With the end of the war, things went from stressful to disastrous. "My father lost everything to communism after the war," Aldo recalled. "The government took our land. We became refugees."

The Andrettis spent seven years in a resettlement camp, living in one room. Seeking a better life, the family emigrated to the United States in 1955, when the twins were fifteen. They settled in Pennsylvania, where Alvise took a job as a steelworker for Bethlehem Steel Co.

"Mario and I had mixed feelings about coming to this country," Aldo recalled. "Other than the Indianapolis 500, you never heard about auto racing in the United States then. In Europe, it was much more of an elite, private sport. We were afraid there would be no way to make a living in racing here."

The teenagers kept their racing pursuits secret from their parents and lied about their ages. A driver had to be twenty-one then to obtain a racing license; the twins were just nineteen when Aldo, always the "hard luck" brother, suffered serious injuries at a racetrack in Hatfield, Pa., in 1959. The crash fractured his skull and left him in a coma for days. But the mishap didn't dent either twin's desire to race.

"If I had stopped and really reflected on the danger just once, I probably never would have stepped back in a race car," Mario wrote years later in *Andretti*. "As realistic as you want to be, you almost didn't want to think about it . . . I was driven by the desire to win at all costs."

Because they shared a car in the beginning, Mario and Aldo seldom competed head-to-head. But Aldo conceded that each twin tried to top the other's successes.

"He was always the target to beat," Aldo said, nodding at a framed photo in his office of a beaming Mario. The photo also depicts the three currently active Andretti drivers: John and Mario's sons Michael and Jeff (born in 1962 and 1964, respectively).

Aldo's move away from Mario to Indianapolis occurred in 1964. Already pursuing auto-related business opportunities, Aldo and his wife Carolyn, known as "Corky," decided it would be convenient to live in the racing "capital."

Aldo's sudden, early exit from driving often is attributed to his two spectacular crashes, the Hatfield accident and a wreck ten years later in Des Moines, Iowa. That 1969 crash caused massive facial injuries.

"I tell my kids, 'I have so much plastic in my face now, I'll never age,' " Aldo quipped, referring to surgeries and implants. "But it's a myth that I got out of racing because of the crashes. They were both near-fatal accidents, and it was publicized that I was on my last legs. But I always knew I was going to make it.

"The truth is, I got out of racing to take advantage of a business opportunity. I didn't even think it would be the end of driving for me. For a while, I assumed I could do both. I soon learned that to be successful in business, you have to devote 100 percent—just like racing demands 100 percent."

Meanwhile, Mario raced. Did he ever. His became a familiar name in record books and in newspapers around the world, particularly after he won the Indianapolis 500 in 1969 and came close to capturing victory at the Speedway several other times during the next twenty-five years. Some highlights: Mario's first Indy Car victory was in 1965 at Indianapolis Raceway Park (the Hoosier Grand Prix); he qualified fourth that year for his first 500, finishing an impressive third and capturing "Rookie of the Year" honors. He won the Indy Car championship that year, repeated in 1966, then ventured into stock cars and won NASCAR's Daytona 500 in 1967.

Ten years later, Mario won the Italian Grand Prix and three other Formula One events. He captured the World Driving Championship at Monza, Italy, in 1978, only the second American to do so.

He remains the only driver to win an Indy Car championship and the world championship. And Mario Andretti is the only person ever named Driver of the Year in three decades (1967, 1978 and 1984).

Mario's major frustration: Never winning a second Indy 500. He almost did so in 1981, when Bobby Unser beat him by a mere eight seconds and was penalized a lap for passing under a yellow "caution" flag. Mario was declared the winner, but an appeal by Unser reversed the decision.

"Only A. J. Foyt can come close to Andretti for longevity and versatility," notes Ralph Hickok in *A Who's Who of Sports Champions.*

Marion's son Michael has roared to the forefront of Indy Car and Formula One racing, winning the Indy Car points championship in 1991. The next year, three Andrettis—Mario, Michael and John—finished in the top ten in Indy Car points.

John's advice for aspiring race drivers: "Be as dedicated as you would be to getting a doctorate in college."

Although he doesn't have a Ph.D., John demonstrated his father's mettle by obtaining a business degree from Moravian College in Pennsylvania after graduating from Ritter High School in Indianapolis, where he met his wife Nancy.

Aldo said he's followed his son's progress in racing with pride. But does he worry while watching John and Michael and his other relatives race? Aldo smiled and spoke softly. "John doesn't know this, but I can feel what he is sensing. I'm not trying to relive my racing through him. But he's my son, and I've been there, so I can feel it as he drives. I am also his biggest fan."

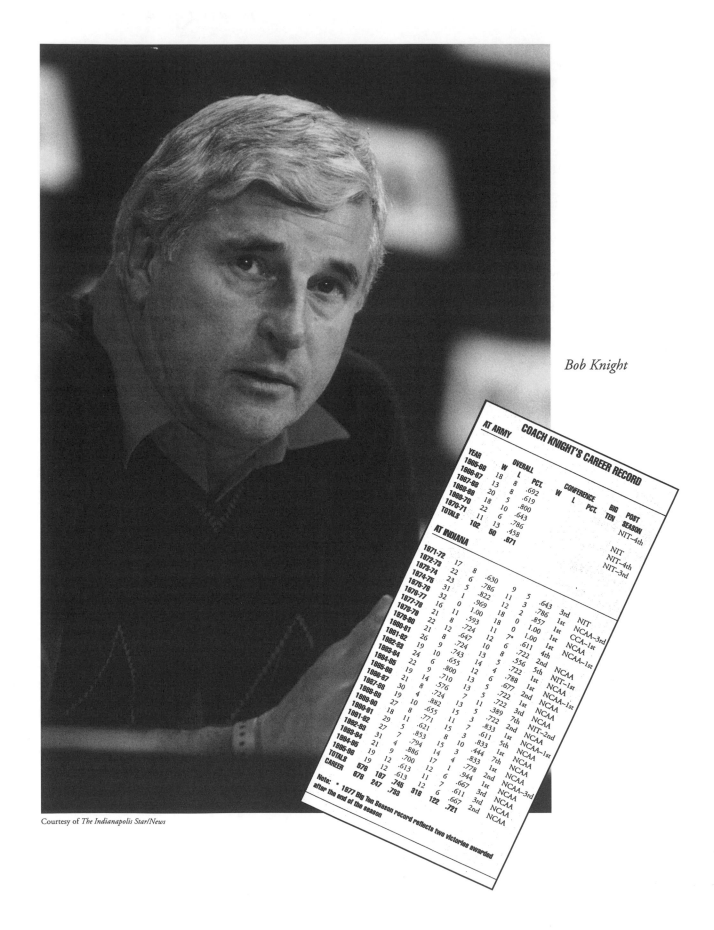

Bob Knight

Courtesy of *The Indianapolis Star/News*

COACH KNIGHT'S CAREER RECORD

AT ARMY

YEAR	OVERALL			CONFERENCE			BIG TEN	POST SEASON
	W	L	PCT.	W	L	PCT.		
1965-66	18	8	.692					
1966-67	13	8	.619					
1967-68	20	8	.800					
1968-69	18	5						
1969-70	22	10	.786					
1970-71	11	6	.458					NIT–4th
TOTALS	102	50	.871					

AT INDIANA

YEAR	W	L	PCT.	W	L	PCT.	BIG TEN	POST SEASON
1971-72	17	8						NIT
1972-73	22	6	.630	9	5	.643	3rd	NIT–4th
1973-74	23	5	.786	11	3		1st	NIT–3rd
1974-75	31	1	.822	12	3	.643	3rd	NIT
1975-76	32	0	.969	18	0	.857	1st	NCAA–3rd
1976-77	16	11	1.00	12	0	1.00	1st	CCA–1st
1977-78	21	12	.724	18	0		1st	NCAA
1978-79	22	8	.593	10	8	.611	4th	NCAA–1st
1979-80	21	12	.647	12	7*	1.00	1st	NCAA
1980-81	26	9	.724	13	5	.722	2nd	NIT–1st
1981-82	24	10	.743	14	5	.556	5th	NCAA
1982-83	22	6	.655	12	6	.722	1st	NCAA
1983-84	19	9	.800	13	5	.788	1st	NCAA–1st
1984-85	21	14	.710	13	5	.677	1st	NCAA
1985-86	30	8	.576	13	11	.722	2nd	NCAA
1986-87	19	4	.724	15	3	.722	1st	NCAA
1987-88	27	10	.882	11	5	.389	3rd	NIT–2nd
1988-89	18	8	.655	15	3	.722	7th	NCAA–1st
1989-90	29	11	.771	8	10	.833	1st	NCAA
1990-91	27	5	.621	15	3	.611	5th	NCAA
1991-92	31	7	.853	14	4	.833	1st	NCAA
1992-93	21	4	.794	17	1	.778	7th	NCAA–3rd
1993-94	19	9	.886	12	6	.944	2nd	NCAA
1994-95	19	12	.700	11	7	.667	3rd	NCAA
1995-96	19	12	.613	12	6	.611	3rd	NCAA
TOTALS	678	187	.746			.667	2nd	NCAA
CAREER	678	247	.733	318	122	.721		

Note: * 1977 Big Ten Season record reflects two victories awarded after the end of the season

Bob Knight

Basketball coach

He strongly and imperatively defines the term "Indiana Legend." Bob Knight books, sweaters, dolls and even decorative coffins are found not only in the Hoosier state, but from just about everywhere from the Atlantic to the Pacific.

Since the volatile, driven Knight became coach of Indiana University's basketball team in 1971, the Hoosiers have captured national championships in 1976, 1981, and 1987. Those accomplishments have been surpassed only by a few other men in college basketball history, including another legendary coach with links to Indiana, Martinsville native John Wooden.

On an international level, Knight coached American teams to gold medals in the 1984 Los Angeles Olympics and the 1979 Pan American Games. At IU, his teams have captured eleven Big Ten titles.

His triumphs haven't been the only source of his notoriety, however. Knight's controversial, intense personality and incidents such as a chair-throwing episode during a loss to Purdue in 1985, have made Bob Knight one of Indiana's most famous residents for more than twenty-five years.

His supporters are every bit as passionate as his detractors. In 1987, IU forfeited a game to a team from the Soviet Union because Knight refused to leave the floor after being ejected. (He had drawn three technical fouls for arguing with referees.) When Knight later was reprimanded by the IU administration, at least as much fury was directed at university officials as at the coach.

Knight is a truly complex individual, far more than just a temperamental disciplinarian and a winning-is-everything stereotype. Having the colorful, quotable Knight as coach has been a roller coaster ride for IU and its fans. Yet even his most vehement critics acknowledge that no one understands the mental and physical dynamics of basketball better than the man in the red sweater.

"Your biggest opponent isn't the other guy," Knight told Sports Illustrated *magazine in 1981. "It's human nature."*

He was born Robert Montgomery Knight in 1940 a few miles from Orrville, Ohio, a town of about forty-four hundred residents. Knight's mother, Hazel Menthorne Knight, was a teacher. His father, Carroll Knight, usually called "Pat," was a railroad man.

"My dad started working on the railroad in Oklahoma in 1920," Knight wrote for a book called *When I Think About My Father* (Sta-Kris Inc.), a compilation of letters from famous Americans edited by Mary Kay Shanley. "He retired in 1962. I don't think he ever earned over eight thousand dollars a year, yet with the exception of a lot and house, he never owed anybody a cent. My dad took out a twenty-year mortgage and gave up everything he liked to do to pay the mortgage off in four years.

"I use this illustration to show that my dad had the greatest single-mindedness of purpose of anybody I know."

Clearly the examples of hard work and self-discipline were picked up by young Bobby. He applied those qualities to high school athletics at Orrville, where he lettered in basketball, football and baseball. (Knight is said to have been an excellent power hitter. In fact, he often has identified slugger Ted Williams as his lifelong hero.)

But it wasn't just the industriousness of his role models that Knight admired. He has referred to his father, who died in 1970, as the "most honest person" he ever met.

"My dad had a tremendous responsibility toward his job with the railroad," Knight wrote in *When I Think About My Father*. "I couldn't begin to count the number of rainy, cold or snowy nights that I walked through the railroad yard with him, holding a lantern so he could check the seals on boxcars to make sure none had been broken into.

"I remember him saying to me, 'If you are going to accept pay for something, do it right.'"

After high school, Knight enrolled at Ohio State University. Although his father hoped he would become an attorney, Bob Knight has said that he was uncertain of his career goals when he showed up on campus.

He majored in education, minored in history and government and played on Buckeye basketball teams that captured three Big Ten titles and the 1960 NCAA championship. But Knight was overshadowed as a player by some of his teammates, including future Boston Celtics star John Havlicek.

After graduating from Ohio State in 1962, he was an assistant basketball coach at Cuyahoga Falls High School near Cleveland, Ohio, then became an assistant coach at West Point. Years later, Knight told *The New York Times* that his stay at West Point gave him an appreciation for discipline—and, as he put it, "a way discipline could be applied to basketball and the players I would teach."

By 1965, he was the head coach at Army. Knight's teams there won 102 games and lost 50; they led the country in defense three times and were invited to the National Invitational Tournament four times. Under Knight, Army beat its arch-rival Navy every year.

Analysts noted that his Army teams usually were at a disadvantage with opponents in height, speed and natural ability. But Coach Knight seemed to pull the full potential from his players, emphasizing the importance of teamwork over the cult of star players. Analysts would say much the same of Knight's teams at IU after he was named head basketball coach in Bloomington at age twenty-seven.

Soon after arriving on campus in 1971, the young coach insisted on pre-practice conditioning routines. They included drills for his players that involved arduous runs up the steps to the top of Assembly Hall.

Although Knight's toughness with his players is well-known, his loyalty and generosity to his friends and former players hasn't drawn the same attention. Many say Knight prefers to keep those aspects of his personality low-key. Certainly he has been outspoken about his dislike of several of the promotional aspects of his job, including dealing with journalists. Yet in some ways he manages to be a reporter's dream because he is so quotable and witty.

"A coach flies off the handle and everyone sees him," he said when asked about his temper by a group of journalists in 1994. "I'd like to be around to see what one of you guys does when somebody changes your copy a little bit."

He consistently has won praise for the purity of his program in Bloomington. While the careers of athletic officials and coaches at colleges across the country have been tainted by scandals involving cash and gifts to lure recruits, Knight and his recruiting techniques never have been questioned.

Some of his greatest triumphs as a coach came in the mid-1970s, and his 1975 and

1976 teams became legendary. The '75 team was undefeated until losing to Kentucky in the regional finals. The next year, IU was undefeated in its regular season and went on to capture the NCAA championship. To a generation of Hoosiers, Knight's players during this era are still heroes: Kent Benson, Scott May, Quinn Buckner, Tom Abernathy and Jim Crews among them.

Meanwhile, Knight had launched his philanthropic effort that has received the most publicity: his unflagging support of the IU library system.

In 1976, he helped create an unrestricted fund so the library could expand its collections. In the years since, he has helped raise more than $5 million, university officials estimate. In 1990, the library started the Bob Knight Endowment; through this fund, the library has been able to purchase everything from videotapes of Shakespearean productions to recordings of African-American musicians.

In 1981, when one of Knight's star players, Landon Turner, was paralyzed in a traffic accident, the coach raised money for a trust fund. Knight personally contributed about fifty thousand dollars to get the fund started, according to *The Indianapolis Star*.

The coach is the father of two sons from his marriage to his first wife, Nancy. (The couple divorced in the mid-1980s. In 1988, Knight married his second wife, Karen Vieth Edgar, a former high school basketball coach in Oklahoma.)

His older son, Tim, obtained an economics degree from Stanford University and has handled his father's marketing and business affairs in recent years; Tim Knight also coordinates motivational seminars and his dad's popular summer camp. Knight's younger son, Pat, played on his father's IU teams in the early 1990s and recently has worked as a regional scout for the Phoenix Suns.

Away from basketball arenas, Knight is an avid fisherman and popular spokesman in TV and radio commercials, many of which poke fun at his intimidating image. For example, in a commercial for NutraSweet, the artificial sweetener, Knight was depicted as being overly kind to his players—that is, artificially sweet.

Though his sense of humor is clearly a trait that's been under-appreciated, Knight obviously is grateful for the widespread respect for his honesty and work ethic.

"It always gives me an extra thrill when a player I have coached says he has learned how to work hard by being a basketball player at Indiana University," Knight wrote in *When I Think About My Father*.

"I'm also pleased when people refer to me as being honest. Such comments are a reflection not on me, but on my dad."

(Top left) David Wolf, the first Indianapolis native in space, signs autographs during a visit to his hometown.

(Above) Gus Grissom

(Left) Hoosier astronaut Jerry Ross received a civic award from Indiana gospel singer Sandi Patty.

Astronauts

Why in heaven have so many American astronauts spent portions of their lives in Indiana? It's primarily because of Purdue University, the college in West Lafayette nicknamed the "Mother of Astronauts." Since the beginning of our nation's exploration of space, almost every NASA mission has had at least one Purdue link. From the first man to walk on the moon, Neil Armstrong (Purdue class of '55) to physician-scientist David Wolf, the first Indianapolis native in space (class of '78), Purdue has influenced the exploration of "the new frontier."

The university wages a perpetual one-upsmanship battle with the Massachusetts Institute of Technology over which school can claim the most Americans selected for space flight. As of 1997, twenty-two Purdue grads have been chosen.

In addition, thousands of Purdue engineering graduates have built the vehicles the astronauts fly. Several Purdue professors have worked at the Jet Propulsion Laboratory, where spacecraft are designed. Even the packaging of the dehydrated food consumed by shuttle crews has been supervised by a Purdue alumna. She is Karen Pearson Ross, a native of Sheridan, Indiana, and the wife of Hoosier astronaut Jerry Ross.

All of this is part of a broader picture—namely, that more Midwesterners have been chosen as astronauts than natives of any other region of the country. "This may sound corny," said astronaut Greg Harbaugh (Purdue class of '78) during an interview in 1989, "but I think NASA craves good, solid Midwesterners, wholesome types raised with the work ethic."

It would be misleading to claim full-fledged "Hoosier" status for astronauts such as Armstrong, Harbaugh and Eugene Cernan (Purdue class of '56), the last man to leave footprints on the moon. Although all of them spent several years in West Lafayette, they grew up in other states.

But why try to claim them? Plenty of other NASA astronauts—men and women with "the right stuff"—have deep Hoosier roots. These space explorers were born and grew up in Indiana before enrolling at Purdue and, in some cases, the Indiana University School of Medicine.

Then they left their home state to, eventually, see the stars.

Virgil "Gus" Grissom

The original group of American astronauts was selected in 1959. Among the seven men was Virgil Ivan "Gus" Grissom of Mitchell, Indiana, a town in Lawrence County about eighty miles south of Indianapolis.

Two years later, astronaut Grissom was on board for the second manned flight of the Mercury program—making him the second American to go up in space.

In 1965 Grissom orbited the Earth in a Gemini spacecraft. Among his distinctions: He became the first person to travel in space twice. Unfortunately, Gus Grissom is remembered not just because of his triumphs as an astronaut, but largely because of his tragic death.

He was killed at age forty on January 27, 1967, in one of the space program's worst tragedies. Grissom was serving as commander of the Apollo 1 spacecraft. With fellow astronauts Ed White and Roger Chaffee (Purdue, class of '57) aboard with Grissom, the Apollo 1 capsule was mounted atop a Saturn rocket for what was supposed to be a routine ground test at Cape Kennedy in Florida.

During countdown, an electrical short in a wire near Grissom's feet sparked a fire. Fed by the pure oxygen in the spacecraft, the blaze engulfed Apollo instantly. Combustible materials inside the capsule released a toxic gas that suffocated all three astronauts.

Born in 1926, the son of a railroad signalman, Grissom was active in the Boy Scouts in Mitchell. He was inducted into the US. Army Air Corps, then enrolled at Purdue. After graduating in 1950 Grissom was an Air Force officer and fighter pilot during the Korean War. But he nearly was rejected from the history-making group of original astronauts when medical tests revealed he suffered from hay fever.

Legend has it that Grissom saved himself with this classic line: "There won't be any ragweed pollen in space."

Despite his engaging personality and considerable achievements, Grissom's image remains controversial decades after his death. That's because of his depiction in *The Right Stuff*, journalist Tom Wolfe's 1969 best-seller (and subsequent movie) about the space program. The book and film imply Grissom panicked when his Mercury capsule splashed down in 1961. Loaded with valuable scientific data, the capsule sank to the bottom of the Atlantic Ocean, although Grissom was picked up by rescuers from a helicopter.

"I was lying there, flat on my back—and it just blew," Grissom explained at the time. Other astronauts said they believed his explanation, but *The Right Stuff* speculates that a panicky Grissom triggered the explosive hatch in the Mercury, causing it to take on water. Whatever the truth, Gus Grissom went on to achieve successes, including his smooth Gemini flight in 1965.

He is remembered as an all-American hero in his home state in several ways; Bunker Hill Air Force Base in north central Indiana was renamed in Grissom's honor.

Even the Apollo disaster that caused his death had positive results. The tragic fire led to changes that many analysts say were crucial to the ultimate success of Apollo, which put men on the moon in 1969.

David Wolf

The first Indianapolis native to go up in space, astronaut David Wolf was one of seven Columbia crew members in 1993 who spent fourteen days in space, then a NASA record.

That's just one of Wolf's claims to fame—and astronaut is only one of his many professions. He's a physician with experience as a flight surgeon. As a medical researcher, he headed a team that developed a widely acclaimed bioreactor, a device regarded as a boon for cancer research. He's also an electrical engineer and a pilot with the Indiana National Guard.

A thrill seeker since his teenage days at North Central High School and Purdue, Wolf is an avid motorcyclist. He's also an aerobatic pilot (NASA asks him to stop competing six months before a launch) who has explored the Arctic Circle and remote parts of the Amazon River, where Wolf delivered medical care to natives.

Born in 1956, young David Wolf daydreamed of becoming an astronaut. "At first, you think, 'Well sure, everyone wants to be an astronaut,' " recalled his father, Dr. Harry Wolf, an Indianapolis physician, during an interview in 1993. "You don't tend to take it seriously. But then you noticed his desire never wavered."

David Wolf said, "I've gone from being thrilled by adventure to loving the technology to the point I'm at now, being most interested in the research benefits (in space) for Earth."

Regarded as a bright young star among American astronauts, Wolf was selected by NASA in 1996 for his biggest challenge ever. He moved to Russia to learn the country's spacecraft technology and language at Star City, the legendary training center for cosmonauts near Moscow. He also went through survival training north of the Arctic Circle in northernmost Siberia.

It was preparation for an overwhelming but exhilarating undertaking, a prime example of the American-Russian cooperation in 1990s space exploration: In late September of 1997 the Hoosier astronaut went up in the space shuttle *Atlantis* to spend more than four months living in the Russian space station *Mir*. At the orbiting outpost, Wolf conducted medical and scientific experiments high above the Earth.

Jerry Ross

He was the astronaut who entertained his earthbound television audience by somersaulting in space in April 1991. And Jerry Ross was the NASA astronaut with the buoyant personality who, when told to come back in the space shuttle *Atlantis* after his somersault, grumbled: "Rats." That prompted TV commentators to liken him to "a boy who hears his mother call for dinner."

In an interview after his return to Earth, Ross, whose sense of humor is legendary at the Johnson Space Center in Houston, commented: "People have told me, 'I'm glad it was 'rats' you said. I tell them, 'Hey, that's just my Indiana way of talking.' "

Born in 1948, Ross grew up in a rural area near Crown Point. As a boy during the *Sputnik* era of the late 1950s, he made scrapbooks about space and, by his own admission, "played hooky from school" to watch space missions on TV. Determined to become an astronaut, he graduated from Crown Point High School and Purdue.

Aside from Ross' somersault, the Atlantis expedition in 1991 also included an emergency spacewalk by Ross to fix an antenna stuck against the side of a $617 million Gamma Ray Laboratory. The trip ended a long hiatus in American spacewalks—a gap of more than five years. Ross had been the last previous spacewalker as well, in 1985. On that foray, the Hoosier walked on a mechanical arm while demonstrating construction techniques in space. For a while, Ross held the record of "spacewalk hours" for any astronaut.

Now a popular public speaker across the country, Ross describes his travels in space this way: "Think of the most awesome, breathtaking sights of your life. Rainbows, sunrises, sunsets, twilights, stars, blue sky. Now glue those scenes end to end and run them fast as you can right after each other, as if through a viewfinder."

Donald Williams

A farm boy from tiny Otterbein, Indiana, near Lafayette, Captain Donald E. Williams grew up to become commander of the crew on the space shuttle Atlantis in 1989.

"When you grow up on a farm, you tend to be interested in how things are put together and how to repair them if they break," Williams said during an interview in 1989. "I never did much observing with a telescope, but I read a lot of science fiction. I used to sit on the farm and watch the night sky."

Born in 1942, Williams is the son of a farmer and an elementary school teacher. He played varsity basketball and ran track at the former Otterbein High School, then enrolled at Purdue shortly after the first group of astronauts was chosen. With his tuition paid by a Navy ROTC scholarship, Williams studied mechanical engineering. During the summer between his junior and senior years at Purdue, he served as a cadet aboard a Navy submarine.

"That's what convinced me I would rather be an aviator," he said, laughing. "Aboard a sub, it's cramped. The hours are long, and it is difficult, if not impossible, to get away from the other people."

The same could be said about space shuttles.

"But there is one *big* difference," Williams commented. "We have windows to look out—and the view is awesome."

A Navy flier and a test pilot who served four tours in Vietnam, Williams completed 330 combat missions. He was selected as an astronaut in 1978, and seven years later was a crew member aboard the shuttle *Discovery*.

With Williams at the controls, Atlantis deployed *Galileo*, a $1.4 million planetary probe, on a six-year voyage to Jupiter. The Hoosier astronaut and his crew also studied the Earth's ozone layer and were monitored for medical experiments.

Other astronauts also have links to Indiana beyond a Purdue connection, including NASA astronaut Mark N. Brown, who was born in Valparaiso in 1951. A graduate of Valparaiso High School and Purdue, Brown became a major in the Air Force and was a mission specialist on a space shuttle in 1989. Aboard the shuttle Discovery in 1991, Brown was the astronaut chosen to dispatch an observatory satellite designed to examine the effects of pollution on the Earth's ozone layer.

Another astronaut with Indiana connections is Janice Voss, a native Hoosier. Although she was born in South Bend in 1956, Voss considers Rockford, Illinois, her hometown. But she has something in common with all of the other Hoosier astronauts: a Purdue education.

Dan Quayle

Vice president

No question, most Americans were surprised in August of 1988 when George Bush announced that forty-one-year-old Dan Quayle, then Indiana's junior senator, would be his running mate on the Republican ticket in the presidential campaign. But James Danforth Quayle has been surprising people most of his life by pulling off unexpected victories. They include his upset of three-term incumbent U.S. Senator Birch Bayh in 1980, a triumph that made Quayle, then thirty-three, the youngest senator ever elected from Indiana.

His youth, good looks and unflagging enthusiasm—while often regarded as assets in a public figure—also may have worked against him. Throughout his career in public office, Quayle has fought a perception that he's an intellectual lightweight; during his term as vice president (1988–92), Dan Quayle jokes were a staple for comedians and talk show hosts like Johnny Carson, Jay Leno and Quayle's fellow Indianapolis native, David Letterman.

"I laughed at the jokes that were funny and ignored the others," Quayle said during an interview in 1997. "My kids did the same thing—they just took their cues from my reactions."

A factor that undoubtedly helps: Quayle enjoys thousands of supporters across America, particularly among social and political conservatives. Sometimes even his critics have reversed themselves.

Consider the Murphy Brown *incident in 1992. As vice president, Quayle made headlines and endured widespread detraction during his unsuccessful re-election campaign when he attacked* Murphy Brown, *a popular TV sitcom. In the episode, the title character, a glamorous broadcast journalist, gave birth to an illegitimate child.*

A few years later, Bill Clinton, the Democrat who defeated Bush, said he agreed with much of Quayle's critique. Atlantic *magazine even published a cover story on the social costs of illegitimate births titled "Dan Quayle Was Right."*

Quayle's redemption in some quarters—and his appeal to many conservative voters—prompted speculation about him as a candidate for the Republican presidential nomination in 1996. But he bowed out of the race early on and said during the interview he has "no regrets" about stepping aside. Later in 1996, Quayle and his wife, Marilyn Tucker Quayle, moved from Carmel, Indiana—their home since leaving Washington, D.C. in 1992—to Arizona, where Quayle had spent some of his teenage years.

He now heads Campaign America, a political action committee dedicated to electing conservative candidates. Quayle, a popular speaker and fund-raiser, crisscrossed the country to appear at political and charitable events, maintaining a fast-paced schedule.

"In April 1997, I was home a grand total of eight days," Quayle said, flipping through a jammed appointment book. "I lead a very fulfilling life. I have many things I want to accomplish."

Do his goals include a run for the White House in 2000?

"I don't have to decide just yet," he replied. "I'm considering it, obviously."

Courtesy of office of former U.S. Vice President Dan Quayle

Dan Quayle

He's also not ruling out eventually moving back to his home state. He was born in Indianapolis in 1947, and has spent most of his life in the state. Stressing that "I'm a Hoosier first and foremost," Quayle did rule one thing out: He says he will never again run for vice president.

"Been there, done that," he explained, laughing.

Dan Quayle once saved a man's life.

The dramatic incident occurred in 1964, when seventeen-year-old Dan Quayle was a high school junior. He was hosting a party for his Spanish class at the Quayle home in Huntington, Ind. His youngest brother, Michael, then eight years old, was scampering about as, in his words, "the typical pesky kid brother."

Outdoors, a seventy-one-year-old man on a tractor was grading the driveway when the vehicle flipped, pinning him underneath. Michael Quayle watched as Dan and his classmates sprinted out the door and hoisted the tractor off the victim.

"Watching Dan and Jerry Franks [a friend] do that was the neatest thing in the world," Michael Quayle recalled in a 1990 interview. "As a little kid, to see someone's life saved by your big brother . . . Well, what can I say? I looked on Dan as a hero."

The brothers' parents are Jim and Corinne Quayle. The family moved back and forth between Indiana and Arizona during the boys' childhoods as James Quayle worked for newspapers owned by Corinne's family, the Pulliams.

"I guess you could call me a newspaper brat," Dan Quayle commented during an interview in 1997. "I was in so many different grade schools that I devised a game. The new kid, always me, would be put in the last row. I tried to see how quickly it would take me to work my way up to the front before we moved again."

The Quayles spent many of Dan's childhood and teenage years in Huntington because Jim Quayle was publisher of *The Huntington Herald-Press*.

The family included three children in addition to James Danforth Quayle. (Always called "Dan," he was named after a longtime family friend killed in World War II.) The other siblings are Christopher, now a free-lance writer, and Martha, Michael's twin; Michael and Martha were adopted as babies by the Quayles.

Almost all of the children, including Dan, were active volunteers in Republican campaigns. As a teenager, Dan was known to cruise Huntington's streets in his car with a license plate that read "AuH20"—the chemical symbol for "Goldwater," as in Barry Goldwater, the 1964 presidential candidate.

At Huntington High School and DePauw University in Greencastle, Indiana, Dan Quayle was, as he has conceded, a mediocre student. Years later that fact would be played up on the national stage. One memorable episode occurred in 1992 when, as a dignitary attending a spelling meet, Quayle "corrected" a child's spelling of potato—by misspelling it himself as "potatoe."

The focus on such episodes, though, has caused many to underestimate Quayle. His passion for golf also probably has been overemphasized, at least as it relates to his goals. In the interview, Quayle denied published accounts that he had considered becoming a professional golfer in 1969 as he was preparing to graduate from DePauw, where he was captain of the golf team. "I love the sport," he said, "but I knew I wasn't good enough to make a living at it."

Rather, Quayle described his entry into politics as much more calculated than many have assumed. At DePauw, Quayle was a political science major. After graduating from Indiana University School of Law in Indianapolis with his wife, Marilyn Tucker Quayle, Dan returned to Huntington. Although he made the move in part to work as associate publisher of the family newspaper and to open a law practice with Marilyn, Quayle said he had other motives.

"I was told northern Indiana was fertile territory for a young conservative Republican with political aspirations," Quayle said.

But he conceded he was thinking of running for the Indiana legislature, not the U.S. Congress. Instead, in 1976 at age twenty-nine, Quayle decided to take on an eight-term incumbent Congressman J. Edward Roush, a liberal Democrat. It was the first of many Quayle campaigns written off by political analysts.

"Really, it wasn't that difficult a race for me, and I knew it wouldn't be," Quayle said. "I grew up with Ed Roush's son. I always knew his father was out of step politically with voters in his district. From Day One, I thought I could win."

He did—and then won re-election in 1978 with the largest margin of victory ever in the northeastern Indiana congressional district. He followed that with his stunning defeat of Birch Bayh in the U.S. Senate race of 1980.

"[Former Indiana Congressman] John Brademas told me later, 'That was *the* upset of the year across the country,'" Quayle recalled. "Again, I have to say it really wasn't that difficult."

Quayle said he enjoyed his years in the Senate much more than those in the House of Representatives. "If you're in the minority party, as I was in the House, it's stampede time," he said. "I was able to accomplish much more as a senator."

He pointed with particular pride to the Job Training and Partnership Act of 1982 that he cosponsored with an unlikely ally, Massachusetts Democratic Senator Ted Kennedy. The legislation reorganized job-training programs, made them more efficient and provided ways for private businesses and state officials to cooperate.

"Public service has been my life," Quayle said. "There have been moments of deep disappointment, but also moments of great satisfaction—and those are the ones I focus on."

Marilyn Tucker Quayle

She's an attorney, a political activist and a "Second Lady" who focused her attention on disaster relief when her husband was vice president of the United States.

While Dan Quayle stood second in command of the most powerful nation on earth and her family lived in the Vice President's House on the Naval Observatory, Indianapolis native Marilyn Tucker Quayle added another, rather surprising credit to her resume: novelist.

With her older sister, Nancy Tucker Northcott, Mrs. Quayle wrote *Embrace the Serpent* (1992), a political thriller that focused on a power play between Cuba and the United States. The sisters followed it up with a fast-paced sequel four years later, *The Campaign*, about a conspiracy to derail a U.S. Senate campaign.

During an interview in 1992, Mrs. Quayle said she based several of her fic-

Courtesy of *The Indianapolis Star/News*

tional scenes on her experiences in Washington, D.C., including visits to the White House and flights on Air Force One.

"The characters are all composites," she stressed. "I certainly would never do anything that would create a problem for my husband . . . He had no direct input, but he read three different versions of the book in progress."

Far from hindering Dan Quayle's career, Marilyn Tucker Quayle usually is characterized as the more ambitious of the two. Although she never has run for political office, Marilyn Tucker Quayle frequently was mentioned as a senatorial or gubernatorial candidate in her home state; the Quayles returned to Indiana after his term as vice president ended in 1992 in part so she could resume her practice with an Indianapolis law firm. Talk about her political aspirations has subsided somewhat since 1996, when the couple moved to Arizona; Marilyn Tucker Quayle is continuing her career as an attorney in the Phoenix area.

Marilyn Tucker was born in 1949 and grew up on the Northside of Indianapolis as the daughter of two physicians. Her father, Dr. Warren Tucker, was a pulmonary specialist. Her mother, Dr. Mary Alice Craig Tucker, reared six children while pursuing a career as a pediatrician; she died of cancer in 1975. Since then Marilyn Tucker Quayle has placed early detection of breast cancer—and raising funds for cancer research—at the top of her list of crusades.

Always achievement-oriented, Marilyn Tucker was an honor student at Broad Ripple High School and was given the lifelong nickname of "Merit" by her sister Nancy because she won so many honor badges in Girl Scouts.

She met Dan Quayle when both were students at the Indiana University School of Law; they married after a ten-week courtship. Marilyn Tucker Quayle took her bar exam just a few days after giving birth to the couple's oldest son, Tucker, in 1974. The Quayles also have two other children, Benjamin (born in 1976) and Corinne (born in 1978).

As the wife of the vice president, Marilyn Tucker Quayle drew both criticism (some denounced her speech at the 1992 Republican National Convention as unnecessarily strident) and acclaim for her forceful image.

She won particular praise for her efforts on behalf of flood, tornado, and hurricane victims. Marilyn Tucker Quayle frequently left Washington to travel to the sites of natural disasters, where she provided relief alongside American Red Cross workers.

David Letterman in the early 1980s.

David Letterman

TV personality and comedian

*In naming him one of the fifty greatest TV stars of all time—along with Lucille Ball, Johnny Carson, and Milton Berle—*TV Guide *credited "loopy" Indianapolis native David Letterman with "moving the talk show closer to being an art form."*

Long a cult favorite among college students and insomniacs because of his caustic humor, Letterman achieved vast popular and critical acclaim in 1993 with the debut on CBS-TV of Late Show With David Letterman. *He was so famous that even his mother, Dorothy, became a national celebrity. A Carmel, Indiana, housewife, she popped up on her son's show with reports from the 1994 Lillehammer Winter Olympics—then received one million dollars to write a cookbook. Her son in 1995 was chosen as the host for Hollywood's most glamorous event, the Academy Awards.*

Born in Indianapolis in 1947, David Letterman had a slow, sporadic rise to fame, beginning with a series of radio and TV jobs in his hometown. They included a stint as a TV weatherman in which the absurdly miscast comedian forecast "hail the size of canned hams."

He was interviewed in 1993 in Broadway's historic Ed Sullivan Theater which, after sitting vacant for twenty years, was renovated for his show. A lifelong lover of fast cars, Letterman mentioned during the interview he had "a small dream" of investing in an IndyCar racing team. A few years later, he became a co-owner of former Indianapolis 500 winner Bobby Rahal's team.

His popular Late Show *continues to duel for late-night audiences with NBC-TV's* The Tonight Show *starring Jay Leno, the successor to Johnny Carson.*

NEW YORK—Midnight is approaching, the end of an exhausting workday. Crowds of shivering teenage autograph seekers wait at every exit.

Their quarry began the morning by cracking his head against a door frame, a mishap that caused blood to pour down his cheeks, required emergency treatment of four stitches, and aggravated an old neck injury.

Despite all that, the man behind the desk—who says he was a child hypochondriac—is smiling, revealing the famous gap between his front teeth.

Who needs the Top 10 explanations for why David Letterman would grin?

The Indianapolis native regularly heads lists of the one hundred most powerful people in the entertainment industry and of the "hottest" celebrities in show business. His annual pay is estimated at fourteen million dollars. The instantaneous critical and popular success of his CBS show startled many—including, Letterman concedes, himself and his staff.

Even the recent World Series was altered to benefit him. Opening pitches were thrown out about twenty minutes earlier so as not to jeopardize the 11:35 P.M. start of *Late Show*.

So, beaming despite a grueling day that involved taping a show, planning a week's worth of programs, and injuring his head, Letterman has slipped into sweatpants, high-tops, and a Newman-Haas IndyCar racing team T-shirt.

The School 55 graduate, former Atlas Supermarket stock boy, and Channel 13 *Clover*

Power host and weekend weatherman is asked if he is the happiest he has ever been.

The forty-six-year-old comedian pauses during an interview that's full of serious, contemplative replies. Without apparent hesitation, Letterman volunteers candid, self-analytical comments—despite his reputation for deflecting personal inquires with devastating zingers.

"Yes," he says, speaking softly and slowly as he stubs out a cigar. "Yes . . . I suppose I am the happiest ever now." The grin reappears. "Everything has come together."

And, he says later, lessons have been learned.

Letterman mentions one of them when reminded about a legendary escapade from his days in Indianapolis broadcasting during the mid-1970s. On the air at WIBC, he announced the "sale" of the Soldiers and Sailors Monument to Guam, which planned to paint the memorial green as a colossal tribute to asparagus.

Rather than smirking at the memory, Letterman says he thinks of it now in serious terms.

"A lesson I've had to learn over and over in my life, I'm sorry to say, is that just because I may think something is funny doesn't mean it's funny to everyone else," he explains.

"People called the radio station very upset because their relatives had given their lives in battle for this country. To them, the Soldiers and Sailors Monument had sincere, symbolic significance."

Similarly sobering lessons persist in his personal life, concedes the middle child of the late Joseph Letterman, a Broad Ripple florist, and his wife, Dorothy.

Letterman mentions his mother, a retired secretary of Second Presbyterian Church who remarried after Joseph Letterman's death and moved to Carmel, Indiana.

"She will say something," he explains, "and I will shoot back with commentary. Ulp. I can tell right away by her eyes. To her, I've thrown a dagger."

His voice softens and he shakes his head, expressing amazement at what he calls his mother's selflessness. During a recent visit, he called to say he would drop over momentarily.

"When I showed up, she said"—his voice softens even more, becoming gentle and whispery—" 'Dave, would you like a nice piece of strawberry pie?'

"Well, I learned later she created and baked the entire pie—from scratch to serving—in between my call and the visit less than an hour later."

For all his appreciation for his mom, the future comedian emulated his father, friends say. Joseph Letterman died at age fifty-seven in 1973, about two years before his son packed up his red pickup truck and headed to California.

The elder Letterman is widely recalled as charismatic and jovial.

"I'd guess Mr. Letterman was the source—or at least a big source—of Dave's humor," says Jeff Eshowsky, forty-six, an Indianapolis building contractor who became buddies with David when they were fifth graders at School 55.

Their friendship evolved from summers as Haverford Little League teammates through Broad Ripple High School (class of '65) and simultaneous, after-school jobs at Atlas.

His friend's wit, Eshowsky says, was always there, if unrecognized. "Dave was sort of a withdrawn individual as a fifth-grader, but he was extremely quick-witted and sarcastic. Despite whatever you may have heard about his grades, he was always sharp in common sense."

Legends about his lackluster academic career at Broad Ripple are not overstated, Letterman says. Saying his marks consisted of "solid C's," he described himself as a floundering teenager.

His mediocrity in school was thrown into sharp relief because his two sisters excelled. Janice, his older sister, is a Carmel resident; Gretchen is a writer and former editor for a newspaper in St. Petersburg, Florida.

Their brother's inspiration finally came during a public speaking class in his junior year of high school.

"I still remember the first speech I had to give," he recalls, grinning. "It was the first pursuit at Broad Ripple that came easily to me. It was so much fun. I thought, 'What could be a logical [professional] extension of this?' "

Letterman is just as effusive about his after-school job as a stock boy at Atlas, an experience he calls a "turning point" in his life. The job came about after he quit the freshman (reserve) basketball team at Broad Ripple.

"I was tired of it, and I knew I wasn't that good," he recalls. "My parents very wisely said, 'Fine. You can quit. But if you give that up, you have to get a job. We don't want you loafing after school.' Well, Atlas was our neighborhood market of choice. It seemed logical to apply there."

The result?

"It wasn't just a job," Letterman replies. "It was a step in social maturation. To this day, the Atlas experience remains one of the most positive influences in my life. It was the first time I was entrusted with real responsibility."

About that time, Letterman joined in a neighborhood football game—and wound up with a broken nose that's never been fixed. As a result, widespread public attention on the gap in his front teeth surprises him, the comedian says. Ever since the Broad Ripple football game, he's considered his most distinctive feature to be his broken nose—something TV viewers will notice easily if they look closely, he adds.

Shortly after the nose accident, Letterman enrolled at Ball State University, where his grades were no better than his marks at Broad Ripple. The words DEDICATED TO ALL C STUDENTS BEFORE AND AFTER ME are inscribed on a plaque in the David Letterman Control Room on the university's Muncie campus.

The broadcast studio is among several donations from Letterman, a 1970 telecommunications graduate. He has given money for video equipment, an annual scholarship and the launching of WCRD, a student-run radio station.

But some say Letterman underestimates his accomplishments on campus.

"His introductory course with me was a large lecture class," recalls Darrell Wible, a professor emeritus of telecommunications who had Letterman in seven classes. "There were seventy students, but three A's. David got one of them . . .

"You never know how talent will evolve or be recognized. I couldn't have predicted his spectacular success, but I remember walking down the hallway with a faculty member who said, 'That Letterman is stupid.'

"I said, 'As far as I'm concerned, David Letterman is a creative genius.' "

Ball State is far from the only beneficiary of Letterman's largesse. Most of his gifts to Hoosier nonprofit agencies, schools, summer camps and social service groups have been granted under demands of anonymity.

Ron Elberger, his Indianapolis attorney, didn't want to reveal dollar totals or the identity of recipients—although he confirmed they range from the Indiana School for the Deaf and the Indiana School for the Blind to the Marion County Children's Guardian Home.

"All I can tell you is his philanthropy has been significant, consistent and innovative," Elberger says. "Indianapolis is home to Dave. He's proud of it. That will never change."

Letterman owns a house in New Canaan, Connecticut. That's about a forty-minute commute from the Ed Sullivan Theater, which now displays Letterman's name on its Broadway marquee. He also has an apartment in the trendy Tribeca neighborhood in lower Manhattan.

Letterman has been married once—during his senior year at Ball State to Michelle Cook, another student. Although they divorced about eight years later, he spoke warmly of her, crediting his ex-wife with giving him the confidence to quit WTNS Radio in Indianapolis and strike out for Los Angeles.

"I knew Dave couldn't stay locked into announcer booths, weatherman jobs, and tight parameters here," recalls Ron Pearson, an Indianapolis advertising executive who met Letterman at Ball State and formed a campus improvisational comedy troupe with him.

"But I worried Dave would ultimately overstep the bounds and spend the rest of his life in Broad Ripple, tending bar and regaling a select group who found him funny."

Actually, Letterman did overstep some bounds—or at least smash conventions. Al Rent, former program director at Ball State's WBST-AM, says he was instructed to fire Letterman after he broadcast fictitious—but hilarious—biographies of classical composers.

Back then, Letterman occasionally sported a full beard and weighed 153 pounds. About a year ago, he was shocked to discover he weighed 205.

"I went to bed hungry every night for a year," says Letterman, who stands more than six-feet-two and looks almost reed thin at his current 175. "It was iron will. I ate one meal a day—lunch."

The same self-discipline is apparent in other ways, friends say. "He's never missed a day of work on his shows," Elberger says. "It's that Midwestern work ethic in him."

How does this square with a tendency to hypochondria, particularly in boyhood? And why did Letterman charge ahead despite his head injury, taping a show (the blood and bandages were concealed beneath a baseball cap) and never mentioning the stitches to a visitor?

"Ahhhh," you don't understand the personality type," Letterman says. "You get a small thing in your mind and seize on it. But the big stuff? No sweat."

He smiles broadly, again revealing his gap. Actually, Letterman reports, there are two gaps in his mouth. He uses a dental device called a spacer to fill the other one.

"The truth is, I never knew I had a gap in my front teeth," he says. "Then, when I was starting out on national TV, I was told [producer] George Schlatter would be interested if I had my teeth fixed.

"I said, 'Uh, what's wrong with my teeth?' . . . So I tried a spacer in front. But I have an overbite, and that amplified the problem. I looked like a duck."

Letterman tosses back his head and laughs. An engaging conversationalist and careful listener, he comes across as low-key and polite, quite a contrast to his image as a master of caustic humor.

As he walks his visitor to an elevator, toting the towel he had used to sop the blood from his head injury, Letterman expresses longings for Hoosier tomatoes and "deep, sincere nostalgia" for his Atlas stockboy days.

But the comedian's joy in his current life also is apparent—and a refreshing surprise, even to him.

"We didn't think our show would be this successful this soon—or maybe ever," he says. "Somehow we hit our stride from the start."

He tosses the towel aside. That way, Letterman can offer a hearty handshake, using both hands in the clasp.

David Anspaugh

Movie director

The man who would direct the best-known movie about Indiana, along with other lyrical, inspirational motion pictures set in his home state, was born in 1946 and grew up in Decatur.

Hoosiers filmmaker David Anspaugh was interviewed in 1991 before receiving the Indiana Governor's Arts Award. He went on to direct Rudy *(1993), which concerned a football legend at the University of Notre Dame, as well as* Moonlight and Valentino *(1995). Also in 1995, Anspaugh married actress Roma Downey, star of the popular TV series* Touched By An Angel. *Their daughter, Reilly Marie, was born in 1996.*

David Anspaugh, forty-four, who was among recipients of the tenth Indiana Governor's Arts Awards, once enjoyed local fame in northeastern Indiana as the starting quarterback for his varsity football team. He also set a county record as a pole vaulter. Earlier, he had been an avid Little Leaguer.

Basketball, for the director of the famous feature film *Hoosiers*, was not tops.

"We had a great football team at Decatur," Anspaugh recalled. "I played guard on the basketball team my senior year, but we had a terrible team."

This from an Emmy Award-winning director known for his $7 million movie about "Hoosier Hysteria," a film inspired by the most dramatic moment in Indiana basketball history.

Anspaugh, an Indiana University graduate who collected his two Emmys for directing *Hill Street Blues* episodes, received the governor's award during a gala at the Indiana Roof Ballroom attended by hundreds of business, civic and arts leaders.

Anspaugh, who also directed the movie *Fresh Horses* (1988) starring Molly Ringwald and Andrew McCarthy, said dozens of high school basketball coaches have told him that to "psych up" players before crucial games, the coaches screen the movie *Hoosiers*. The film is based on the legendary upset victory of Milan High School in the 1954 state championship.

"I've even had [former Chrysler Corp. chairman] Lee Iacocca tell me, David, that he has viewed *Hoosiers* over twenty times for inspirational purposes," former Indiana Governor Evan Bayh reported as he presented Anspaugh with the state's top arts award.

Even in the Soviet Union, where basketball has only recently generated interest, *Hoosiers* hits home.

"Next to the world premiere in Indianapolis, my trip to the Soviet Union has been the most satisfying experience with *Hoosiers*,' " said Anspaugh, who was invited to Moscow last winter. The Soviets selected *Hoosiers* as one of the few American movies shown at a film festival.

"I walked into Moscow's largest theater," Anspaugh recalled. "When the movie was shown, the Russian people cheered and laughed and cried. Afterward, I stood on the stage

David Anspaugh

and answered questions. A Russian woman in the audience told me, 'People don't realize how similar we all are in our life experiences. I *knew* all those characters in the movie.'"

Since *Hoosiers*, Anspaugh has encountered some frustrations. "I spent a considerable amount of time preparing two movies that collapsed."

One of them also was set in Indiana. Anspaugh planned to direct *A League of Their Own*, a movie about a forgotten chapter of baseball history—women's professional teams in the 1940s. With Twentieth Century Fox as distributor and Penny Marshall as producer, the movie was to be filmed near Evansville.

"Three weeks before filming was to begin, it all fell through. Needless to say, it was very disappointing."

(Penny Marshall eventually completed *A League of Their Own* as both director and producer.)

"Deep down, I think David always dreamed of making movies," said his father, Lawrence Anspaugh, seventy-one, a portrait photographer. His studio in Decatur recently celebrated its forty-fifth anniversary.

"He kept his ambitions very much to himself. He seemed to know that if you are a kid from a small town in Indiana, especially back then, and you tell people you want to be a Hollywood movie director, they would think you were foolish."

The elder Anspaugh is past president of the Professional Photographers of America, the world's largest association of professional photographers.

"I was inspired by an artist in my family—my father," David Anspaugh said. He confided that he used to peek through his dad's cameras on tripods, pretending he was on location with movie cameras.

"He was always so involved in sports that he never spent huge amounts of time at the studio," Larry Anspaugh recalled. "Whatever he wanted to do was fine with his mother and me.

"David was an excellent athlete. I didn't want to squelch that or require him to come to the studio. The work I do and the way I do it requires a complete love. He would have to discover the excitement on his own.

"I don't know what the future holds for David, but in my opinion there will never be another *Hoosiers*," Larry Anspaugh continued. He admits to choking with emotion every time he views the film.

"I know I'm biased, but I think it is flawless in capturing the Hoosier character. In my opinion, the movie is a classic."

Author Nelson Price interviewing screenwriter Angelo Pizzo in 1992 on the campus of the University of Notre Dame, which served as the set for the movie Rudy.

Photos courtesy of *The Indianapolis Star/News*

Angelo Pizzo

Screenwriter

Interviewed on the University of Notre Dame campus during the filming of Rudy *(1993), charismatic screenwriter Angelo Pizzo has provided the ideas for Hollywood's most critically and commercially successful movies about Indiana.*

Along with his former Sigma Nu fraternity brother at Indiana University, director David Anspaugh, Pizzo created Hoosiers *(1986). Born in Bloomington in 1948, Pizzo followed the heartwarming* Rudy *with two joyous events in his personal life—and also endured a natural disaster.*

In 1994, he married actress Greta Lind, who had a featured role in Rudy. *Also that year, the couple's home in Santa Monica, California, was near the epicenter of a devastating earthquake, but both escaped unharmed. At the end of 1994, Lind gave birth to the Pizzos' first child, Anthony.*

SOUTH BEND, Indiana—Maybe more than anyone else, a grandson of Sicilian immigrants is shaping how Hoosiers are depicted in the movies.

As a boy in Bloomington, Angelo Pizzo never dreamed his life would unreel this way.

He yearned for a career in the foreign service or as a politician like his father, a Democratic state legislator and Monroe County coroner. Dr. Anthony Pizzo, a Tech High School and University of Chicago graduate, also is a pathologist and the director of laboratories at Bloomington Hospital.

Angelo, the eldest of seven Pizzo siblings, was studying political science at Indiana University during the Vietnam War.

Disillusioned with public officials—but armed with the support of his father—he scuttled his plans, became a conscientious objector and drifted, temporarily settling in Aspen.

Still youthful-looking, darkly handsome and exuding the fitness of a former marathon runner, Pizzo, forty-four, commands attention—in his own personable, nonthreatening way—on the set of a $14 million movie being made for Columbia TriStar Pictures.

He is the co-producer and screenwriter of *Rudy*, a film-in-the-making at the University of Notre Dame about a Hoosier sports legend. Pizzo has a track record on this terrain, along with the fellow Hoosier he calls a "blood brother."

The director of *Rudy* is David Anspaugh, his former Sigma Nu fraternity brother and Colorado roommate. Also as co-producer/screenwriter and director, Pizzo and Anspaugh created *Hoosiers* (1986), the sleeper hit based on the most famous moment in Indiana high school basketball history, the upset victory of Milan High School.

"You know something?" Pizzo asked during a break from filming.

"Even as a kid who wanted to be in politics, I was *passionate* about films. My father will tell you stories about how, when I wouldn't show up until 10 or 11 o'clock, my folks knew I could be found at a theater."

But as Dr. Pizzo recounts the episodes, they sound more like cliff-hangers than heart-tuggers.

"Angelo and two friends disappeared once when he was not more than eight or nine years old," Dr. Pizzo recalls.

"I had all of the police, firefighters and security guards in the city of Bloomington searching for him. I finally found Angelo and his friends at a cowboy movie—in the front

row."

For six years, South Bend resident Daniel E. "Rudy" Ruettiger was convinced that no one but Pizzo could write his story for the screen.

"Angelo understands the struggles you confront in life," said Ruettiger, also forty-four, whose unlikely quest to play football for the Fighting Irish is the basis for *Rudy*. This is the first time that Notre Dame administrators have allowed filming on campus since Ronald Reagan urged teammates to "win one for the Gipper" in *Knute Rockne, All American* (1940).

"What can I say about Angelo? Talent aside, he is a warm, caring person," Ruettiger said. "He *understands* human relationships."

Listen to the writer known for character development and "small" stories about Mid-westerners. Note how he describes the movies that captivated him in those Bloomington theaters.

"I loved Westerns, big epics—anything sweeping and larger than life. That's the romance of youth."

Pizzo paused, glanced across a windswept lake at Notre Dame and managed to smile at an obvious irony.

Because of Hollywood's preoccupation with current versions of the blockbusters that dazzled him as a boy, several of Pizzo's screenplays have failed to obtain financing. Even those projects that have reached the cameras—including *Rudy*—barely survived.

"Just a month ago," Ruettiger confided, "this movie was dead in the water."

Pizzo is philosophical.

"It's hard to get financing for *anything* unless you have Tom Cruise or Arnold Schwarzenegger. But I'm determined to write movies I would want to see. I knew we would have a long, uphill struggle with *Rudy*. But we did with *Hoosiers*, too."

Pizzo's first influential piece of prose came before he graduated from IU in 1971. It was his ninety-page application for conscientious objector status.

"I wrote not from a political standpoint, but from a passionate, humane approach," Pizzo recalled. "I prevailed. I was one of the very, very few young men in Indiana who applied for CO status and actually got it."

By then Pizzo had become a voracious reader—something that may have provided him an edge on a pilot for the TV game show, which was never broadcast.

That came after a year in Aspen spent—in Pizzo's words—"finding myself." Next he and Anspaugh decided to attend film school at the University of Southern California.

A stranger met Pizzo near campus and handed him a questionnaire. The result: an invitation to appear on *The World Quiz Show*, a prospective series.

Sitting in the audience, TV personality Allen Ludden was impressed by Pizzo's mastery of answers. He introduced Pizzo to his partner, Grant Tinker, who arranged an internship with *The Mary Tyler Moore Show*.

A career in the entertainment industry was launched.

Inspired to create *Hoosiers* after picking up his brother Seth at a high school basketball game, Pizzo wrote the screenplay in longhand at his parents' cabin in northern Indiana.

The lyrical film went on to be hailed as a classic of small-town life, the triumph of the human spirit, the importance of second chances—and as a portrait of the residents of Pizzo's home state. Coaches, business leaders and politicians around the world have used it to inspire people confronting challenges.

To create *Rudy*, his next movie, Pizzo spent several weeks at Notre Dame last fall.

"I didn't take a single note," he recalled. "I soaked up feelings. I talked to football players, coaches and students. I walked around campus endlessly. I read in the student lounge for hours."

To write the screenplay, Pizzo, who now uses a computer, holed up in a friend's cabin near Aspen. He returned to Notre Dame with the film crew in mid-October. The *Rudy* team will travel to Whiting, Indiana, and Chicago to capture other footage.

After *Rudy*, Pizzo hopes to become a director.

"This may sound strange," he confided, "but even now I don't think of myself as a writer. I see myself as a filmmaker . . . If I direct, David would produce. We share similar sensibilities and values. On the set, we speak in shorthand."

Those values—and the lyrical way his movies convey them—have touched the man who once searched for his son at Bloomington theaters.

"The feelings of compassion, decency and understanding—those are what shine through Angelo's work," Dr. Pizzo said, his voice softening.

"As an artist, he stays true to himself. You can't ask more than that."

Mark Spitz regarded his performance at the 1968 Mexico City Olympics as a failure because he won only two gold medals. He rebounded with a bang at the 1972 Munich Olympics where he won seven gold medals.

Mark Spitz

Olympic gold medalist

The winner of an unprecedented seven gold medals at the 1972 Olympic Games in Munich (he set a world record in each of his seven victories, a feat many consider the most outstanding achievement in Olympic history), Mark Spitz was born in California. And most of the superstar swimmer's adult life has been spent in southern California.

So what makes Spitz a Hoosier?

It's the fact that the world's premier aquatic athlete lived in Indiana during the years of his history-making accomplishments. In January 1969, Spitz enrolled as a pre-dental student at Indiana University, then at the peak of its fame as a swimming power under legendary coach James "Doc" Counsilman.

The coach and the handsome, record-smashing swimmer remained a team for nearly the next four years, during which Spitz captured the Sullivan Award as the nation's outstanding amateur athlete in 1971. With his IU teammates, Spitz won NCAA championships and just about every other possible victory in his sport.

Born in Modesto, California, in 1950, Mark Andrew Spitz was the oldest of three children in a family of competitive swimmers. Swimming almost before he could walk, Mark spent a few of his early years in Honolulu when his father, a steel company executive, was transferred there. By the time he was ten years old, Mark Spitz held seventeen national age-group records.

After graduating from IU in 1972 and becoming internationally famous for his Olympics triumphs, Spitz was admitted to the IU School of Dentistry. But he abandoned plans to become an orthodontist, signed a contract with a Beverly Hills talent agency, posed for a poster with his seven gold medals (it set world sales records for an Olympic athlete) and moved to California.

"He's still the Babe Ruth, the Joe Montana, the Michael Jordan, the Muhammad Ali of the wet set," Swim magazine noted twenty-three years later.

America's most decorated Olympian was interviewed in March of 1992 in the wake of a failed comeback attempt. At the "ancient" age of forty-two, Spitz tried to make the American team for the Barcelona Olympic Games. The U.S. Olympic Swimming Trials that year were held at the Indiana University Natatorium, not far from his old stomping (or splashing) grounds.

The athlete whose accomplishment is considered the greatest individual achievement in Olympic history will not be in the water at the Indiana University Natatorium this week.

Mark Spitz, who turned forty-two three weeks ago, failed to qualify for the U.S. Olympic Swimming Trials under way on the campus of Indiana University-Purdue University at Indianapolis.

That sinks any hope that Spitz, who won an unprecedented seven gold medals and set seven world records twenty years ago, will be competing in the Summer Olympic Games in Barcelona.

Obviously, it also torpedoes any future Olympic dreams for the aging former IU standout. Attempting to swim in the 1996 Atlanta Olympics when Spitz will be forty-six is unrealistic, he concedes.

"I'm still swimming, though," Spitz says. He trains two-and-a-half hours daily at the UCLA campus near his home in Beverly Hills.

"I have a meet in Italy in April with what are being billed as European superstars. There are a lot of offers on the table for me to compete."

Most of the offers, he concedes, are from overseas. Spitz says he hasn't decided how many to accept. His much-heralded comeback, which included races televised live in 1991 on ABC's *Wide World of Sports*, was promoted as an attempt to prove that athletes aren't washed up after thirty.

But if Mark Spitz can't make an Olympic team, can any forty-two-year-old?

"Maybe not in swimming," he replies. "Boxing is not judged on your performance in hundredths of a second. You could get hit, scramble back up and knock the other boxer out. But can you make it in a speed sport like swimming? Maybe not."

Spitz says he recently was analyzed by an international group of physiologists who told him that, after thirty-five, the average man loses one percent of his muscle strength annually.

"I was gaining one percent, which means I'll never get faster," says the six-foot-tall, dark-haired athlete. "That just keeps me even. I would have to be gaining two percent muscle per year, which for anyone my age is almost impossible. I'm fighting something unavoidable and not exclusive to me. It's called old age."

When Spitz announced his comeback in September of 1989, his old Hoosier coach was flooded with phone calls. Ironically, it was the tenth anniversary of James "Doc" Counsilman's own history-making, age-defying performance: In September 1979 Counsilman shattered an age barrier by becoming the oldest man to swim the English Channel. He was fifty-eight.

Known as something of a loner during most of his early career, Spitz married Susan Weiner in 1973. They have two sons, Matthew and Justin. Matthew is not interested in following his dad's footsteps. "He's into baseball and sports like that," Spitz reports.

After the 1972 Olympics, Spitz' appearances in TV specials, comedy programs and other shows were poorly received. He says he has no aspirations in the entertainment industry now. He is a spokesman for Clairol hair products and various pool products, but his primary business interests are in California real estate.

Until he announced his comeback, Spitz had been out of competitive swimming for nearly eighteen years. Some analysts contend that the long layoff was more of an obstacle than his age.

"That may be right," Spitz comments. "But I'm not living my life through conjecture . . . And I have a lot of fond memories of the Olympics, of Indiana University and living in Indiana. No one ever can take that away from me."

Jane Pauley

TV newswoman

Her pregnancies drew national attention. So did her hairstyles, her marriage and her values.

In fact, just about every aspect of Indianapolis native Jane Pauley became fodder for public scrutiny beginning in the mid-1970s. It's not a surprise considering that her face was one of the first things millions of Americans saw when they woke up. Pauley was co-host of NBC-TV News' The Today Show, serving in that capacity for thirteen years, longer than any other woman broadcaster affiliated with the top-rated morning news program.

A pioneer TV newswoman, Pauley has been in the public eye since her early twenties—first with WISH-TV, Channel 8, in her hometown, and then for a year with a Chicago television station. She really made headlines when, just shy of her twenty-sixth birthday, she was chosen to replace the venerable Barbara Walters on Today *in 1976.*

Despite all of that—and perhaps because of her wholesome image and the warmth Pauley conveys—many Hoosier friends still call her "Janie" nearly thirty years after their graduation from Warren Central High School. Born in Indianapolis in 1950, Pauley was interviewed at her NBC News office in late 1990. Her father, whom she frequently referred to as a significant influence, died three years later.

Although Real Life With Jane Pauley—*the show that followed her stint with* To-day—*was short-lived, the Hoosier broadcaster followed it up in 1992 by becoming co-host of* Dateline NBC, *a prime-time NBC newsmagazine. By the mid-nineties* Date-line *was so popular it was broadcast three nights a week.*

Famous for her self-deprecating humor, Pauley claims to have invented the term "bad hair day." She lives in New York City with her husband, Pulitzer Prize-winning "Doonesbury" cartoonist Garry Trudeau, and their three children.

NEW YORK—On the fifth floor of Rockefeller Center, a few feet away from her Emmy award, Dick Pauley's daughter is warming her coffee in a microwave.

She is a $1.4 million-or-so queen of live TV who, according to broadcast executives, be-comes "one" with a camera "more than anyone else."

She used to break out in hives.

She is a forty-year-old dubbed the heroine of her generation by *The New Republic*—"the first baby boomer they tried to put out to pasture . . . and failed."

She used to get vicious calls from female viewers.

The Warren Central High School grad, class of 1968, is "an American icon," according to *Ladies Home Journal*, which put her on its cover. So have—in the last year alone—*Life* magazine; *New York* magazine (which called her "The Loved One" and "Saint Jane"); *Good Housekeeping*; *TV Guide* (as one of the most beautiful women on TV); *Esquire* (as one of the

Indianapolis native Jane Pauley hugs her former Warren Central High School speech coach, Harry Wilfong, when The Today Show *broadcast from her hometown in May of 1986.*

one hundred best wives of all time); *People* (on the cover twice, although she shared one with New Kids on the Block), *US* and *Savvy*.

In some of those stories, Jane Pauley described herself as "pathologically nice."

Now she corrects that.

"I am a kind person," she says slowly, walking past a framed fingerpainting, the handiwork of her youngest son, four-year-old Tommy.

"I am *not* a pathologically nice person. There is a difference between nice and kind. Nice implies a selfless quality I just don't have. I will be kind in your presence, but . . . nice . . ."

Pauley, who is prone to long, reflective pauses as well as sudden hoots of laughter, indulges in the former.

The five-foot-four-and-a-half mother of three is wearing her light brown hair pulled back while clad in a beige jacket, black slacks and flats. Crisp, but unpretentious. Nine hours later, by the time Pauley slips behind The Desk for *The NBC Nightly News*, she will have switched to anchorwoman red.

Pauley mentions her father, a retired sales executive for a milk company.

"Now *there* is someone who is pathologically nice," she says. Her hazel eyes shift to a corner of the office. Her distinctive, manicured voice softens.

"The neighbors admired Dick Pauley. They knew they could count on Dick Pauley. They knew Dick Pauley would do the honest and right and decent and *nice* thing."

She resumes eye contact. "I always thought my dad looked like Jimmy Stewart."

Pauley notes that native Hoosiers Dick and Mary Pauley moved in the mid-1980s to a condominium near Tampa, Fla. The move came after Dick Pauley retired as a sales manager for Dean Foods and Mary Pauley suffered a stroke. Told by some of her friends that her father had been compared to a diplomat, she smiles—but disagrees. "That implies aloofness," Pauley explains. "It misses the warmth."

Another pregnant pause. "I would compare my dad to a minister . . ."

She won't identify her least favorite guests during her record-breaking, thirteen-year stint on *The Today Show*.

Pressed, she will describe them only as "a prominent financial analyst" and "an academician-politician." Pauley says she disliked their abrasiveness.

She will identify the most difficult show to get through.

"The morning after John Lennon died," Pauley responds without hesitation, referring to the ex-Beatle gunned down in 1980. Later, she confirms that she wept recently when she and her husband attended a Paul McCartney concert.

"You talk to any girl, woman, who was at Woodview Junior High or Warren Central with me—all of us would react the same," she adds. "The Beatles are special to us."

Lee Giles remembers her hives.

The news director at WISH-TV, Channel 8, in Indianapolis hired Pauley for a television job in 1972 when she was a twenty-one-year-old beginner. Make that utter novice.

"I interviewed her several times because she kept seeking a job," Giles recalls. "We finally had an opening, and I called Jane back. In the interview phase, she was by far the most articulate, the brightest and the most enthusiastic. The hitch was her total lack of broadcasting experience.

"I asked Jane, 'Will you audition? This is make-it-or-break-it time.' Then—well, she and the camera became one. Never before or since have I seen someone jump out like that."

Although she lacked journalism experience when she applied at Channel 8 as a recent Indiana University graduate, Pauley already was a seasoned veteran at thinking on her feet.

At Warren Central, her mentor was Harry Wilfong, a speech and debate teacher. Pauley won the state championship in girl's extemporaneous speaking. In 1967, she was elected governor of Indiana Girls State, a major coup for a Hoosier teenager.

But despite her poise, professionalism and on-camera presence at Channel 8—or perhaps because of all that—Pauley became a target.

"I haven't talked about this much before, but Jane did get a great deal of criticism from viewers," Giles says. "We thought she was great, yet there would be scathing calls and letters from women—almost a jealousy factor. Maybe she somehow was threatening, too pretty and too articulate. These were 'Who do you think you are?' calls.

"Jane would shrug her shoulders and go back to typing a story. I thought, 'Wow, I've never seen anyone handle this so well.' Internally, though I think the calls devastated her. Even though she was adept at keeping her nerves to herself, I remember seeing her break out in hives."

Not only are Pauley's hives history, her on-air unflappability is legendary. And in recent years, she's become known for her fortitude—particularly during the much-publicized brouhaha at *Today* over the ascendancy of Deborah Norville, a younger, blonde TV personality.

Amid widespread perceptions that network executives were positioning Norville as a replacement, Pauley stunned her bosses in the fall of 1989 by announcing she wanted to leave *Today*.

The Hoosier's popularity immediately skyrocketed. One of the results: the blizzard of "Saint Jane" and "The Loved One" cover stories extolling Pauley's decency.

The hive problem had its origins in her days at Eastridge and Moorhead elementary schools. How shy was Margaret Jane Pauley, born in Methodist Hospital on Halloween of 1950? So timid that—in a story she delights in telling now, with typical self-deprecating wit—she was called "Margaret" her entire second-grade year. She was too meek to correct the teacher, who incorrectly addressed her on the first day.

Later that year, Mrs. Pauley took her youngest daughter to a specialist who announced that Jane was a nervous child who would "have to be careful her whole life."

Pauley, whose fame has come from live TV, cracks up after quoting the doctor's advice—but then becomes contemplative.

"I see in my own kids that it's possible to be both shy and want to be noticed. I had the same simultaneous, contradictory impulses."

She notes that her seven-year-old twins Ross and Rachel (born in 1983) are nothing alike in personality. Asked to elaborate, Pauley is analytical but protective.

"None of my kids are extroverted," she says. "But they are all kind. That pleases me immensely. Little children are not always kind. Part of my role as a parent, the duty of civilizing them, involves bringing the kindness out. What a relief it already seems to be there."

Pauley's husband is the controversial, Pulitzer Prize-winning cartoonist Garry Trudeau, creator of the influential *Doonesbury* comic strip. In addition to the twins, Pauley and Trudeau are the parents of a son, Thomas, born in 1986; it's his fingerpainting that's framed in his mother's office.

Despite being the offspring of two *Who's Who* superachievers, none of the three Trudeau-Pauley children is precocious, their mother says. "But they all have artistic flair."

When the conversation turns to Trudeau, Pauley attributes to her husband the same qualities she ascribed to her father. She praises his neighborliness. "Garry is a *much* better neighbor than me." She lauds his even disposition. She bristles when asked if he is cynical. "He is very much a grown-up, a mature, responsible person and hard worker. He is *another* pathologically nice guy."

Asked if culture clashes pop up between an upper-crust, East Coast prep school grad/ Yale alumnus and a Hoosier product of public schools, she shakes her head.

"I think Garry wanted a Midwestern girl," she says, flashing the familiar Pauley smile— broad and disarming. "Probably a reaction to his prep-school background."

Judy Smith Abbett, an old Warren Central and IU classmate, says, "Janie has always been fun and a wonderful friend. But over the years she has become even better in terms of being sensitive and caring. I attribute that to Garry and the children."

Basketball Legends

The surprise isn't that the state famous for "Hoosier Hysteria" has produced so many basketball heroes. The surprise is in the diversity of Indiana's legendary figures of the sport.

Hardwood heroes range from a shy, small town resident-turned-National Basketball Association champion and coach (Larry Bird) to a city kid and pioneer for African American high school athletes (Oscar Robertson) to a coach whose influence stretches beyond the basketball court (John Wooden).

Simply put, if you grow up in Indiana, basketball is bound to touch your life. To begin with, "Hoosier Hysteria" most likely affected the size of your high school gymnasium. Of the ten largest high school gyms in the country, nine are in Indiana, according to the Indiana High School Athletic Association. (New Castle High School's gym is Indiana's—and the nation's—largest.) In Indiana, gyms are built to accommodate basketball spectators—lots and lots of them.

The state's infatuation with the sport certainly helps define young Hoosiers' role models—often the latest college or high school hoops sensation or the coach with the most wins. Among those who have become folk heroes:

Larry Bird

Many analysts say the most famous native of French Lick, Indiana, was the greatest passing forward ever in the National Basketball Association—and the most versatile player in the history of the league.

And five years after retiring as an NBA player, Larry Bird accepted a new challenge: "Larry Legend" returned to his home state in 1997 to coach the Indiana Pacers.

As a sensational pro player, Bird—all six feet nine inches and 220 pounds of him—led the Boston Celtics to NBA championships in 1981, 1984, and 1986. Before that, Bird electrified the Terre Haute campus of Indiana State University by taking the Sycamores to an undefeated regular season (1978–79) and a berth in the NCAA finals.

The NCAA title that year was won by a Michigan State University team led by Bird's career-long rival and friend: Earvin "Magic" Johnson, a legendary player who, with the remarkable Bird, is credited with lifting the NBA to new levels of public popularity and athletic achievement during the 1980s. Hailed as unselfish players, they established a new style of team-oriented play that emphasizes the pass.

The man with blond bangs and a Hoosier twang named *Sports Illustrated*'s 1986 "Sportsman of the Year" and the NBA's most valuable player for three years in a row (1984–86) was born in French Lick in 1956. Growing up in the southwestern Indiana town previously famous for its health spas, Larry Joe Bird was "painfully shy and backward," as sportswriter Bob Williams put it in *Hoosier Hysteria*.

Bird even began calling himself "The Hick from French Lick." The fourth of six children in the Bird family, Larry was obsessed with basketball as a boy, devoting almost every spare moment to perfecting his shooting skills.

"I played when I was cold and my body was aching and I was so tired," Bird told *Sports Illustrated* years later. "I don't know why. I just kept playing and playing . . . I guess I always wanted to make the most out of it."

At Springs Valley High School, he set nearly every record imaginable and won a coveted basketball scholarship to Indiana University in 1974. But the sprawling campus in Bloomington overwhelmed him, and Bird returned to French Lick after only about a month.

He briefly attended a junior college in Orange County, but struggled with personal problems, including the collapse of a marriage to a childhood sweetheart and the suicide of his father. Bird even took a job in his hometown that would became the stuff of folklore: The future multimillionaire worked as a garbage collector.

Lured to Indiana State by coaches who knew of Bird's spectacular basketball talents, he had to sit out (or "redshirt") his first year because of NCAA rules. Then came the fireworks. Bird averaged more than 30 points a game for two years; in one game at Butler University's Hinkle Fieldhouse, he scored an amazing 47 points. America paid heed: Bird began his junior year by being featured on *Sports Illustrated*'s cover billed as "Basketball's Secret Weapon."

The Boston Celtics of the NBA chose Bird as its first draft pick in 1978, but he opted to finish his physical education degree at ISU. His incredible senior year culminated with a career-high—and school-record—single-game scoring outburst of 49 points against Wichita State University.

Although his Sycamores lost to "Magic" Johnson's Michigan State in the final game of the NCAA tournament, the Boston Celtics came calling again. Bird signed a five-year contract reported at more than $3.25 million, making him the highest-paid rookie in the history of professional sports at the time. His impact on the team was dramatic and immediate. He led Boston to the greatest one-season turnaround in NBA history. The Celtics went from a 29–53 record to 61–21 in Bird's first season. To no one's surprise, Bird was named Rookie of the Year.

Some other stats from his pro career: In 897 regular season games, Bird scored 21,791 points (an average of 24.3 per game) and had 8,974 rebounds and 5,695 assists. He led the NBA in free throw percentage four times and was elected to NBA All-Star teams 13 times. Bird also won an Olympic gold medal as part of America's "Dream Team" during the Barcelona Olympic Games in 1992, the year he retired from the NBA.

A golf lover and frequent TV commercial spokesman, Larry Bird played himself in the movie *Blue Chips* (1994). He was living in Naples, Florida, and devoting much of his time to fund-raising for charities when the offer to coach the Indiana Pacers came up. In May of 1997, the Pacers signed "The Hick from French Lick," who had never coached before, to a multi-year contract at an annually salary estimated at $4.5 million; the contract also gives Bird partial ownership of the team.

Oscar Robertson

A member of the National Basketball Hall of Fame almost in a class by himself, Oscar Robertson initially shot to prominence as a trailblazer in Indianapolis, leading the first team of black players to win the state high school championship.

Robertson, known as the "Big O" to generations of fans, attended legendary Crispus Attucks High School. Not only was his the first African-American team to capture the tournament title, his was the first team from any Indianapolis high school to do so. His back-to-back state titles occurred in 1955 and 1956—an era of pervasive racial segregation.

"Big O" went on to become college's all-time leading scorer as a superstar at the University of Cincinnati. He stayed on top—the very top—as a key player on the gold medal-winning team at the 1960 Summer Olympics and as a pro with the Cincinnati Royals, enjoying a triumphant, fourteen-year NBA career.

Robertson wasn't born in Indiana. He was born in 1938 in Charlotte, Tenn., but his family moved to Indianapolis when Oscar was a child. He grew up on the near westside in Lockefield Gardens, then a poverty-stricken housing project—or, as Robertson put it in *Echoes from the Schoolyard* (1977)—"a ghetto."

"I used to look up at airplanes and wonder where in the world they were going," he wrote, recalling his days as a seven-year-old. ". . . But at that early age I didn't have anything to dream about. When you live in a ghetto, man, you've got to fight. It's a way of life."

Always proud and outspoken, Robertson began playing basketball for Crispus Attucks in 1952. (Only four years earlier, IU player Bill Garrett had become the first black starter in the Big Ten.) Attucks had hoops heroes before, during and after Robertson; they included his older brother, Bailey Robertson, as well as Hallie Bryant, Willie Merriweather and Willie Gardner.

But none approached the status enjoyed by "Big O." A brilliant, six-feet-five guard who was coached by Ray Crowe, Robertson led Attucks to an amazing run of forty-five straight victories. The team captured its first state championship by beating another all-black high school, Gary Roosevelt, in 1955.

At the University of Cincinnati, Robertson was the first sophomore to lead the nation in scoring and the first player to be a scoring leader three times. He was an All-American in 1958, 1959 and 1960, remaining college basketball's all-time leading scorer (2,973 points) for ten years, until Pete Maravich of Louisiana State University finally broke his record.

By then Robertson had achieved many other successes. He traveled to Rome in 1960 as co-captain of the U.S. Olympic team, winning the gold medal. Playing for the Cincinnati Royals, he led the NBA in assists and won honors ranging from Rookie of the Year to Most Valuable Player.

After ten seasons with Cincinnati, Robertson was traded to the Milwaukee Bucks in 1970. Teamed with a rising superstar named Lew Alcindor (later known as Kareem Abdul-Jabaar), Robertson helped propel the Bucks to an NBA championship. He retired as a player in 1974.

Robertson makes his home in Cincinnati, the city of his triumphs as a college and pro player, where he owns a chemical company and is a civic leader.

He made headlines in 1997 with an altruistic act. "Big O" donated one of his kidneys to his daughter, Tia, who suffers from lupus, a disease that affects the body's organs and tissues. Roberston and his wife, Yvonne, have two other daughters, Shana and Mari.

John Wooden

He was the first man named to the Basketball Hall of Fame as both a player and a coach.

When you think about what's been called one of the most incredible dynasties in all of sports—the ten NCAA championships won by John Wooden-coached UCLA teams—it's hard to argue with the assessment of Dale Ogden, author of *Hoosier Sports Heroes*, that Wooden deserves to be called "the best basketball coach who ever lived."

Legendary as a high school player in Martinsville and as a college student at Purdue University, Wooden became known far beyond sports as a motivator and a kind of folk philosopher. Thousands of Americans have used as a blueprint his "Pyramid for Success;" its cornerstones are "Industriousness" and "Enthusiasm," with the pinnacle of the pyramid being "Success." ("Faith" and "Patience" are in between.)

Born in Martinsville in 1910, Johnny Wooden grew up on his family's sixty-acre farm. Their home had no electricity or indoor plumbing. Near bankruptcy, the Woodens left the

(Above) Three "Mr. Basketballs" together in 1956 (left to right) Bob Masters, Oscar Robertson, and Bobby Plump—at Robertson's ceremony.

(Right) Larry Bird in the mid-1980s during his glory years as a Boston Celtic.

(Below) At half time in the locker room, Johnny Wooden coaching the Indiana State University basketball team during a national tournament.

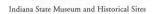

farm and moved into the city of Martinsville. Even though Martinsville High School already was well-known for its excellent basketball teams, Johnny Wooden set a new standard, making the All-State team three times. At Purdue, he was a three-time All-America player.

After graduating in 1932, Wooden coached at a high school in Kentucky, then returned to his home state and spent eleven stellar years as the coach of South Bend Central High School, chalking up a 218–42 record. World War II called him away; Wooden served in the U.S. Navy as a physical education instructor.

Upon his return, he coached for what was then called Indiana State Teachers College; its first team under Wooden was invited to a national tournament, but the coach refused to go because organizers barred black players, including one on Indiana State's team.

The University of California at Los Angeles—then the weakest team in its conference—hired Wooden in 1948, a move which led to his greatest glory. The coach known as "Saint John" always had a winning season. UCLA's Bruins won their first NCAA championship in 1963–64, capping an undefeated season. Wooden coached such future superstars as Lew Alcindor (Kareem Abdul-Jabaar) and Bill Walton and won seven consecutive NCAA championships from 1967 through 1973, a record most say will never be broken.

Wooden retired from coaching in 1975, but accelerated his career as a motivational speaker and elder statesman of his sport. For years he carried with him a motto written for him by his Hoosier father:

Be true to yourself. Make each day a masterpiece. Drink deeply from good books. Make friendship a fine art. Build a shelter against a rainy day.

Steve Alford

Sometimes he seemed too good to be true. Polite, clean-cut, diligent, humble, personable, wholesome and respectful—Steve Alford of New Castle possessed every ingredient to become one of the most popular high school and college basketball players in Indiana history.

Never for a flicker of a second did Alford seem to rebel or drop his straight-arrow, all-American image. This despite the fact that Steve was coached by two demanding masters of the game: his dad Sam Alford at New Castle High School, and legendary Bob Knight at Indiana University.

"Steve has always been laid-back, very capable of handling advice," his brother, Sean Alford, recalled during an interview in 1988. A year earlier, his big brother led IU to an NCAA championship, solidifying his status as a hero to thousands of Hoosiers.

"For my first birthday, I got—what else—my first basketball and hoop set," Alford noted in *Playing for Knight* (1989).

As the title of his autobiography implies, Alford was shaped by Knight—and not only during his four years as an outstanding IU player. (Alford was named the team's "Player of the Year" each of those years.)

He also was coached by Knight on the gold-medal-winning U.S. team in the 1984 Los Angeles Olympics and on IU's around-the-world tour in 1985. So Alford enjoyed the last laugh at the expense of his Olympic teammate, future superstar Michael Jordan, who bet him a hundred dollars that he would never last even four years with the volatile Indiana coach.

Born in Franklin, Indiana, in 1965, Steve spent some of his boyhood years in such Hoosier towns as Monroe City (he learned to count as a toddler by watching the scoreboard in the gym there) and Martinsville as Sam Alford advanced through the high school coaching ranks. But Steve will forever be identified with New Castle High School, where the Alfords made an unstoppable coach-player combination.

In *Playing for Knight*, Steve wrote that he took one glance at the huge New Castle arena—the New Castle Chrysler High School Fieldhouse seats about ninety-five hundred—and instantly vowed to fill it. That he did, becoming a star shooting guard and Indiana's "Mr. Basketball" in 1983.

As a freshman at Indiana, Steve led the nation in free-throw percentage (.913), a distinction Sam Alford had achieved thirty years earlier at Franklin College. Steve became a two-time All-American at IU, scoring 2,438 points during his four years, one of the highest totals in Big Ten history. The NCAA championship in 1987 was the ultimate capper to his college career.

Alford then played in the NBA for the Dallas Mavericks and the Golden State Warriors. Befitting his boy-next-door image, he married his high school sweetheart, Tanya Frost. After four years as a pro player, Alford became a college coach. He started as head coach at Manchester College in North Manchester, Ind.

He currently is the head coach at Southwest Missouri State University. In a classic role reversal, his assistant coach—at Steve's request—is his father, Sam Alford.

Damon Bailey

The frenzy over an athlete from tiny Heltonville, Indiana, began when he was just a junior high school student.

Damon Bailey, a southern Indiana farm boy, became the subject of national curiosity when Indiana University coach Bob Knight visited Shawswick Junior High School to see him play. As quoted in John Feinstein's national best-seller *A Season On The Brink* (1987), Knight remarked, "Damon Bailey is better than any guard we have right now. I don't mean potentially. I mean today."

Well. The hoopla over Bailey (born in 1971) has never waned. It even acquired a name: "Damonmania."

Bailey fulfilled at least some of the exalted expectations. As clean-cut and hard-working as Steve Alford, the high school and IU star of half a decade earlier, Bailey led Bedford North Lawrence High School to four straight appearances in the "Final Four" of the state tourney. He became the all-time leading scorer in Indiana high school history.

Through it all, Bailey's small-town, boy-next-door image captivated fans across the state. As he wrote in his autobiography, *Damon: Living A Dream*, Heltonville "is small town America. It might have five hundred residents if census takers counted far enough beyond the town limits. The post office does not have enough business to stay open eight hours a day, and the only place to buy a Coke or a sack of groceries is at the store owned by Larry 'Bonehead' Faubion."

In his senior year of 1990, Bailey and his teammates won the state championship at the Hoosier Dome, now the RCA Dome. Many analysts suspected the state championship was moved from Hinkle Fieldhouse, its longtime home, to the huge domed arena primarily because of Damon Bailey—that is, to accommodate the thousands of Hoosiers who wanted to watch him play his final games of high school hoops.

After the *Season on the Brink* prelude, it was almost a foregone conclusion that Bailey would attend IU and play for Knight. But it was in Bloomington where Bailey failed to meet the expectations of some fans. Bailey, who is six-feet-three, certainly maintained, if not polished, his golden boy image. Without fail, good-looking Damon came across as modest and courteous; Bailey and his family also received tremendous public sympathy when Hoosiers learned his sister, Courtney, was battling leukemia while he was playing for the Cream and Crimson. (Her disease now is in remission.)

But his career as an IU shooter disappointed some. Even before Bailey arrived on campus, his four years were being called "The Damon Era." As Bailey writes in his autobiography, "I was expected to take IU to greater heights, and I had yet to play a single game. It may have been the first time Coach Knight had been overshadowed by an eighteen-year-old freshman."

IU's teams during "The Damon Era" certainly were nothing to be ashamed of. For example, in the post-season NCAA tournament of Bailey's sophomore year in 1992, the Cream and Crimson smashed once-mighty UCLA by an astonishing 27 points. The next year, IU won 17 Big Ten games, the most for the Hoosiers since the mid-1970s. Some analysts—and Bailey himself—speculated the team might have gone all the way to the national championship if his teammate Alan Henderson had not been injured.

But the fact is that none of the IU teams with Bailey won an NCAA championship or even advanced to college basketball's "Final Four." Distracted by his sister's illness, battling progressive pain in his knees and exhausted from the (by then) years-long hype and relentless demands on his time, Bailey did not match his high school successes.

After graduating from IU in 1994, Bailey signed a contract with the Indiana Pacers. But he sat out a year for surgery on both knees. In the fall of 1995, he was released by the Pacers without playing a regular-season game. On a happier note, Damon married his longtime girlfriend, Stacey Ikerd, a former Bedford North Lawrence cheerleader.

With his dream of playing in the NBA still on hold, Bailey played for the Fort Wayne Fury of the Continental Basketball Association. He left for Europe in the spring of 1997 after signing a contract to play for a pro team in France.

Before going overseas, Bailey voiced the hope of thousands of Hoosiers: that someday he would return to Indiana to play pro basketball.

George McGinnis

In 1969, many sports analysts considered George McGinnis the best high school athlete in the country.

That was the year the Indianapolis-born power forward propelled a legendary Washington High School team to an unbeaten season and the state championship. His 35-point scoring "eruption" during the title game at Hinkle Fieldhouse instantly became part of "Hoosier Hysteria" folklore.

The state's "Mr. Basketball" of 1969 went on to triumphs at Indiana University. In his second year on campus, McGinnis led the Big Ten in scoring and rebounding, becoming the first sophomore in the league's history to do so.

As an outstanding pro player in the 1970s, McGinnis led the Indiana Pacers, then part of the American Basketball Association, to two league titles. "Big Mac", who is six-feet-eight, shared with superstar Julius Erving the league's MVP award and won the league scoring title in 1975.

Even several years after his pro career ended, McGinnis drew crowds of admiring Hoosier children to watch pickup hoops games he played with other former stars. They competed at McGinnis' alma mater, the gym of his beloved Washington High.

"If a guy scores ten points off me now, I can laugh about it," McGinnis said during an interview in 1987. "We just do this for the fun and fellowship . . . We probably undo any

(Left) Steve Alford playing for New Castle High School in the semi-state game of 1983's state tournament: During this game against Broad Ripple High School of Indianapolis, Alford scored fifty-seven points.

(Below) Washington High School graduate George McGinnis playing for the Indiana Pacers in the early 1970s.

Indiana Basketball Hall of Fame

Indiana Basketball Hall of Fame

Damon Bailey celebrating after his Bedford-North Lawrence High School team won the state championship in 1990, his senior year of high school.

Indiana Basketball Hall of Fame

good the workout does with the cold beer and pizza (afterward)."

Sound mellow? Well, McGinnis, who was born in 1950, once was known for his fierce intensity. "Big Mac" and his Washington Continental teammate Steve Downing have been called Indiana high school basketball's most intimidating front line ever.

In his stellar year of 1969, McGinnis set a state tourney record by scoring 148 points in the final four games—a record that still stands.

"Big Mac" won thousands of fans as a Pacer for four seasons (1972–75); he left to play for pro teams such as the Philadelphia 76ers before returning to the Pacers in 1979.

Since retiring as a player three years later, the personable McGinnis has remained in the public eye as an Indianapolis-based business executive. He also is a TV and radio sportscaster every basketball season.

Bobby Plump

Is there a Hoosier youngster who has not heard the legend about the "Milan Miracle?"

Milan is a tiny Ripley County town in southeastern Indiana. In 1954, Milan was one of the smallest schools in the state, with 162 students and a class of twenty-seven seniors.

One of them was Bobby Plump, whose life would forever be changed that year by "the shot"—a stunning, fifteen-foot jump shot he scored against seemingly invincible Muncie Central High School just before the buzzer sounded at the 1954 state championship. That year in Indiana, "David" slew "Goliath."

The storybook upset victory by the "Mighty Men of Milan"—Plump, teammate Ray Craft and others—became the defining moment of "Hoosier Hysteria" and the inspiration for the movie *Hoosiers* (1986). However improbable, achieving another mythic "Milan Miracle" instantly became the dream of young boys in small towns across Indiana.

At the center of the legend was Plump, who actually grew up in Pierceville, a town smaller than nearby Milan—so small it didn't have a high school. According to town folklore, Plump (born in 1936) and teammates such as Gene White and Roger Schroder used to play barnyard basketball until midnight by hanging a light bulb from a shovel handle with a tin reflector.

At Milan High, the teenagers were coached by a new faculty member named Marvin Wood. A disciplinarian with radical (at least for southeastern Indiana) ideas about how to play high school basketball, Wood coached the five-foot-ten-inch Plump and his similarly small Milan teammates (the tallest was Ron Truitt at six-feet-two) to the state finals in 1953. They were eliminated by eventual champion South Bend Central.

But the small team with a big heart returned to the tournament the next year and made a miracle. When the buzzer sounded after Plump's historic, last-second jumper, Milan had toppled Muncie Central 32–30.

In recent years, Plump has been an outspoken advocate of the open high school basketball tournament that made the "Milan Miracle" possible. The founder of a group called "Friends of Hoosier Hysteria," he led the crusade against multiple-class basketball.

His crusade was only partially unsuccessful: A new tournament system for high school basketball, with four classes based on school size, is set to begin in 1998. But the new system will include a "tournament of champions" in which the four class champions will take on each other, Goliaths vs. Davids, just as they did in Plump's heyday.

John Mellencamp

Rock star and songwriter

Often called "rock music's poet of the American heartland," John Mellencamp is as thoroughly "Hoosier" as any international celebrity to emerge from Indiana.

His songs—from teen anthems like "Jack and Diane" to such social commentaries as "Pink Houses" and mournful tunes like "Lonely Ol' Night"—describe the frustrations and dreams of the Midwest, particularly its small-town residents.

A lifelong Hoosier and champion of the underdog, the scrappy, youthful-looking Mellencamp is known almost as much for his unwavering convictions as for his musical triumphs.

Among the latter: His American Fool *album racked up sales of three million in 1982, becoming the year's biggest-selling album. The simultaneous success of two of its hit songs, "Hurts So Good" and "Jack and Diane," made Mellencamp the first rock artist since the Beatles to have two singles in the Top Five at the same time.*

His stance against corporate influences on rock music is the stuff of folklore. For example, Mellencamp turned down millions of dollars for the use of his hit songs "Small Town" and "Pink Houses" (with its "Ain't that America" refrain) in TV commercials and political campaigns.

Deeply moved by the plight of Midwestern farmers, Mellencamp and country music star Willie Nelson organized the first Farm Aid concert in 1985. The concert has become an annual event and usually is described as a fund-raising benefit. But Mellencamp always emphasizes his primary purpose is to influence farm policy legislation.

A sports lover since boyhood and an ardent fan of Indiana University's teams, Mellencamp has donated more than $1.5 million to IU for an indoor athletic facility. His continues to live near near Bloomington, his home for most of his adult life.

To paraphrase lyrics from one of his best-known songs, he was born in a small town, and he lives in a small town.

In October of 1951, John Mellencamp was born in the southern Indiana town of Seymour (population then: about fifteen thousand).

He was the second of five children of Richard Mellencamp, an electrician who became vice president of Robbins Electric Company, and Richard's wife, Marilyn, a Miss Indiana runner-up.

As a rebellious senior at Seymour High School, John Mellencamp eloped with his girlfriend, Priscilla, who was pregnant and three years older than her new husband.

For a time, the young family lived with Mellencamp's in-laws while he worked a series of odd jobs and played guitar in rock bands. The Mellencamps became the parents of a daughter, Michelle.

Eventually John Mellencamp enrolled at Vincennes University and began to write music. Thanks to some demonstration tapes, Mellencamp was signed in 1975 by rock star man-

Rock star John Mellencamp's recording studio is in scenic Belmont, a small town in Brown County.

ager Tony DeFries, a hype-oriented, hard-driving promoter who previously had guided the career of British rocker David Bowie.

DeFries dressed a reluctant Mellencamp as a glitter rocker and billed him as "Johnny Cougar."

Mellencamp and his first album, **Chestnut Street Incident** (named for a street in Seymour) were widely panned. Breaking with DeFries, Mellencamp went to Los Angeles and London to pursue new opportunities.

He retained the "Johnny Cougar" name for a while, but began phasing it out in the early 1980s and eventually dropped it completely.

About this time, Mellencamp and Priscilla divorced on friendly terms. The rock singer married a Los Angeles fashion model, Vicky Granucci, in 1980.

He then recorded his breakthrough album, *Nothin' Matters and What If It Did*. One of its songs, the soulful "Ain't Even Done With the Night," became a hit. Mellencamp then topped himself, creating a sensation in 1982 with his *American Fool* album.

With "Jack and Diane," a song about youthful passion between "two kids growin' up in the heartland" who discover after their teenage years that "life goes on, long after the thrill of livin' is gone," Mellencamp won critical respect as a songwriter.

His subsequent albums, *Uh-Huh* (1984), *Scarecrow* (1985) and *Lonesome Jubilee* (1987), not only contained songs that reflected his social concerns, they also featured instruments seldom heard in rock music, including violin, accordion, mandolin and dulcimer.

"He reinvented folk rock with his innovative integration of acoustic guitar in a hard-rock format, creating a haunting new sound by combining fiddle and accordion," *Playboy* magazine raved.

With Vicky, Mellencamp had two daughters, Teddi Jo and Justice. But life for Mellencamp during the 1980s was a blur of touring and recording. He has estimated he spent eight years of the decade on tour—and the other two writing music or in the studio.

In 1992, Mellencamp even directed and starred in a movie, *Fallen From Grace*, which was filmed in Seymour. Playing opposite Mariel Hemingway, he portrayed a country music singer who returns to his hometown and reopens family wounds.

During all of this activity, his second marriage collapsed. But what the onetime "road warrior" has called his true "wake-up call" came while touring in August 1994. Then, at age forty-two, Mellencamp suffered a heart attack.

"Up until that time, I thought I was bulletproof," he told TV personality Charlie Rose.

Mellencamp reacted to his health crisis by slowing the pace of his schedule, taking up a fitness routine and spending more time at his Bloomington home with his third wife, fashion model Elaine Irwin, and their young sons, Hud and Speck.

In 1996, Mellencamp released his fourteenth album, *Mr. Happy Go Lucky*. Lauded by many critics as among his best work ever, the album has produced a hit single, "Key West Intermezzo (I Saw You First)."

The Hoosier rock star—now famous for nearly twenty years—told music critic Marc Allan of *The Indianapoilis Star*, "I don't know if I'm happier now . . . but I'm trying to have more fun."

Photos courtesy of *The Indianapolis Star/News*

(Above) Evan Bayh surrounded by family memorabilia in his Indianapolis law office in 1986.

(Right) Twelve-year-old Evan Bayh with his father, Birch, then a U.S. senator, in 1968 during a visit to Indiana and the State Fair.

Evan Bayh

Governor

The Bayh name has dominated Democratic politics in the Hoosier state for nearly four decades.

First came Birch Bayh, descended from a family that had settled in Indiana about the time it won statehood in 1816. Folksy and ambitious, Birch Bayh twice served as speaker of the Indiana House of Representatives, then went on to a long, high-profile career (1962–1980) as a U.S. senator. He ran for U.S. President twice and was the author of two amendments to the U.S. Constitution; they dealt with the order of presidential succession and the extension of voting rights to eighteen-year-olds.

His son, Evan, born in 1955, was interviewed at the very start of his political career in early 1986. Not only did he go on to capture the secretary of state's office, Evan Bayh became a two-term governor. His election in 1988 made him the nation's youngest governor at age thirty-two. Known for his balanced budgets and business-oriented approach to government, Evan Bayh served from 1988 to 1996 as one of the most popular Democratic leaders in Indiana history; he won a second term with the largest margin of victory for a gubernatorial candidate in this century.

Evan Bayh and his wife, Susan, became the parents of twin sons, Nicholas Harrison and Birch Evans "Beau" Bayh IV, in 1995. The next year Evan Bayh was chosen to deliver the keynote address at the Democratic National Convention that renominated his friend and occasional golfing buddy, Bill Clinton, for the presidency.

Bayh's term in the governor's office ended in January 1997. Although he joined an Indianapolis law firm and the faculty of the Indiana University School of Business, Bayh primarily seems to be focusing on a run for the U.S. Senate in 1998—the very seat once held by his father. In any national list of rising stars in the Democratic Party of the late 1990s, Evan Bayh's name is always included.

Style. That's what hit you first about the father—an aw-shucks campaigner with a flair for flesh-pressin', winkin' his blue eyes and slippin' in stories about the Hoosier hogs at his Shirkieville farm.

And style is what hits you about the mother—a poised, polished perfectionist who charged through public appearances with chin up, a polite smile and, as her husband used to say, "a hundred-mile-per-hour engine in a thirty-mile-per-hour chassis."

Style is also obvious in their son, a young man described by lifelong acquaintances as respectful, well-groomed and courteous almost from the day he could form his first word.

"He is very much his mother's son, far more like Marvella than Birch," observes Larry Conrad, former Democratic secretary of state whose friendship with the family stretches back to Birch Bayh's first U.S. Senate campaign in 1962. "Evan has always been unfailingly polite, kind of the perfect child, the kid you always hoped your own children would behave like."

Birch Evans Bayh III, known as Evan, lives in an immaculate downtown Indianapolis condominium with furnishings that include a framed print of the signing of the Declaration of Independence and a sign on his desk that insists SOMETHING GOOD IS GOING TO HAPPEN TO YOU.

None of this, however, is what you notice first.

Second only to his startling good looks (one local Republican gripes that Evan and his blonde bride "remind me of Ken and Barbie dolls"), you notice the framed photographs.

There is Marvella Bayh with Birch. Marvella with Lyndon Johnson. Marvella by herself. Marvella in profile.

With mention of her name, young Bayh's voice softens. He talks extensively about his trip to Scandinavia and the Soviet Union, a jaunt shared just by the two of them.

"It was a special journey between two compatible friends," his mother, a second-generation Norwegian, wrote in an autobiography published posthumously in 1979. Her life and death had an incalculable impact on him.

"Evan is a gentle person," says Sally Kirkpatrick, press secretary to John Livengood, chairman of the Indiana Democratic Party. "But I don't think gentleness or compassion should be confused with weakness. He is firm in knowing what he wants."

What Evan Bayh wants, at age thirty, is to be secretary of state. An attorney with the Indianapolis law firm of Bingham Summers Welsh and Spilman, he has been spending many of his evenings and weekends on what politicos call the rubber-chicken circuit.

Gordon Durnil, chairman of the Indiana Republican Party, professes not to be worried about young Bayh: "His father never won an election by any large margin, and, in fact, was defeated the last time he ran (by Quayle in 1980). Plus, the liberal perceptions of his father might be more of a negative.

"Indiana voters are more Republican and more conservative now than they were. I want to add that we're not like the South, where there are political dynasties based on name. You don't just get Indiana votes based on a last name."

Born in Terre Haute, Evan Bayh moved to Washington, D.C., at age seven when his father stunned Indiana politicians by narrowly defeating Republican Senator Homer Capehart. At St. Albans, a private prep school in the Georgetown area of the nation's capital, Evan's classmates included Marvin Bush, son of future President George Bush.

His parents—young, energetic and attractive—were linked closely with the Kennedys, particularly after a 1964 airplane accident in which Birch pulled Ted Kennedy from the wreckage and was credited with saving the senator's life. The Bayhs also were close to the Lyndon Johnsons.

Intertwined with the glamour, however, were bouts with tragedy. In Oklahoma, Evan's grandfather married a second wife younger than daughter Marvella. He attempted suicide and eventually succeeded, shooting his young bride and himself in a scandal that became front-page news in Indiana.

As the son of a controversial politician, Evan also learned to cope with—although he says he never accepted—vituperative attacks on his father. Here is Marvella's account of one such incident, which occurred while she and Evan were home alone watching TV commentator Eric Sevareid laud Birch as a "Midwestern John Kennedy":

"The phone rang, and Evan answered it. A man's voice said, 'You tell your father that if he is going to be a Midwestern JFK, I am going to be another Lee Harvey Oswald.' "

Although Mrs. Bayh wrote that Evan begged his father not to run for president in 1972 (Birch bowed out after the diagnosis of Marvella's breast cancer), young Bayh stresses that he enthusiastically supported the 1976 attempt—and even left IU for a semester to campaign.

Noting that Birch finished second that year to an unknown named Jimmy Carter in

Iowa, Evan says he still believes if his father had entered the race a few weeks earlier—and pushed a smidgen harder—the outcome (and, perhaps, national history) would have changed.

Stung by the loss, Evan signed up as a deck hand on an American freighter bound for Germany.

"People don't realize this, but I am no stranger to hard physical labor," he says, noting he worked heavy construction jobs during summers as a teenager. A tackle on the St. Albans football team, Evan also considered suiting up in the mid-1970s for Lee Corso, then IU's football coach.

"I have a lot of interests, and we both enjoy meeting people," Evan says, referring to his father. "Maybe it is true, that I am more reserved than he is. He is easygoing, and I tend to be a perfectionist, to pay attention to details."

Observing Evan on the campaign stump last May, political reporter Ed Ziegner of *The Indianapolis News* wrote: "There was no 'raw meat' in the speech, something which the elder Bayh almost always got in . . . Evan needs more rapport with his audiences, some jokes to toss in here and there. He is a bit too sober-sided."

"I think I've livened up since then," Evan responds. "For someone to expect me, at age thirty, to be the same finished product as my father, well, that's a bit rough on me. If I came across as a jokester, people would say, 'Who does this young guy think he is?' "

Now married to a former ABC News official and the father of four-year-old Christopher, Birch Bayh is an attorney in private practice in Washington, D.C. He was best man at Evan's wedding in 1985.

Although Marvella wrote extensively about her husband's absences from family activities because of his hectic schedule, Evan shares different memories:

"I remember when there would be only two parents at a Little League game—and he would be one of them. I never felt neglected. We talk on the phone all the time. Mostly about fundamental values, about how all-consuming public life can be, about how nothing is worth neglecting your family."

Susan Bayh, an associate with the Indianapolis law firm of Barnes and Thornburg, says she enthusiastically supports Evan's candidacy.

"When you marry someone, you marry the whole person," she explains. "Part of that person is his aspirations and dreams."

Asked about political aspirations, Evan says, "I have no agenda beyond secretary of state. I have seen too many people in the public eye become captives of their own ambition."

He shifts gears and talks about his image. "People sometimes say to me, 'No one can be polite all the time.' I do have moments where I fall short. But growing up in the public eye, you always know that you are a reflection of your parents. I never wanted to let them down."

There is silence for a moment. His thoughts seem to stray.

Evan Bayh is staring at the pictures on the wall, the photographs of a delicate but driven woman. A woman who won honors for courage, whipped her husband in college speaking contests, coped with car wrecks, a plane crash, and cancer—and shaped a son.

Atkinson-Muse Public Relations

Sandi Patty

Sandi Patty

Gospel singer

Although Sandi Patty is a native of Oklahoma, she has lived almost all of her adult life in Anderson, Indiana.

Patty, one of the most honored vocalists in contemporary Christian music, has chosen to live in the town of her young adulthood (she graduated from Anderson University in 1979) even after achieving national fame.

Blessed with a soaring voice, Sandi Patty has won five Grammy Awards, the recording industry's highest award, and thirty-three Dove Awards, which are presented for outstanding achievements in gospel music. Her renditions of the national anthem, Christmas music and songs associated with her native state, including "Indianapolis Indeed!," have been heard everywhere from presidential inaugurations in Washington, D.C., and the Miss America pageant in Atlantic City to major civic and sporting events in Indiana, including the 1991 World Gymnastics Championships and the Indianapolis 500.

Her albums, including "Mornings Like This" and "Another Time . . . Another Place," have sold several million copies around the world.

Sandra Faye Patty was born in July 1956 in Oklahoma City, but her family only lived there about two years. Her parents had happened to settle in Oklahoma while they were on tour.

Sandi's father, Ron Patty, sang with the Christian Brothers Quartet. Her mother, Carolyn, often was the quartet's accompanist; Carolyn Patty was said to be so talented she could have been a concert pianist. After Oklahoma City, the Pattys lived for much of Sandy's childhood in Phoenix.

Since then, her life has been full of triumphs and sorrows. In the early and mid-1990s, the gospel singer went through a series of struggles—very publicly.

In April 1990, an arson fire in her Anderson headquarters caused $650,000 in damage and destroyed four of her five Grammy Awards and several of her thirty-three Dove Awards.

While she was rebuilding her offices, Patty's marriage of thirteen years to John Helvering, her manager, unraveled. The couple had met at Anderson University and married in November 1978 during Sandi's senior year.

Years later, Sandi Patty conceded that she had had an extramarital affair with Don Peslis, a former backup singer. In a statement she released in 1995, Patty said: "I admit that I have sinned and have made mistakes. I have been seeking counsel from my pastor and from my church, and through this process I feel I have made significant progress toward wholeness, both personally and with the body of Christ." (Patty and Peslis were married in August 1995, about two years after her divorce from Helmering.)

Sadly, there were other tribulations as well. Patty's young son had to undergo brain surgery. One of her three daughters battled a life-threatening illness.

In 1993, Sandi Patty publicly revealed she had been abused as a child by a family friend. She said the abuse occurred while her parents were touring as gospel musicians.

Her childhood clearly had joyous moments, too. In an authorized biography, *Sandi Patti: The Voice of Gospel* (1988), she shared memories of singing with her parents and her brothers, Michael and Craig. When Sandi was eight and Michael and Craig were six and three, they performed as a trio called the Patty Kids.

Sandi has often recalled her father's musical advice: "Make every minute of a song be worth something."

(The book was called *Sandi Patti* because, although her family has always spelled the surname "Patty," a publicist misspelled it "Patti" early in Sandi's career. She lived with the misspelling for fourteen years, finally reverting to "Patty" in 1994.)

Her father was the minister of music at a church in Phoenix; Sandi participated in children's choir and rhythm band. After coming to Indiana in the mid-1970s to attend Anderson University, Patty met Bill Gaither, the Hoosier who would provide her big break.

A native of Alexandria, Indiana, Gaither was an Anderson University graduate who, with his wife Gloria, has carved out a spectacular career in gospel music. They have written over five hundred gospel standards, including Elvis Presley's 1969 hit, "He Touched Me."

Gaither made Sandi Patty part of the Bill Gaither Trio. About that time, she also recorded her first album, *Sandi's Song*. Spectacular success followed. The Gospel Music Association named Sandi Patty the top female vocalist of the year eleven straight times.

"I often have a hard time expressing myself when meeting new people, but I've felt that music is an outlet for me," Patty told *Christian Review* magazine after winning one of her Dove Awards. "It helps me to express emotions that I have a hard time expressing otherwise."

The mother of three daughters and a son from her marriage to Helvering, Patty always has emphasized her devotion to her four children. For example, in an interview at the Indianapolis Motor Speedway in 1991, she explained why she hadn't participated in the 500 Festival Parade with other celebrities on the previous day: "I was organizing a birthday party for my seven-year-old."

Several times Patty has identified Gloria Gaither as her role model in combining a musical career with motherhood. One of Patty's biggest challenges in managing to do both came in 1985 when, during a heavy series of scheduled concerts, her infant daughter Anna was hospitalized after a severe reaction to medication. Anna was not yet even one year old; after every concert, Sandy flew home to be with her at the hospital until she recovered.

Although an intensely private person, Patty has occasionally made public reference to her series of struggles.

"I looked like I had it all together," Patty said, referring to her early image. In promotional material for an album in 1994 called *Le Voyage*, she added, "Not that what I've shared in the past hasn't been me . . . but I've unintentionally given sort of a fairy tale portrayal of my life."

For *Storms of Perfection*, a book about the tribulations of famous Americans, Patty told author Andy Andrews that she has tried to learn from her sorrows.

"The struggles seemed to put things into perspective and help me realize that of all the things that grab for my attention on a daily basis, it is my faith, my friends and my family that hold the true importance," she said.

"In many ways, I've made some good choices in my life and I've made some choices that were not so good. I'm proud of some of the things I've done and ashamed of some of the things I've done. But in the midst of it all, God has been at work in my life. He continues to be at work in my life. That's enough for me."

Reggie Miller

Pro basketball star

Thanks largely to him, Indiana—fabled for its "Hoosier Hysteria" surrounding every aspect of high school and college basketball—finally became a state of pro basketball enthusiasts. And Reggie Miller became the first genuine NBA superstar of the long-suffering Indiana Pacers.

But the name "Reggie Miller" was booed and jeered by thousands of fans attending a draft party in 1987 when he was announced as the team's Number One selection.

That's because Miller, a California native and a sensation as a guard at UCLA, was drafted by the Pacers over popular Hoosier Steve Alford, the clean-cut star of an Indiana University team that had won the NCAA championship earlier that year. Undoubtedly many of the Pacers fans who initially booed Miller were among the thousands chanting "Reg-gie! Reg-gie! Reg-gie!" in 1994 as Miller led the team to its first-ever second-round victories in the National Basketball Association playoffs.

In the process, Miller became a media sensation by taking on the New York Knicks and publicly feuding with that team's Number One fan, filmmaker Spike Lee. During the electrifying fifth game of the playoffs at Madison Square Garden in New York, Miller had one of the best performances in NBA playoff history, scoring twenty-five points in the fourth quarter. He hit five three-pointers in the fourth period, an NBA record.

Throughout the early and mid-1990s, the lanky, ever-grinning Miller seemed to be everywhere. His giant-sized likeness adorned Market Square Arena, welcoming spectators from above like Zeus. He appeared in TV commercials and dozens of national talk shows, from The Tonight Show *with Jay Leno to* Live With Regis and Kathie Lee.

On the basketball court, Miller became the first Pacer ever to start an NBA All-Star Game and set a Pacers record for three-pointers (with 195) during the 1994–95 season. He also chalked up the longest active streak of consecutive starts in the NBA, with 345.

He described his sensational 1994-95 season in his book I Love Being the Enemy *(Simon & Schuster, 1995). Miller also endorsed everything from Nike shoes to McDonald's hamburgers and Marsh supermarkets. He was chosen for Dream Team III, the squad of NBA superstars that won the gold medal at the 1996 Olympics in Atlanta.*

He also married. Miller, who was born in 1965 and grew up in Riverside, California, wed glamorous model-actress Marita Stavrou in 1992.

He was interviewed in 1990 on the set of one of his first forays into TV, a short-lived, teen-oriented talk show.

Under the booms, cameras, ladders, and TV lights, the six-foot-seven pro basketball star sprawls on a sofa.

His clothes—a burgundy cardigan; pleated, charcoal slacks, and tasseled, imported loafers—are casual and hip.

So is his conversation.

Inside, though, the Indiana Pacer is a bundle of nerves, Reggie Miller confides later.

"Carson, Letterman . . . I don't even know how those guys do this every night," he says.

Reggie Miller

He chats as crew members at Comcast Cablevision string a microphone to his chest, tuck wires under his cardigan and tell the twenty-four-year-old UCLA graduate where to stand. How to walk. When to pivot. Where to look—all as he prepares to banter. Spontaneously. To a studio audience of about forty central-Indiana teenagers.

This will be witnessed by Hoosiers who tune in to *Teens Are Talking With Reggie Miller*, a show that premiered a month ago. The Pacers' Number 31, an explosive guard and the first Pacer chosen for the NBA All-Star team in thirteen seasons, is a fan of TV personality Arsenio Hall.

"Arsenio has a say-what-you-feel approach," Miller explains. "That's how I treat my guests. C'mon over. Have a good time. Be yourself. Be loose."

His style may be Arsenio-loose, but his subject matter is Oprah-serious. Teen pregnancy. Drug use. Rap music. All have been explored on his taped, biweekly program.

"Some of these shows become exploitative," Miller says, referring to the glut of syndicated talk shows such *Donahue, Geraldo!,* and *Sally Jessy Raphael.* "I want to be informational."

The native Californian, second in scoring at UCLA only to Lew Alcindor (Kareem Abdul-Jabaar), also wants his show to be a springboard. When his legs give out or his hustle wanes, Miller says he would like to be a TV personality—preferably a talk show host rather than a sportscaster.

The Pacers' Number One pick in the 1987 draft is using his celebrity contacts to pull in headliners for taped interviews as they pass through Indianapolis. Guests on *Teens Are Talking With Reggie Miller* have included basketball legend Magic Johnson, teen rockers New Kids on the Block, and Florence Griffith Joyner, the flamboyant Olympic gold medal-winning track star.

"I've known Reggie since his rookie year in town here," says Sharma Wise, the show's co-host and executive producer. A veteran of WFYI-TV (Channel 20), she created the concept of a Reggie Miller talkfest.

"I remember thinking, 'Who is this guy with the big ears and the gorgeous eyes?' Then I noticed how outspoken and articulate he was."

Miller guffaws, kicks off his loafers, props up his stocking feet and relaxes, upbeat but drained after a taping for the half-hour show. The taping drags on for nearly three hours.

He also spends more than forty-five minutes signing autographs for members of the studio audience and crew—and for several of the guests, including teenagers who reveal that they have coped with severe alcohol and drug problems. Among them is a pale, brown-haired teen who says she smoked marijuana as an eight-year-old. With a baby sitter.

Explaining that he is "blown away" by the tragedy of her story and the honesty with which she recounted it, Miller bends down and hugs her. The hug comes after the taping stops, the lights are flicked off and while cables are being unhooked and dismantled.

Paces away, other teens rave about the spindly, affable host.

"We can open up to Reggie," says Nicole Reid, seventeen, a Broad Ripple High School senior in the studio audience. "He's at ease and relaxed. We can talk to Reggie about things we can't talk to our parents about. Some athletes shy away from the media. He's the opposite."

Another audience member, Sue Knox, a seventeen-year-old junior at Lawrence North High School, agrees. "Reggie is great. Kids open up to him, but he also knows how to handle them. If they act up, he calms them down."

Told of those comments, Miller downplays any magnetism and attributes his appeal to his youth. "Five or six years ago, I was them. I know how they feel."

Each show opens with a bouncy, fast-paced theme song that includes the lyrics: "Reggie Miller, he's the talk of the town . . . You can tell him the troubles you have."

Entering to cheers, whistles and shouts as the music builds, Miller asks the audience, "How's everyone doin' tonight? Havin' a good time?"

"Yes!" the teens shout.

"Any Pacer fans?"

Hearty applause. Miller grins.

"Put on your thinking caps and have an inquisitive mind," he instructs, explaining that the show's topic will be drug abuse. "I want you to ask all the questions in the world."

One of his guests, a former teen drug and alcohol abuser, reveals that she once downed five beers before getting behind the wheel of her car—and colliding with a sedan containing a family of four. The mother was hospitalized and died of complications from the accident a month later.

Asked later about his own teen years, Miller describes them as relatively trouble-free. But he says that empathizing with the angst of teenagers comes naturally.

The fourth of five children, Miller grew up in a medium-sized, suburban city near Los Angeles in a close-knit, two-parent, middle-class family. But he was born with an open chest cavity and "pronated hips," a condition in which the leg bones force the ankles inward.

Doctors told the family that Reggie might never walk unassisted, let alone play basketball. He wore steel braces at night until he was four. After that, Reggie wore corrective shoes. At one point his mother, Carrie Miller, had to wake him up once an hour at night to turn him so his leg bones would rotate.

In addition to all of that, Reggie grew up in the shadow of an older sister, Cheryl Miller, regarded by many as the best women's basketball player ever. A year older than Reggie, Cheryl Miller was a four-time high school All-American who led the U.S. women's team to an Olympic gold medal in 1984. She later became a TV basketball commentator (and in 1997, was named a head coach in the Women's NBA).

But Reggie puts a positive spin on all this. Coming from a large family, and one in which another member had experienced the stresses of public life, were assets, Miller says. "There was always someone who had gone through the same thing," he explains. "I didn't really feel alone."

The basketball star becomes unusually quiet. He's clearly preoccupied by the revelations of his teenage guests. Long after the taping has wrapped, Miller is still pondering what he has heard.

"I hate to see these awful things happen to kids," he says. "I can see pain in their eyes."

Somehow, he adds, he wants to reach out and help.

Joshua Bell

Violinist

By age twenty-two, charismatic Joshua Bell already was being called "the preeminent violinist of his generation" by, among others, the music critic for Esquire *magazine .*

Born in Bloomington, Indiana, in 1967, Bell exhibited extraordinary musical talent as an elementary school student—and was blessed with an internationally renowned maestro in the neighborhood to nurture it. Josef Gingold, the legendary Indiana University music professor, took on Joshua as a student when the boy was twelve.

Bell was interviewed in 1990, five years before Gingold's death. A few years after the interview, Bell replaced his distinctive, guitar-shaped 1726 Stradivarius violin with a later model—a 1732 Stradivarius once owned by Paganini.

Now booked years in advance, he performs more than a hundred concerts annually with the world's major orchestras at concert halls and music festivals from Milan to Tokyo. He's recorded thirteen albums and is one of the first classical musicians to be the focus of a music video.

Prodigy turns poster boy.

The temptation is to sum up the twenty-two-year-old international violin star from Bloomington that way.

After all, there is his ebony Porsche, his Manhattan co-op, his appearances on Johnny Carson's *Tonight Show* and the splashy promotional campaign. The promos, criticized by purists as "tasteless" and "teen meat" in approach, capitalize on the classical musician's blue-green eyes and striking looks.

"Sex & Violins," proclaims *Esquire* magazine, which features a full-page close-up of a smoldering Joshua Bell, "heartthrob."

But there is another, quieter Bell.

This is the low-key Josh who loves Indiana University basketball. The one who reads Tolstoy on airplanes, catches Woody Allen movies between concerts and can't stand to listen to his own records, even though he draws raves from Seattle, Hong Kong and Honolulu to New York, Naples and Tokyo. This Josh, the one away from the posters and publicity agents, is a whiz at physics, likes Beatles music, describes himself as "addicted" to golf and totes his own luggage.

But his prized possession is not the sports car; it's his 1726 Stradivarius with a guitar shape—no corners opposite the scrolls.

That makes the instrument one of a kind, just like its owner. He is a graduate of Bloomington North High School who has performed with the Boston Pops, will fiddle on the steps of the U.S. Capitol and tour the Soviet Union in 1990 and who made his Carnegie Hall debut as a soloist at seventeen.

"From the time he was a tiny boy, Josh wanted to master anything new in his environment," noted Shirley Bell, a mental health worker who teaches at IU and helps manage her son's finances. His career also is handled by a New York agency.

Heavily marketed as a young heartthrob, international violin star Joshua Bell says, "Marketing is harmless and might even accomplish something. To get young people into classical music is terrific. These are the audiences of the future."

"Computers, physics, tennis—Josh would take off on tangents and exhaust each endeavor," Shirley Bell recalled. "The violin was the one constant."

Private lessons began at age five. By the time he was twelve, Joshua had captivated the world's wizard of violin teaching. The revered Josef Gingold, distinguished professor of music at IU, had never accepted a student so young.

Typically, the day before the crucial concert that convinced the maestro to take on the young charge, Josh was out tossing boomerangs—one of which returned to bonk him on the chin.

"Only inches more to the left," Joshua says now, "and it would have wrecked the way I rest the violin."

Gingold, who speaks of his prize pupil with unabashed adoration, probably would have heard his potential regardless.

"Joshua was *born* with great talent," says Gingold, whose eightieth birthday in 1989 included a bash with Bell on the bill. "He later developed a tremendous desire to work toward perfection. Joshua always has been a joy to teach. After a while he was more a colleague than a student. He was that good.

"Now, of course, Joshua is a violinist of the elite, one of the top talents in the world."

At the moment, the top talent is disembarking at Indianapolis International Airport, clad in a leather jacket, blue jeans and sneakers.

Returning after a week of performances in Houston, three hours of sleep and a plane grounded for ninety minutes with mechanical problems, Josh is yawning but upbeat. Ever determined to improve himself, he has been reading *Anna Karenina*. He is booked solid more than two years in advance. Bell performs a hundred concerts a year, the limit that travel schedules and stamina permit.

He is a pinup boy, featured in a Steve Alford-type poster that depicts a wholesome-looking, brown-haired Midwesterner. But instead of a basketball, a Strad is tucked under his arm.

Fresh off the plane, Bell wants to talk about hoops, particularly his beloved Hoosiers. "I missed watching the game on TV last night because of my concert," he says, groaning. "Did you catch it?"

Make no mistake, though. In a field dominated by Asian, Israeli, and Russian artists, most much older than this Hoosier virtuoso, Bell is serious about music. A sampling of the critical hosannas from just a six month-period:

The Detroit Free-Press: "Bell's talent is extravagant. He is clearly going to be one of the handful of truly great violinists of this century—and maybe the next as well."

The Arizona Republic: "The Indiana-born violinist has it all. His technique is phenomenal, his tone warm and silky smooth and his musicianship unquestioned."

The Charleston (South Carolina) *News and Courier*: "His is a major talent that captures the audience not only with his exquisite tone, but with his unassuming, winsome personality on stage."

The few salvos have come as a result of the matinee-idol marketing push. "Bell's record label is tastelessly promoting him in a full-color, teen-meat brochure," *The Boston Globe* complained. "We see Bell in improbable postures with his violin, sitting on the hood of his new Porsche, wearing stone-washed jeans."

But even traditionalists concede his talent is so overwhelming that the marketing becomes irrelevant.

"London Records' crass campaign to sell Bell as an all-American teen hunk was tasteless enough for me to toss his debut discs unheard into the discard pile," reported critic Peter

Davis of *New York* magazine. But coaxed by friends who extolled the violinist, Davis retrieved them and pronounced Bell "a musician of distinction, wise beyond his years."

But the violin has never been the all-in-all; his interests and talents are multidimensional, and include basketball and tennis.

"Josh never spent hours and hours in the practice room because he always had so many other interests," Shirley Bell says. "My husband and I never blocked him from doing anything he wanted to do, including skiing and driving fast cars—as much as I would have liked him to stop. We just thought having other interests was healthy."

A middle child, Joshua has sisters, Toby and Rachel, who also play classical music but pursue other endeavors. Their father, Alan, is a psychologist on the faculty at IU.

"There is a wonderful, close relationship between Joshua and his family," Gingold comments. "His parents were cooperative, but not pushy. For his part, Joshua is honest, highly intelligent, charming and loyal to all of us."

In 1987 Bell, then nineteen, became the first violinist in ten years to sign an exclusive contract with Decca/London Records. The agreement called for two records a year for five years. The first was *Presenting Joshua Bell*, the cover of which depicted the boyish musician in casual attire gazing at the camera.

"I can't listen to my own records," Bell confides. "Like most musicians, I'm self-critical. I keep wishing I had done it a different way."

He also concedes to jitters before his two appearances in the seat next to Johnny Carson. But the warmth of the talk show host and fellow guests Michael Keaton and Garry Shandling calmed him.

"My nervousness is a positive thing, a high rather than a fear," he says. "I hope I always have it."

Bell also expresses relief that he has outgrown his prodigy label. He always felt the emphasis on his youth drew attention away from the music.

Any advice for budding Bells?

"Concentrate," he replies. But he adds a second recommendation:

Nurture other passions.

Ryan White

Teenage crusader, AIDS activist

AIDS victim Ryan White was interviewed in early 1986 in the middle of his crusade to attend school in tiny Russiaville, Indiana, near Kokomo. Ryan, who was born in 1971, was just fourteen.

Within a year, he had become an international symbol of courage, dedication and tolerance in the face of the devastating AIDS epidemic. Ryan testified before government panels, crusaded with celebrities, and appeared on national TV talk shows. In travels around the country, he spoke to thousands of young people about acquired immune deficiency syndrome, bigotry and simply overcoming obstacles in life, whatever their nature. In 1990, at age eighteen, Ryan died in Riley Hospital for Children in Indianapolis.

His mother, Jeanne, became what TV talk show host Phil Donahue calls a "guerrilla fighter" for humanitarian causes. Carrying on her son's crusade, she began the Ryan White Foundation, a nonprofit, Indianapolis-based agency dedicated to worldwide AIDS education. Testifying before public officials and speaking at fund-raisers, Jeanne White maintains a hectic schedule of advocacy. At her urging, the U.S. Congress passed—and President George Bush signed—the Ryan White CARE Act in 1990; it authorizes up to $8.75 million in funding for programs to help people who test positive for HIV, the virus that causes AIDS.

Two years after her son's death, Jeanne married a Cicero neighbor, Roy Ginder, a former auto mechanic who had befriended Ryan.

KOKOMO, Indiana—Right from the start, Jeanne Hale White knew something was terribly, unalterably wrong with her son.

"After he was circumcised, he bled for three days," recalls the moon-faced, controversial woman whose recent family life has become a network news soap opera.

"Ryan has less than one percent clotting in his blood, so the doctors began labeling him a 'severe hemophiliac.' I thought, 'Please, God, no; not this.' "

As grave and unusual as Ryan's health was at birth, the Whites did not suspect the tiny boy's physical condition would one day pit the family against strangers, neighbors and friends in Howard County. Nor did they realize Ryan would prompt stares when they enter movie theaters and glares when they dine in restaurants, plus hundreds of unsolicited packages and letters, requests for autographs and the characterization of Jeanne White as a stage mother *par excellence*.

They did not know Ryan's health would force major adjustments upon his sister Andrea, a roller-skating champion whose rink successes had previously catapulted *her* into the position of family celebrity.

"You would not believe the questions we get asked," Mrs. White, thirty-eight, says during an interview in her modest, single-story frame house on Kokomo's outskirts.

"Tell everyone I wash my dishes just like everyone else. I wash them by hand because my dishwasher has been on the blink most of the time we've lived here.

"And Ryan doesn't have a [special] drinking glass. We share the same toothpaste. We had

Ryan White with his mother, Jeanne, in 1986 during his crusade to attend school in Russiaville, Indiana.

one guy—a *Newsweek* writer—who spent three days here, went in our bathroom and nosed around to see if we shared toothpaste.

"The guy kept saying, 'This is for a cover story. This is for a cover story.' Ryan said, 'So what? I've already been on the cover of national magazines.'"

That incident points up an aberration in the White household. Those who know the family well—including some who have clashed with the Whites—point out it is Ryan rather than his mother who issues the commands and makes decisions on his behalf, both major and minor.

The fourteen-year-old AIDS victim, now repeating seventh grade at Western Middle School in nearby Russiaville, appears much more diminutive and frail than his televised images suggest.

Although Ryan is barely four-feet-eleven and seventy-six pounds, Mrs. White says he is healthier now than at any time in his life. And—depending on your viewpoint—he is driven by a character that remains strong, steadfast or stubborn.

"Ryan White is the man in that house," observes Charles R. Vaughan, a Lafayette attorney who has represented the Whites in their court battles to return Ryan to the classroom. "A decision that affects Ryan is made by Ryan. He absolutely calls all the shots. Every time you ask Jeanne anything, she turns her head and looks at Ryan for the decision as to what to do."

"Instead of a stage mother, she is almost like a secretary," says an Indiana journalist who has covered the Whites for months. "Ryan tells her what he will and will not do, and she follows his orders."

Mrs. White, who divorced Ryan's father eight years ago, is in constant motion, attempting to sew beads on a skating costume for her daughter, answer a continually ringing telephone, pack for a trip later this week to New York City, get Ryan measured for a tuxedo and tend the family pets—all after putting in an exhausting eight-hour shift at a General Motors plant.

"They want to know how many pictures, Ryan," Mrs. White says, yelling from an interview in the living room with a reporter and photographer.

No reply emanates from Ryan's bedroom, a tiny room full of Marvel comic books, GI Joe toys and photographs of TV actor Michael J. Fox.

Nibbling on a fried chicken drumstick, Mrs. White scurries from the room, consults with her son in whispered tones and returns. "He says you can take five pictures," she reports. "Three of him. Two of me and him."

She sighs. "Personally, I would rather have given it up [the fight for Ryan to attend school] a long time ago. It would have been a lot easier on me and a lot easier on the rest of the family . . . But this is what Ryan wants to do, and I want what he wants."

What is Ryan's prognosis?

"Who knows?" Mrs. White responds, her voice softening. "I certainly don't know. They gave him three to six months after he was first diagnosed. (Ryan was told he had AIDS in December 1984, following a transfusion of contaminated blood.)

"But he is healthier now than ever. Last fall, he was down to fifty-four pounds. Now he is about right, except for the fact he is so small for his age. He eats everything. He even has developed a little tummy. I have given him two IV's twice a week since he was four or five. The most now is an occasional fever, and that hasn't happened at all this month . . .

"Sure, sometimes I get scared. And so does Ryan. Last summer, he was out in the sun all day and at night we noticed great big red spots all over him. He said, 'Mom, I'm really scared.'

"I said, 'Ryan, I am too.' But by morning all the spots were gone. He has no lesions at all now, and energy that just won't quit. He'll stay up to midnight or 1 A.M., going constantly."

The Whites concede they don't strictly follow doctor's orders. Pets, for example, were forbidden because Ryan's physicians at Riley feared household animals could spread disease.

Yet Ryan has both a dog—a mixed-breed mutt called Wally Waldonado ("Channel 8 in Lafayette named him, for what I don't know," Mrs. White says)—and a cat, Chi Chi.

"Ryan said, 'It's my life, and I want a pup,'" Mrs. White recalls. "He said, 'I want a pup that likes no one but me.'"

Nor does Ryan lack human companionship. His best friend, a sixth-grader named Heath, lives across the street. Heath and other pals still play with Ryan, sleep overnight at the Whites' house and swap comic books.

But that reaction has not been universal. Dozens of Hoosiers demonstrated and picketed to show their support for Western School Corporation officials following the announcement that they would bar Ryan from attending classes. The educators said the health risk for other children was too great—despite top Indiana health officials arguing otherwise.

Although Ryan won his court battle to attend classes, many of his friends shun him. Some teenagers taunt him with ugly names or obscene gestures. They even have ridiculed classmates who stick by Ryan during the controversy.

During an interview, Ryan answers most questions in monosyllables or short sentences. The Cubs are his favorite baseball team. He likes to swim, although for a while he was barred from many Kokomo pools.

Ryan considers himself a "slightly below average" student, but Mrs. White disagrees, reporting that her son rarely achieves a grade lower than a C.

His eyes sparkle, however, when asked to talk about Heath, roller skating ("I'm getting ready to go to a skating party right now") and comic books featuring the X-Men.

"Someone sent him a rare sixty-dollar comic book the other day," Mrs. White says, sighing. "*Sixty dollars* for a comic book. That's crazy—can you imagine what we could do with sixty dollars?"

Isn't she afraid Ryan will catch an infection—flu, pneumonia, or even a potentially devastating common cold—from his classmates?

"Once I asked about putting Ryan in a bubble," she replies. "He [a physician] said that would not help. We can't live just in a protected world. I think it's very important to keep his body healthy and active, to keep his strength up."

Has she ever considered moving to a more receptive community?

Mrs. White nods, then pauses. She looks around her living room, cluttered with suitcases, letters, framed photos of Ryan and Andrea, a poster of Italy, yellowing Indiana newspapers and potted houseplants.

There are two problems with moving, she said. Money is one of them. The second is even more practical.

Who, Mrs. White asked, would want to buy the AIDS house?

Her question eventually was answered. The Whites were able to sell their home and move to Cicero, Indiana, in 1987—thanks to proceeds from a TV movie, The Ryan White Story.

Other Legends

George Ade—humorist, journalist and playwright

The writer known as the "Aesop of Indiana" was born in 1866 in Kentland, Indiana. Shunning farm work, George Ade attended Purdue University and became a reporter for newspapers in Lafayette and Chicago. He began writing a popular column for *The Chicago Morning News* that introduced the type of writing that won him fame: modern fables.

His first book, *Fables in Slang* (1899), became a best-seller. Ade told moral tales using everyday language. In "The Fable of the Good People Who Rallied to the Support of the Church," he described the lengths to which churchwomen went to decorate for a raspberry festival; when the hoopla was over, the church had raised $6.80. Ade concluded by noting that people will do anything to avoid putting money in an offering basket.

In 1904 he returned to Indiana, moving to an idyllic estate called Hazleden about fifteen miles from his birthplace in Kentland. Hazleden and its elaborate gardens became the setting for literary parties and the sightings of celebrities such as Theodore Roosevelt, Calvin Coolidge, Damon Runyan, and Will Rogers. Meanwhile, Ade turned out a string of popular plays and comic operas, including *The Sultan of Sulu* and *Peggy from Paris*.

Ade died in 1944. Hazleden, which is open to the public by appointment, is on the National Register of Historic Places.

Garo Antreasian—printmaker

Internationally renowned printmaker Garo Antreasian is credited with changing the world of art—and he got his start in Indianapolis. Antreasian, who was born in the Hoosier capital in 1922, pursued his passion for art at Arsenal Technical High School and the Herron School of Art.

He became a master of lithography, the process of drawing images on polished limestone and eventually imprinting the image on paper, foil, cloth or plastics. As a founder of the Tamarind Lithography Workshop in Los Angeles in 1960, Antreasian was a major catalyst for the rebirth of printmaking in the United States. He has lived in Albuquerque, New Mexico, since 1964.

Mike Aulby—bowler

He was born in Indianapolis in 1960, graduated from Franklin Central High School in 1978 and went on to become, as most sports analysts saw it, the "bowler of the decade" of the 1980s. Mike Aulby's first major win was the Professional Bowlers Association (PBA) National in 1979; also that year he was named "Rookie of the Year" by the PBA.

During the 1980s, left-handed Aulby swept three major tournaments—the PBA National (1985), the U.S. Open (1989), and the ABC Masters (1989). Aulby was the top money-maker on the pro bowling tour in 1985 and 1989; he also set an earnings record of $298,237 in 1989. Known for his compassion, Aulby serves as his sport's goodwill ambassador to several charities, including the Children's Miracle Network. Aulby and his wife, Tami, live in Carmel with their son, Christopher. Mike Aulby was inducted into the PBA Bowling Hall of Fame in 1996.

Babyface—pop singer and songwriter

Kenneth "Babyface" Edmonds was born in Indianapolis in 1958 and graduated from North Central High School in 1976. Known as "Kenny" to his boyhood Hoosier friends, he played guitar and sang as a counselor at central Indiana summer camps; also as a teenager, he performed at local nightspots with a band called Tarnished Silver.

As "Babyface," the youthful-looking Edmonds has become a veritable "hit machine" of the 1990s. Since 1987, Babyface has turned out sixteen Number One records and one hundred Top Ten records as a singer, songwriter or producer. In 1997, Babyface was nominated for twelve Grammy Awards, tying a record set by his boyhood idol, Gary native Michael Jackson. Babyface and his wife, Tracey, have a son, Brandon.

David Baker—jazz musician and educator

His career has had several high notes. David Baker, born in Indianapolis in 1932, conducted the first orchestra funded by the Smithsonian Institution. Since 1966, he's been a professor at the Indiana University School of Music, where he heads the jazz department. He's also composed music played by the Indianapolis Symphony Orchestra. Baker is credited with pioneering the use of cellos in jazz music.

The Ball Brothers—glass canning manufacturers and philanthropists

The clear, glass jars used across the nation for canning vegetables and fruits have had a Hoosier name on them: Ball. The Ball name has been particularly prominent for generations in Muncie. The five Ball brothers moved there in 1886 to run their business, which became the nation's largest manufacturer of home-canning jars.

The enterprising Ball brothers were Lucius, William C., Edmund Burke, Frank, and George. Their father, Lucius Stiles Ball, was a farmer in Ohio, where the boys were born. When the brothers were teenagers, the Ball family moved to upstate New York. In the late 1870s, two of the brothers, Edmund (1855–1925) and Frank (1857–1943), formed a partnership and opened a small factory in Buffalo that made tin oil cans. By 1884, they had added glass fruit jars and been joined by their brothers.

The Balls moved to Muncie when the city offered them a seven-acre site and five thousand dollars in moving expenses. Their factory opened in 1888 and achieved astounding success, particularly with its famous Mason jars. The eldest Ball brother, Lucius (1850–1932), who had graduated from medical school in Buffalo, also became a doctor in Muncie. William (1852–1921) remained in Buffalo several years, overseeing a branch of the company there before he, too, moved to Muncie.

Eventually the Ball Brothers Co. became Ball Corp. The brothers—particularly Frank and George (1862–1955), the youngest—used their wealth to benefit their adopted hometown. In addition to funding Ball Memorial Hospital and many public and private institutions in Muncie, the brothers developed Ball State Teachers' College, now Ball State University.

Richard Bennett—stage actor

Although four generations of his family operated sawmills, Richard Bennett (born in 1872 in Bennetts Mills, Indiana) had other dreams. After attending Logansport High School, he took to the stage, rising to the top rank of theater stars after the turn of the century.

His triumphs included *They Knew What They Wanted* (1924). Bennett's daughters, Constance and Joan, became top Hollywood stars of the 1930s and '40s. Richard Bennett died in 1944.

The Bettenhausens: Tony, Gary, and Tony Jr.— race car drivers

The star-crossed racing family started out in the Chicago area, where Melvin Eugene (Tony) Bettenhausen Sr. was born in 1916. He began racing midget cars in the late 1930s. After service in World War II, Tony made his Indianapolis 500 debut in 1946; he was forced out by mechanical problems after forty-seven laps. That kind of thing became a pattern; Tony Sr. didn't finish a 500-Mile Race until 1958.

Meanwhile, he won two national driving championships. In the 500-Mile Races of 1958 and 1959, Bettenhausen not only finished, he captured fourth place both times. Then tragedy struck. A couple of weeks before the Indianapolis 500 of 1961, he agreed to test drive the car of a fellow driver and suggest improvements. The car crashed at the Speedway, killing Bettenhausen.

His oldest son, Gary, was born in 1941. He lives in Monrovia, Indiana, and has followed his father's career path. Gary raced midget and sprint cars in the 1960s, and in 1969 was USAC's most active driver. Although he is known as a fierce competitor, Gary drew praise for his compassion during a race in 1971 when he stopped his car to help a rival, Mike Mosely, who was pinned in a burning car.

In 1972, Gary nearly won the Indianapolis 500; he was enjoying a comfortable lead at 175 laps when he was forced out with ignition problems. He suffered serious right arm injuries during a USAC dirt race in 1974, but continues to compete and has started in twenty-one Indianapolis 500 races. His kid brother Tony Jr. (born in 1951) lives in the Indianapolis area; in 1981, his rookie year at the Indianapolis 500, Tony Jr. finished seventh. Also that year, Tony Jr. placed second—and nearly won—the inaugural Michigan 500.

Bill Blass—fashion designer

His specialties are elegant evening wear for women and men and women's classic sportswear and daytime suits. Thanks to his creations, "Bill Blass" has been one of the best-known names in popular fashion for nearly forty years.

Blass was born in Fort Wayne in 1922. He left his home state in the early 1940s to study fashion at Parson's School of Design in New York. His mentor in the fashion business was another Hoosier: the late Norman Norrell, a designer from Noblesville. Consistently respected for his styles, Blass has won the fashion industry's Coty Award three times (in 1961, 1963, and 1970). He also has been inducted into the Fashion Hall of Fame.

Otis Bowen—governor and Cabinet member

Although Otis "Doc" Bowen was born in Rochester, Indiana, in 1918, he is associated with the northern Indiana town of Bremen. That's where Bowen, a graduate of the Indiana University School of Medicine, became a family physician after World War II.

His political career began as Marshall County coroner in 1952. Four years later Bowen, a Republican, was elected to the Indiana General Assembly. He was elected governor in 1972, then became the state's first chief executive to benefit from a change in Indiana law that allowed a governor successive terms; Bowen won re-election in 1976. Popular because of his "family doctor" image and stance against property tax increases, "Doc" Bowen resumed his medical practice after leaving office. He re-entered public life when President Ronald Reagan named him Secretary of Health and Human Services. Bowen served in the Cabinet from 1985 to 1989, then returned to Bremen to live.

Mordecai "Three-Finger" Brown—baseball pitcher

The greatest pitcher in Chicago Cubs history was born in 1876 in Nyesville in western Indiana. Mordecai Peter Brown's famous nickname derived from a childhood accident with a corn shredder in which he lost part of his right hand. Ironically, his reshaped hand became an asset: "Three-Finger" Brown was able to throw a curveball with an exceedingly sharp downward break.

Initially a third baseman with a coal mining team in southern Indiana, Brown made his debut in the big leagues as a pitcher with the St. Louis Cardinals in 1903. But his national fame came as a Chicago Cub beginning the next year. As the leading pitcher, Brown was the star of a Cubs dynasty from 1906 to 1910 that included three pennant wins and a World Series championship in 1908. His lifetime ERA of 2.06 is the third best in baseball history.

In 1913, with the Cubs dynasty crumbling, Brown was traded to Cincinnati. He rejoined the Cubs in 1916, then ended his career in the minor leagues with the Terre Haute Tots. "Three-Finger" Brown retired in 1920 and died in 1948. The next year, he was elected to the Baseball Hall of Fame.

Tom Carnegie—sportscaster

With his rich, booming baritone, Tom Carnegie became an institution on Indiana television and at the Indianapolis Motor Speedway, where he has been track announcer more than forty years.

The "Voice of the 500"—a broadcaster forever associated with the phrase "It's a new track record!"—was born in 1919 and grew up on a farm near Kansas City. A polio-related virus in Carnegie's teens ended his days as an athlete, so he became a broadcaster. He moved to Indiana in 1942 to take a job with WOWO Radio in Fort Wayne. In the 1950s, Carnegie was chairman of Butler University's radio and TV department.

But his greatest fame came at the Speedway (he began announcing at the track in 1946) and as sports director for WRTV-Channel 6 in Indianapolis. For decades he covered or announced nearly every major sporting event in the state, including the boys high school basketball tournament.

Schuyler Colfax—vice president

The first of five Hoosiers who became vice president of the United States was born in New York City in 1823. Schuyler Colfax' father and older sister died when he was a child, so he was reared by his widowed mother. At age ten, he quit school to work as a store clerk. A few years later his mother remarried, and in 1836 she and thirteen-year-old Schuyler moved with her new husband to St. Joseph County in Indiana.

When Schuyler's stepfather was elected county auditor, the family settled in South Bend. Colfax worked as a clerk for the Indiana Senate and as a Statehouse correspondent for a newspaper. In 1855, he was elected as a Republican to the U.S. House of Representatives. Always ambitious and gregarious, he was elected Speaker of the House twice.

In 1868, Colfax won a fierce battle among several prominent Republicans to be the running mate of Civil War hero Ulysses S. Grant. Soon after the Grant-Colfax ticket won the election, the Hoosier began laying the groundwork for a presidential campaign of his own. But his career was derailed by accusations that he had financial dealings with a company connected to building the massive Union Pacific Railway. Impropriety by Colfax was never proved, but he was compelled to testify before congressional investigatory committees. When Grant decided to seek re-election in 1872, delegates to the Republican National Committee chose Henry Wilson of Massachusetts as his running mate.

After leaving office, Colfax became a popular public speaker. He died at a train station in Minnesota while on a lecture tour in 1885.

James "Doc" Counsilman—swimming coach

His world fame didn't derive only from coaching Mark Spitz and forty-seven other Olympians. James "Doc" Counsilman, the legendary coach at Indiana University, "re-invented swimming for all of us," as *Swim* magazine once put it.

Counsilman, born in Alabama in 1920, re-invented the sport by applying scientific principles to analyze and enhance swimming strokes. His book, *The Science of Swimming*, has been translated into more than twenty languages. One example of the way Counsilman dominated the sport: In the 1964 Summer Olympics, his athletes captured nine of eleven gold medals; the other two went to Australians coached by him at I.U.

After decades of coaching others (he joined the IU faculty in 1957) and designing training equipment used around the world, Counsilman set a record of his own. In 1979, at the age of fifty-eight, he became the oldest person to swim the English Channel. Counsilman retired as Indiana University's swim coach in 1990. (For more details, see "Mark Spitz" in the "Legends of Our Own Day" section.)

Dan Patch—racehorse

"The Patch," as the harness racing horse was nicknamed, became nationally famous at the turn of the century for his amazing speed and stamina. Some analysts considered Dan Patch of Oxford, Indiana, to be the greatest athlete of his era—human or animal.

The story of Dan Patch began in far western Indiana when Dan Messner, an Oxford shop owner, bred a mare he bought at an auction with a famous racehorse named Joe Patchen. Born in 1896, Dan Patch was ridiculed as a colt because he was gangly. But "The

Patch" silenced his critics in 1900 when he won his first race by an incredible 225 yards at the Benton County (Indiana) Fairgrounds.

After Dan Patch won twelve races, his success unnerved Messner, who feared a rival owner might poison his horse. He sold Dan Patch for twenty-thousand dollars to an entrepreneur from Buffalo, New York. Dan Patch then competed on the grand circuit; he never lost another race. His dominance hurt the wagering at racetracks because everyone knew which horse would win. After Dan Patch was purchased by Minneapolis businessman Marion Willis Savage in 1902, the horse's name and likeness were used to sell everything from dog food to sleds and washtubs. In 1916, both Dan Patch and his owner were stricken with heart failure; the horse died July 11, and Savage passed away the next day.

Jim Davis—cartoonist

Jim Davis grew up on a farm near Marion, Indiana, surrounded by his family's twenty-five cats. So perhaps it was inevitable he would create the most popular comic strip cat in America.

Davis was born in 1945. His famous creation, the mischievous, lasagna-loving "Garfield," was born in 1978. Childhood asthma prevented young Jim Davis from participating in much farm work, so he spent hours doodling. Later, Davis decided to study art at Ball State University.

Early jobs included assisting an advertising firm in Muncie. Initially, Davis created a cartoon strip about a gnat named "Norm." (When the idea proved unmarketable, he ended the strip by drawing a giant shoe squashing the gnat.)

Then Davis turned to "Garfield"—and a supporting group of characters including nerdish owner "Jon Arbuckle" and doggy pal "Odie." Even Davis has said he was astonished at how rapidly the strip caught on with newspaper readers. Today, "Garfield" is read by more than 200 million people in twenty-five hundred newspapers. The cat also has been the subject of thirty-three books and thousands of products ranging from stuffed toys to underwear. The headquarters of Paws Inc., Davis' company, is on a farm outside Muncie.

Anita De Frantz—Olympics organizer and medalist

She wasn't an athlete at Shortridge High School because, unless you count cheerleading, there were no organized sports for girls when Anita DeFrantz (class of '70) attended the Indianapolis school.

But DeFrantz, who was born in Indianapolis in 1952, went on to become, as *The Sporting News* put it in 1996, "the most powerful woman in sports." Her first fame came as a bronze medalist in rowing at the 1976 Montreal Olympics.

Then she managed the athletes' village for the 1984 Los Angeles Olympics. But DeFrantz truly attained power in the mid-1990s as the only American—and the only woman—on the executive board of the International Olympic Committee. Her international clout is a major reason the 1996 Summer Olympics were held in Atlanta and the 2002 Winter Games will be in Salt Lake City.

Carl Erskine—baseball pitcher

When the legendary Brooklyn Dodgers moved to Los Angeles in 1958, a Hoosier was chosen to pitch the opening game before eighty thousand eager California fans. Carl Erskine pitched a winning game. It was typical of his twelve-year career as a Dodger.

He was born in Anderson, Indiana, in 1926 and, as he grew up there, advanced through the ranks of sandlot, high school and amateur baseball. A scout for the Brooklyn Dodgers noticed the young hurler during a Summer American League game and offered Carl a first-class train ticket to Brooklyn and a hundred-dollar bill. After a brief stint in the Navy, Erskine signed with the Brooklyn Dodgers. He spent some time in the team's minor league system in Danville, Illinois, and Fort Worth, Texas.

Erskine eventually became the star pitcher for the Dodgers during the Jackie Robinson era, playing from 1948 to 1959. He pitched for the team in five World Series and hurled two no-hitters during his career. During his best season in 1953, Erskine led the National League in winning percentage (.769) and set a record in the World Series for striking out fourteen New York Yankees in one game.

He retired from the sport at age thirty-two and moved back to Anderson. In his home-town, Erskine has been an active civic leader. For several years he was president of an Anderson bank and a board member of the city's largest hospital. In the mid-1990s, the Carl D. Erskine Rehabilitation and Sports Medicine Center was dedicated in Anderson.

Chad Everett—TV star

The handsome, dark-haired actor was born in South Bend in 1936. Chad Everett is best known for his leading role as the heroic young surgeon in the TV series *Medical Center* (1969–76). Everett, whose real name is Raymond Lee Cramton, also has acted in several movies, including *The Singing Nun* (1966) and *The Impossible Years* (1968).

Crystal Gayle—country and pop singer

She is the kid sister of country music superstar Loretta Lynn, who will forever be identified with Kentucky. Crystal Gayle (real name: Brenda Gail Webb) was born in Paintsville, Kentucky, in 1951, but grew up in Wabash, Indiana. Searching for jobs, the family moved to the Hoosier state when Crystal was just three years old.

In Wabash, Crystal's mother worked in restaurants while her father, a former coal miner, lost a battle with black lung disease. After graduating from Wabash High School, Gayle lived in Bloomington and began singing in local clubs. She toured periodically with her sister, who by then was the queen of country music.

Gayle enjoyed a huge hit in the mid-1970s with "Don't It Make My Brown Eyes Blue," a soulful tune that topped both the pop and country charts; it also won Gayle a Grammy Award.

She lives near Nashville, Tennessee, with her husband, Bill Gatzimos, who grew up in Logansport, Indiana. "We're Hoosiers through and through," Gayle says.

Jeff George—football quarterback

Immensely talented, strong-armed and controversial—Jeff George has been called all of those during a football career that won him national attention as a teenager in Indianapolis.

The youngest of three sons of David and Judy George, Jeffrey Scott George was born in 1967 and demonstrated phenomenal ability as a quarterback at Warren Central High School. A three-sport letterman, George led the football team to back-to-back state championships (in 1985 and 1986) and generally was considered the best high school quarterback

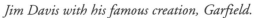
Jim Davis with his famous creation, Garfield.

Jeff Gordon in his moment of triumph in 1994 at the inaugural Brickyard 400 at the Indianapolis Motor Speedway.

The Jackson Five in 1972 included (left to right) Jackie, Jermaine, Marlon, Michael, and Tito. Not pictured is Randy, who later replaced Jermaine in 1976.

The Ball brothers (left to right): George A., Lucius L., Frank C., Edmund B., and William C.

in the nation. Courted by colleges from coast to coast, George chose to play for Purdue University, but left after a year when his coach was fired. George eventually ended up at the University of Illinois.

He returned to his hometown in 1990 when the Indianapolis Colts made him the Number One pick in the 1990 draft. His $12 million contract made George the highest-paid rookie in National Football League history to that point. But Jeff George's stint with the Colts was rocky. Among other factors, his holdout from training camp alienated team management and many fans. After four tumultuous seasons with the Colts, George left to quarterback the Atlanta Falcons. He led Atlanta to the playoffs in 1995, but following a sideline dispute with his coach, he parted ways with the team and signed a five-year contract in 1997 with the Oakland Raiders.

Josef Gingold—violinist and music professor

A paternal figure to dozens of acclaimed musicians who studied at the Indiana University School of Music, Josef Gingold also was known as the "father" of the International Violin Competition in Indianapolis.

Yet the maestro's own family background was turbulent. Gingold was born in 1909 in what is now Belorus; his family was forced to flee at the outbreak of World War I. German soldiers ordered the Gingolds to live in an armory behind barbed wire. Five-year-old Josef played his first "concerts" there when his fiddle playing captivated the guards. After playing with Arturo Toscanini's NBC Symphony Orchestra and serving as concertmaster with orchestras in Detroit and Cleveland, Gingold was lured to the IU faculty in 1960.

A collection of three hundred orchestral repertoire excerpts that he compiled is a standard text for students and symphony players around the world. Gingold founded the International Violin Competition in Indianapolis in 1982. (For more details, see "Joshua Bell" in the "Legends of Our Own Day" section.) Gingold died in 1995.

Jeff Gordon—stock car champion

It was almost too perfect: The winner of the inaugural Brickyard 400 at the Indianapolis Motor Speedway was a clean-cut, handsome NASCAR driver with Hoosier roots who is married to a beauty queen he met on Valentine's Day—and Jeff Gordon won the stock car race in 1994 a few days after his twenty-third birthday.

His triumph at the Brickyard turned out to be just a warm-up. The affable young driver, born in 1971, has enjoyed stunning, rapid success in Winston Cup racing. Since his Winston Cup debut in November 1992, Gordon has won twenty-six races, including the Daytona 500 in 1997 and, also that year, a thrilling Coca-Cola 600 during which he came from behind to snatch victory.

Jeff Gordon's passion for vehicles began in 1975, when his mother and stepfather bought four-year-old Jeff a miniature race car. Four years later, he was a national champion among quarter-midget drivers and followed that up by winning dozens of GoKart events. In part to help Jeff pursue his love of racing, his family moved from California to Pittsboro, Indiana, when he was thirteen. Jeff Gordon is a graduate of Tri-West High School.

Gordon, who is attracting thousands of new spectators to NASCAR events with his charisma and his rainbow-colored cars, enjoys a fifteen-thousand-member fan club and vast celebrity endorsements. He and his wife, Brooke Sealey, a former Miss Winston, now live in a spacious lakeside home near Charlotte, North Carolina.

Michael Graves—architect

"In a land of brand names, Michael Graves is the Coca-Cola of American architecture," *The New York Times* once declared.

He was born in Indianapolis in 1934, graduated from Broad Ripple High School in 1952 and studied architecture at the University of Cincinnati and Harvard University. Graves is known as a pioneer of post-modernist architecture. His home in Princeton, New Jersey—an architectural wonder he calls "The Warehouse"—is a national tourist attraction, with Italianate gardens, wisteria vines, gridded latticework and tiled bricks.

For his hometown, he has designed the Indianapolis headquarters of Thomson Consumer Electronics and the Indianapolis Arts Center in Broad Ripple. Graves has taught at Princeton University since 1962.

Bob Griese—football quarterback

He is in both the College and Professional Football halls of fame for his spectacular successes as a quarterback for Purdue University and the Miami Dolphins.

Bob Griese was born in Evansville in 1945. At Purdue, he was a two-time All-America selection and guided the Boilermakers to a Rose Bowl victory in the 1966–67 season. He was drafted by Miami in 1967 and played fourteen seasons for the Dolphins, leading the team to two Super Bowl championships in the 1970s. Griese retired as a player after the 1980 season, but remains active as a TV analyst and a civic leader in Miami.

Halston—celebrity fashion designer

Roy Halston Frowick was born in Des Moines in 1932, but he grew up in Evansville. He graduated from Bosse High School, attended Indiana University and got his start designing hats for Bergdorf Goodman in New York. Halston first made news by creating Jacqueline Kennedy's pillbox hat for the presidential inaugural ceremony in 1961.

In the early 1970s, Halston was the best-known designer in the world. His fame came not just from his designs (which included long cashmere dresses and wraparound dresses) and his celebrity clients such as Elizabeth Taylor and Liza Minnelli, but for his fast-paced life-style. Halston was at the center of the New York club scene of the 1970s. He died of AIDS in 1990.

Tony Stewart—race driver

By the late 1990s, Tony Stewart—who was born in 1971 and grew up less than an hour's drive from the Indianapolis Motor Speedway—was being called "America's most diverse race car driver." That's because handsome, charismatic Stewart has competed with distinction in seven dissimilar racing series, from sprint cars, midgets and NASCAR to Indy cars.

In 1997, Stewart, only twenty-six, won the Indy Racing League points championship and became something of the poster boy for the league. That year he led the Indianapolis 500 for sixty-four laps—more than any other driver—before brushing the fourth turn wall and finishing fifth. At the 1998 Indianapolis 500, Stewart roared to the lead, but his dreams of victory evaporated with a blown engine; he finished last.

Even so, the Hoosier is considered one of auto racing's brightest new stars. Having grown up in Rushville and Columbus, Ind., Stewart practically was born, as Indianapolis Monthly magazine put it, "with 10W40 in his veins." As a teenager, Tony won national go-kart championships; he has said that winning the 500 always has been "the Number One goal in my life."

In 1996, his debut year at the 500, he captured Rookie of the Year honors. Stewart has chosen to continue to live in Columbus since reaping fame—and even bought back his boyhood home.

Tom Harmon—football player

Born in Gary in 1919, Tom Harmon became a football star and a state champion hurdler in the 1930s at Gary Mann High School. He followed that up with national fame as a running back at the University of Michigan, winning the Heisman Trophy in 1940. (So far Harmon is the only native Hoosier to win the Heisman.)

Harmon was the first player chosen in the 1940 NFL draft, but instead played one season for the New York Americans in a rival league. While serving in the Air Force during World War II, Harmon's plane was shot down over China. He suffered serious burns on both legs and was awarded the Purple Heart. He still managed to play two more seasons of professional football in the 1940s with the Los Angeles Rams. When his playing days were over, Harmon enjoyed a successful career as a TV and radio sportscaster.

He married movie actress Elyse Knox; their son, Mark Harmon, is a popular TV star. Tom Harmon died in 1990.

Billy Herman—baseball player

Billy Herman, a rookie, was up to bat for the Chicago Cubs in 1931. He hit the ball, which hit the ground behind home plate, ricocheted up and struck Herman on the head. It knocked him out cold.

It was an embarrassing way to start as a pro, but Herman's career was far from shameful. Born in New Albany in 1909, Herman became one of the greatest hit-and-run hitters of all time. Playing for teams from Chicago, Brooklyn, Boston and Pittsburgh from 1931 to 1947, he had a lifetime batting average of .304.

Herman often led the National League in hitting categories and was a ten-time All Star. His best year was 1935 while playing for the Chicago Cubs. That year he led the league in double plays, hits and doubles. Herman took two years off baseball to serve in the Navy during World War II. When he returned to the sport, he played for various teams, then was a manager and scout. He retired in 1975 and died in 1992.

Tony Hinkle—college coach

At Butler University in Indianapolis, his name was synonymous with athletics for generations. While coaching at the small, private university, Tony Hinkle took Butler's basketball team to a national championship in 1929. He coached baseball and football as well as basketball, eventually chalking up a combined total of more than one thousand victories at Butler.

Paul Daniel "Tony" Hinkle was born on a farm near Logansport in 1898. A gifted athlete, he earned nine varsity letters at the University of Chicago—three each in basketball, football and baseball. He came to Butler in 1921 and was a coach and teacher nearly fifty years, retiring in 1970. (Four years earlier, the athletic fieldhouse on campus had been re-named Hinkle Fieldhouse.) A beloved figure on campus for two more decades as special assistant to the president, Hinkle died in 1992.

Two fascinating bits of trivia about Tony Hinkle: It apparently was his idea that basketballs should be orange. And aside from his longtime wife Jane, Hinkle had only one girlfriend in his life: In Chicago, he dated a woman who later married baseball legend Lou Gehrig.

Gil Hodges—baseball player and manager

The hard-hitting first baseman for the Brooklyn (and later Los Angeles) Dodgers was born the son of a coal miner in Princeton, Indiana, in 1924.

Gil Hodges attended St. Joseph's College in Rensselaer, where he quickly became the star baseball player. In 1943, he began playing baseball in Indianapolis for the P. R. Mallory team. His talent got him noticed by the Brooklyn Dodgers. Hodges played eighteen seasons in the major leagues, batting .273 overall and hitting 370 home runs. During his career, Hodges hit 14 grand slams, a record.

Eventually the Dodgers traded Hodges to the New York Mets, and when his playing days were done he became manager of an expansion team, the Washington Senators. In 1968 he was named manager of the Mets, then in a deep slump and the laughingstock of the league. A year later, Hodges led the "Miracle Mets" to a World Series championship. His career as a manager was tragically brief. In 1972, Hodges died of a heart attack while playing golf in Florida.

Kin Hubbard—cartoonist

"You can take a voter to th' polls, but you can't make him think."

So quipped cartoon character "Abe Martin," a crackerbarrel philosopher created by Frank McKinney "Kin" Hubbard. The cartoonist was born in Bellefontaine, Ohio, in 1868, but moved to Indiana in the 1890s to work for *The Indianapolis News*. Hubbard began as a police reporter and sketch artist. "Abe Martin," a fictional resident of Brown County, made his debut in 1904.

His homespun wisdom became enormously popular, resulting in national syndication. Twenty-six books of "Abe Martin" witticisms were published. Hubbard died of heart disease at the peak of his success in 1930.

Tony Hulman—Speedway owner and entrepreneur

Anton J. "Tony" Hulman, Jr., who became one of Indiana's wealthiest men, was born in 1901 in Terre Haute. The son of a prosperous grocer, Hulman was educated at private prep schools in the East, including Lawrenceville Academy and Worcester Academy. An avid sportsman from boyhood on, Tony Hulman was named the nation's best high school hurdler in 1919 and the country's top prep pole vaulter in 1920.

During World War I, he served with the American Red Cross ambulance corps. When Hulman returned from overseas, he enrolled at Yale University, where he competed on the crew, track and football teams.

Returning to Terre Haute, he joined his family's grocery business and Clabber Girl baking powder mill. Under his guidance, the company grew and diversified tremendously, and

Hulman became a multimillionaire. His holdings at various times included newspapers and radio stations in Terre Haute, a gas company and the city's largest hotel.

Outside his hometown, though, Hulman primarily became known as "Mr. Speedway." In November 1945, he bought the Indianapolis Motor Speedway, which had deteriorated after years of neglect during World War II. Hulman immediately launched a modernization and improvement effort, plowing millions of dollars into the world-famous track. He oversaw the Indianapolis 500 for more than thirty years until his death in 1977. In the 1990s, the world's greatest race has been overseen by Hulman's grandson, Tony George.

Robert Indiana—sculptor and painter

By far Robert Indiana's most famous works are his LOVE sculpture and painting, which brought him international acclaim. (Unfortunately for Indiana, he initially neglected to copyright the image, which has been "pirated" extensively.)

At his birth in New Castle in 1928, his name was Robert Clark. But he eventually had his name legally changed for marketing purposes and to reflect his heritage, saying he was inspired by legendary playwright Tennessee Williams.

Before Clark/Indiana turned seventeen, his family had moved twenty-one times. But he spent most of his youth in the Indianapolis area; his artistic talents became apparent at Tech High School. He served in the Air Force in the 1940s, then studied art in Chicago, England and Scotland.

Since 1978, Indiana has lived a secluded life on a small island off the coast of Maine. His LOVE statue is near the entrance to the Indianapolis Museum of Art.

The Jackson Five—pop singers

Gary resident Joe Jackson and his wife, Katherine, had nine children, several of whom have achieved worldwide fame as solo performers in pop music. First, though, five of the brothers (actually six, with one Jackson sibling replacing another) enjoyed broad, international appeal as the Jackson Five.

Their story began when Joe Jackson, a crane operator at a steel mill, found a gig for his five oldest sons. They are Jackie (born in 1951), Tito (born in 1953), Jermaine (born in 1954), Marlon (born in 1957), and, of course, Michael, who was born in 1958. When their parents discovered the brothers had musical talent, they started training them. Tito, one of the most ambitious of the brothers, persuaded his siblings to form a group. The brothers began performing at nightspots and talent competitions in northwestern Indiana and across the state line in Chicago.

The Jacksons' big break came when they performed at a campaign benefit for Gary Mayor Richard Hatcher. Pop star Diana Ross was there. Impressed by their talent, she brought the brothers to the attention of Motown Records boss Berry Gordy. Gordy felt they had tremendous potential, particularly nine-year-old Michael. The Jackson Five's debut single, "I Want You Back," was a smash hit in 1970. More attention followed thanks to an album called *Diana Ross Presents the Jackson Five*.

Jermaine left the group in 1976 and was replaced by the youngest brother, Randy (born in 1962). Meanwhile, Michael Jackson had launched a phenomenally successful solo career beginning at age thirteen with the 1972 pop hit "I'll Be There." By then, the Jackson family had left Indiana for southern California.

The popularity of the Jackson Five eventually receded, but Michael Jackson has remained one of the biggest—and most controversial—entertainment personalities in the world. In 1982, he released the biggest-selling album in history, *Thriller*. Two of the Jacksons' sisters, Janet (born in 1966) and LaToya (born in 1956), also have enjoyed success in solo singing and/or acting careers.

Jonathan and Ann Jennings—Indiana's first governor and first lady

Both Jonathan Jennings and his wife, Ann, were transplanted Hoosiers. The son of a Presbyterian minister, he was born in New Jersey in 1784 and grew up in Pennsylvania. She was the daughter of prosperous surveyor and grew up in Kentucky, where she was born in 1792.

Jonathan Jennings moved to the Indiana Territory to study law in Jeffersonville. A strong opponent of slavery, he was elected territorial delegate to Congress in 1809, defeating a pro-slavery candidate. Jennings then became a crusader to win statehood for Indiana.

He married Ann in 1811. While her husband campaigned for Congress, she often nursed victims of malaria, then an epidemic. Jennings was only thirty-two when he began his first term as governor; he was elected to a second term, but left in the middle of it (in 1822) to take a seat in Congress.

Ann died in 1825. Jonathan Jennings remarried and continued to serve in Congress until 1830, but developed a drinking problem. Defeated in his last campaign, he died in 1834.

His annual salary as governor in 1816 was a thousand dollars. Most of it went to pay the cost of entertaining at the governor's residence in Corydon, Indiana's first capital.

Emily Kimbrough—author

Emily Kimbrough became famous with her best friend, actress-author Cornelia Otis Skinner, thanks to a book on which they collaborated, *Our Hearts Were Young and Gay* (1942). A witty reminiscence of their youthful adventures during the early 1920s on an ocean liner and a vacation in Europe, the book became a national bestseller and was made into a movie in 1944.

Born in Muncie in 1899, Kimbrough attended Bryn Mawr College in Pennsylvania, where she met Skinner. According to their book, "Emily had an inborn faculty for attracting disasters minor and major." One example: She hit a drowning man with a chair, which she had thrown to him instead of a life preserver.

During her career, Kimbrough served as fashion editor, then managing editor, of *Ladies' Home Journal* magazine. She wrote fourteen books, including a sequel to her bestseller, *We Followed Our Hearts to Hollywood*, and an exuberant account of life in Muncie at the turn of the century, *How Dear to My Heart*. Kimbrough died in 1989 at her home in New York City.

Greg Kinnear—movie actor and TV talk show host

The cheerful, boyish-looking TV personality was born in Logansport in 1963 and spent his summers at a cabin in Lake Wawasee. Kinnear's family left Indiana when he was nine because his father, the president of a vending business in Logansport, became a diplomat with the State Department. Consequently, Greg spent his teen years in Beirut and Athens.

Kinnear came to national attention as host of cable TV's *Talk Soup* in the early 1990s. In

Country singer Crystal Gayle (top) and actress Shelley Long.

Thomas Marshall, vice president under Woodrow Wilson.

Jonathan Jennings, Indiana's first governor.

1994, NBC selected him as the host of *Later*, a late-night (actually, early-morning) talk show; Kinnear starred on the program for two years. His jaunty, appealing personality won him a leading role in his first movie, a remake of *Sabrina* (1995) with Harrison Ford. Kinnear followed that up with a comedy, *Dear God* (1996), and *As Good As It Gets* (1997) with Jack Nicholson.

Alfred Kinsey—sex researcher

He was a zoologist by training, but Alfred Kinsey of Indiana University became world famous for his controversial studies of human sexuality.

The conservative-looking, bow-tied scientist was born in Hoboken, New Jersey, in 1894. Kinsey didn't come to Indiana until 1920, when he obtained a teaching job at IU. The idea to study human sexual behavior occurred to Kinsey while, as a zoologist, he was analyzing the mating habits of insects—specifically, wasps.

He and his staff interviewed hundreds of people for the best-selling books *Sexual Behavior in the Human Male* (1948) and *Sexual Behavior in the Human Female* (1953), which together became known as "The Kinsey Report." In August 1953, Kinsey was the cover subject of *Time* magazine, which hailed him as the "Columbus of Sex" for his pioneering research.

His studies indicated that people were much more sexually active than believed and that a significant number had homosexual experiences. Several Indiana legislators sought to shut down Kinsey's work, but IU President Herman B Wells protected his research, stressing the need for "academic freedom." Some of Kinsey's conclusions about sexual activity and his methodology have been challenged in recent years. Kinsey died in 1956.

Kenesaw Mountain Landis—baseball commissioner and federal judge

Because he led his sport with an iron fist through several difficult periods, Kenesaw Mountain Landis has been called "the most successful dictator in United States history."

He was born in Millville, Ohio, in 1866, but moved to Logansport with his family when he was seven. Landis dropped out of high school during his sophomore year and never finished, much to the dismay of his father. He eventually became a reporter for the *Logansport Journal*. Landis also played on amateur and semiprofessional baseball teams. Then he studied at a law school in Chicago, graduating in 1891.

Once a Democrat, Landis switched to the Republican Party and later to the Bull Moose Progressives. In 1905, President Theodore Roosevelt appointed him federal judge in northern Illinois. Landis became a national figure when he levied a $30 million fine against Standard Oil of Indiana for unethical business practices.

When baseball was disgraced in 1919 by bribes from gambling interests in what became known as the "Black Sox Scandal," the sport's leaders searched for a someone who could restore order. Eleven club owners asked Landis to become the sport's first single commissioner, replacing a three-man panel. Landis was given sweeping powers, including the authority to investigate any act detrimental to baseball and to impose any punishment he considered necessary on players or teams. One of his first acts was to ban eight "Black Sox" players permanently from the sport.

For a few years, Landis tried to be both a judge and baseball commissioner; he retired from the bench in 1922 to focus on the baseball job. In that year, Landis suspended legendary Babe Ruth and two other players for going on a barnstorming tour after having played in the World Series. An intimidating man, Landis was considered by the press to be harder to approach than the U.S. President. He died in 1944.

Mark Lenzi—Olympic diver

Olympic gold medalist Mark Lenzi was born in Fredericksburg, Maryland, in 1968 and periodically has lived in Michigan. But he won medals in two Olympics while living and training in Bloomington, Indiana.

After high school, Lenzi came to Indiana University to train under legendary diving coach Hobie Billingsley. An underdog, Lenzi surprised sports analysts by capturing the gold medal in three-meter springboard diving at the 1992 Barcelona Olympics. Afterward, Lenzi endured highly publicized struggles with depression and financial problems. But the IU graduate rebounded. Again coached by Billingsley, whom Lenzi calls "a second dad," he won a bronze medal in springboard diving at the 1996 Atlanta Olympics.

Bobby "Slick" Leonard—Indiana Pacers coach

The colorful coach of the Indiana Pacers in the old American Basketball Association was born in 1932 and grew up in Terre Haute. A scrappy, fierce competitor, Bobby "Slick" Leonard was a star player at Terre Haute Gerstmeyer High School and Indiana University, where he was a member of the 1953 national championship team. He played pro basketball with the Lakers in Minneapolis and Los Angeles.

But his biggest fame came as the coach of the Pacers from 1968 to 1980. With a rallying cry of "no tears, no fear," he guided the team to 598 victories. In recent years, Leonard has been a radio and TV sports commentator, and in July 1997, he was named the ABA's all-time leading coach.

Little Turtle—Native American commander

One of the greatest military leaders in Native American history was born in 1751 near the present city of Fort Wayne.

A Miami Indian, Little Turtle rose to prominence in 1780 when a Frenchman named La Balme, inspired by George Rogers Clark's capture of Vincennes, attacked the Miami and other tribes living near the Maumee River. Hearing of the unexpected invasion, Little Turtle rallied an army of Miami warriors to pursue La Balme and his men. Although greatly outnumbered, the Indians prevailed by surrounding the camp and attacking after nightfall; they killed La Balme and his entire brigade.

Little Turtle repeated the feat in 1790 when he and his warriors killed 680 soldiers led by Brigadier General Josiah Harmer. In response, Congress ordered General Arthur St. Clair, governor of the Northwest Territory, to raise a force to destroy the Miami. Little Turtle and his warriors prevailed again in 1791, turning back St. Clair's force and killing about 900 men. Little Turtle's victory was the largest single battlefield defeat of U.S. soldiers by Native Americans.

But then "Mad Anthony" Wayne (who had analyzed Little Turtle's warfare strategies) and a force of five thousand men took on the Miami in a battle not far from Fort Wayne.

The Indians fought courageously in the Battle of the Fallen Timbers of 1794, but the might of Wayne's force eventually forced them to flee. Little Turtle subsequently struck a friendly alliance with the Americans and discouraged the Native American initiatives that led to the Battle of Tippecanoe. Little Turtle spent his last years urging improvements in the morals and quality of life of Native Americans. He died in 1812 at his lodge.

Ross Lockridge, Jr.—novelist

Ross Lockridge's only novel, *Raintree County*, was published to tremendous acclaim. It became the most popular book of 1948, selling more than 400,000 copies that year alone. The historic saga tells the story of southern Indiana resident John Shawnessy, who fights in the Civil War, writes poetry on the banks of the serene Shawmucky River and courts beautiful women.

Lockridge was born in Bloomington in 1914. He attended Indiana University, married and fathered four children. Then he spent seven years behind a typewriter, slaving over his masterpiece until its publication in 1948. That same year, Lockridge took his own life. *Raintree County* became a popular Hollywood movie in 1957 starring Montgomery Clift and Elizabeth Taylor.

In 1994, one of Lockridge's sons, Larry, wrote a biography of his father. Larry Lockridge analyzed the novelist's frustrations, including a deep depression over editorial revisions in *Raintree County*, which probably contributed to his suicide.

Shelley Long—TV star

The Emmy Award-winning actress was born in Fort Wayne in 1949 and grew up there, competing against another future TV star (Jane Pauley of Indianapolis) in high school speech contests. Shelley Long has starred in movies, including *Night Shift* (1982) and *The Money Pit* (1985), but is best known for her leading role as Diane, a snobby waitress on the popular TV series *Cheers*. She played the character from 1982 to 1987.

In the film version of *The Brady Bunch* (1995), Long updated the "Brady mom" role made famous by another Hoosier actress, Florence Henderson.

Thomas R. Marshall—vice president

"What this country needs is a really good five-cent cigar."

That's the remark most people associate with Thomas R. Marshall, a Democrat from Columbia City, Indiana, who became vice president of the United States. He served under President Woodrow Wilson from 1913–21.

Because of the quip about cigars and his other wisecracks, Marshall primarily is remembered for his wit. But recent analysts have commended his self-restraint. During Wilson's second term, the president suffered a serious stroke; many felt he was unfit to finish his term. Marshall was in a position to grab power. He declined, explaining that ascending to the highest office in the land by invoking the Constitution would shake the nation.

Marshall was born in North Manchester in 1854. He studied at Wabash College and became a lawyer in Columbia City. Because of his wit, Marshall was a popular speaker. Democratic boss Thomas Taggart of Indianapolis recruited Marshall to run for governor; he was elected in 1909. Another of his famous remarks is: "Once there were two brothers. One ran away to sea, the other was elected vice president, and neither of them was heard from again."

Marshall died in 1925.

Don Mattingly—baseball player

As a three-year-old boy in Evansville, Don Mattingly received a New York Yankees baseball cap from a neighbor. He grew up to cause a sensation in the 1980s as a Yankees first baseman.

Mattingly, who is left-handed, was born in Evansville in 1961. According to family folklore, a high school coach said Don had a perfect swing as an eight-year-old. At Reitz Memorial High School, he was a star pitcher and led his team to a state championship. (A gifted athlete, Mattingly also was quarterback for the football team and point guard on the basketball team.) The Yankees drafted him after graduation, and he spent a few years in the minor leagues.

In 1984, his first full season in the majors, Mattingly led the American League with 207 hits, 44 doubles and a .343 batting average. He was named the league's most valuable player in 1985. The next year Mattingly won a one-year salary of $1.975 million, the largest in arbitrated baseball history to that point. Recurring back problems hurt his career in the early 1990s, but he remained a fan favorite until his retirement in 1995. A quiet, unassuming man, Mattingly returned to Evansville to live.

Paul V. McNutt—governor, federal administrator and presidential hopeful

Supporters of a Paul McNutt for president crusade in 1940 had their hopes pinned on one thing: that fellow Democrat and incumbent President Franklin D. Roosevelt would not seek a third term. When FDR decided to make the unprecedented attempt, McNutt bowed out of contention and urged delegates at the Democratic National Convention to unify behind the president.

The son of an attorney, Paul Vories McNutt was born in Franklin, Indiana, in 1891. He attended high school in Martinsville and was president of his class and a pitcher on the baseball team. At Indiana University (class of '13), where he was a rival of classmate Wendell Willkie, McNutt reaped amazing success; he served as class president, editor of the newspaper and attained almost every other major leadership role on campus.

He graduated from Harvard Law School in 1916 and practiced law in Martinsville with his father for one year. After a stint in the Army, McNutt became a law professor at IU Named dean of the law school at age thirty-four (he was the youngest dean in the school's history), McNutt eventually won the post of national commander of the American Legion. He was elected governor in the Democratic landslide of 1932. After his term expired, McNutt spent two years as high commissioner of the Philippines. Upon his return to the United States, he was appointed the administrator of the Federal Security Agency.

When World War II broke out, McNutt served as chairman of the War Manpower Commission. After the war, McNutt became the first ambassador to the Philippines. In 1947, he set up a law practice in New York City. McNutt died there in 1955.

J. Irwin Miller—business executive and philanthropist

A native son of Columbus, Indiana, Joseph Irwin Miller reshaped the town literally. It's not just that Miller for more than fifty years has been at the helm of Cummins Engine, a Columbus-based manufacturer of diesel engines and a Fortune 500 company. Thanks to Miller's vision and generosity, Columbus (where he was born in 1909) has become nationally known for its diverse contemporary architecture.

Marilyn Miller—musical comedy star

She was born in 1898 in Evansville, and by age four was in vaudeville billed as "Miss Sugar Plum." Marilyn Miller became a star in Ziegfeld stage productions such as *Ziegfeld Follies of 1918* and *Sally* (1920). She died in 1936.

Sherman Minton—U.S. Supreme Court justice

Sherman Minton as born in 1890 to a poor, hardscrabble farmer's family near the Ohio River in southern Indiana. His family moved to Texas, but he returned to Indiana to become a student leader at Indiana University, where he completed law school in 1915.

After performing brilliantly in advanced work at Yale, Minton began a distinguished career in politics. Elected as a Democratic senator from Indiana in 1934, Minton become one of Franklin D. Roosevelt's leading lieutenants in Congress, spearheading New Deal legislation. Another young senator, Harry S Truman, worked with "Shay" Minton to pass FDR's key legislative programs. They became lifelong friends.

Eventually, Truman appointed Minton to the U.S. Supreme Court, where he served from 1949 until 1956, thus becoming the only Hoosier so honored. Minton died in 1965.

Oliver Perry Morton—governor

The dignified statue of Indiana's Civil War governor Oliver P. Morton stands on the Statehouse lawn looking in the general direction of the Soldiers and Sailors Monument. That statue at the hub of Monument Circle honors the veterans of the war (1861–65) in which Morton played an important part.

Born in Wayne County in 1823, Morton practiced law in Centerville. He was one of the original supporters of the Republican Party and was nominated for governor in 1856. When Governor Henry Lane resigned to run for the Senate in 1861, Morton, who was by then lieutenant governor, became governor.

Word of the firing on Fort Sumter, South Carolina, reached Indiana in April 1861, and Morton moved to raise all the troops President Lincoln called for in an emergency—and more. An avid Northern partisan and Lincoln supporter, Morton worked tirelessly during the war to equip and outfit soldiers, provide ammunition from an armory in Indianapolis—anything and everything to support "our Indiana boys." He even raised money himself to fund state affairs when he ran into trouble with the Democratic legislature.

He was known as the "soldier's friend" and used unique methods to take care of Hoosier soldiers. He even ventured to Washington to personally request that Lincoln intervene and supply shivering southern Indiana soldiers on Cheat Mountain in West Virginia who were without overcoats—and trousers—as the snow fell.

Ever the strong-minded politician, Morton drew criticism when he exaggerated the presence of the Knights of the Golden Circle and other Southern-sympathizing groups in Indiana late in the war. Morton was encouraged to run for the presidency in 1876, but Rutherford B. Hayes was named the nominee by Republicans. Morton died the next year.

Meredith Nicholson—writer

'Tis morning, and the days are long. It is always morning and all the days are long in Indiana.

So wrote one of the fabled "Big Four" of the golden age of Indiana literature shortly after the turn of the century: Meredith Nicholson. (The other three were James Whitcomb Riley, Booth Tarkington and George Ade.)

A writer who described his home state with tremendous affection, Nicholson was born in Crawfordsville in 1866. He attended public schools in Indianapolis, but quit when he was fifteen, later explaining that he was not suited for formal schooling. (But Nicholson was an avid reader and taught himself Latin, Greek, French, and Italian.)

He initially worked as a legal clerk in the office of Lew Wallace's brother, William. But Nicholson eventually found an outlet for his writing, beginning as a reporter with *The Indianapolis Sentinel* and graduating to literary editor and editorial writer with *The Indianapolis News*. A professor at Columbia University asked Nicholson to write a cultural history of Indiana. Called *The Hoosiers*, it was published in 1900.

For the next twenty-five years, Nicholson turned out a book nearly every year. They included a best-selling novel, *The House of a Thousand Candles* (1905) set in northern Indiana. An outspoken Democrat, Nicholson served on the Indianapolis City Council from 1928 to 1930 and ran unsuccessfully for a State Senate seat. His biggest political involvements came between 1933 and 1941, when he served as a diplomat to Paraguay, Venezuela and Nicaragua. He died in 1947, having advised aspiring writers to "stay in your own hometown."

Jaycie Phelps—Olympic gymnast

At age sixteen, the five-foot-tall, ninety-seven-pound gymnast won international attention as one of the "Magnificent Seven" athletes who captured America's first Olympic gold medal for women's team gymnastics.

The road to Jaycie Phelps' triumph at the 1996 Atlanta Olympics was rough. In her early teens, Jaycie and her mother moved from her hometown of Greenfield to Scottsdale, Arizona, then to Cincinnati, Ohio, in search of better coaching. Her father and brother usually remained in Greenfield. Jaycie, who was born in 1979, always says that she considers Greenfield home.

Eugene C. Pulliam—newspaper publisher

He was a self-made man who became an influential media titan in Indiana and Arizona, one of the last of a breed of crusading newspaper publishers.

The son of a Methodist minister, Eugene C. Pulliam was born in western Kansas in 1889. Pulliam came to Indiana to attend DePauw University. On the Greencastle campus, he and other students founded the organization that became the country's largest journalism group, the Society of Professional Journalists (called Sigma Delta Chi for several decades).

By 1948, Pulliam was publisher of the two largest newspapers in the state, *The Indianapolis Star* and *The Indianapolis News*. He also owned major dailies in Phoenix and smaller newspapers in Muncie, Vincennes and Lebanon. Although usually associated with fiery conservative views, Pulliam was not easy to stereotype. He stood up to the Ku Klux Klan and pioneered the concept of an opposite-editorial ("op-ed") page in newspapers. He died in 1975. His son, Eugene S. Pulliam, succeeded him as publisher of the Indianapolis newspapers.

Ernie Pyle—journalist and war correspondent

Ernest Taylor Pyle was born on a farm near Dana, Indiana, in 1900. He attended Indiana University and was editor-in-chief of the campus newspaper, but left without graduating. Pyle worked on newspapers in LaPorte, Indiana, and Washington, D.C., where he met his wife, Geraldine.

They married in 1925, pooled their money, quit their jobs, bought a Ford roadster and took to the back roads of America for adventure. Ernie Pyle eventually became a "roving human-interest columnist" for the Scripps-Howard newspaper syndicate. He reported everywhere from Chesapeake Bay in Maryland to Good News Bay in Alaska, often filing stories as "The Hoosier Vagabond."

But his lasting fame began as America moved toward involvement in World War II. Even before Pearl Harbor, Pyle was in London covering the European conflict. Soon newspaper readers across the country were captivated by Pyle's accounts. He wrote the soldier's story. Pyle ventured to the front lines, rotated among the various branches of service, shivered in foxholes and joined U.S. troops fighting in North Africa, Europe and the Pacific.

In 1944, Pyle received the Pulitzer Prize for his stories and columns. He was killed in April 1945 as the war wound down; on Okinawa, Pyle and four officers were traveling in a jeep that came under fire from a Japanese machine gunner. A plaque at the site reads: "At this spot the 77th Infantry Division lost a buddy Ernie Pyle 18 April 1945."

Johann George Rapp—spiritual leader and communal living advocate

Johann George Rapp was born in Iptinger, Wurtenberg, Germany, in 1757. Rapp objected to the orthodox Lutheran church and was forced to leave his homeland because of his strong denunciations of the church. He arrived in America in 1803 and organized other dissidents from Germany; the "Rappites" eventually began a colony in southern Indiana they called New Harmony. (For more details, see "Robert Owen" in the "Legends of History" section.) Rapp died in 1847, more than twenty years after he left Indiana.

Knute Rockne—University of Notre Dame football coach

Win just one for the Gipper.

That's the phrase forever linked with legendary coach Knute Rockne, as spoken to him by George Gipp, a football player at Notre Dame who was dying of pneumonia. But Rockne was a folk legend for many reasons other than his association with the famous deathbed request. Above all else, he accumulated an astounding string of victories as coach of the Fighting Irish.

Rockne was born in Voss, Norway, in 1888. He was five years old when his family came to America, settling in Chicago. Knute played football as a student at Notre Dame (class of '13), then stayed on as a chemistry teacher and assistant football coach.

Rockne became head coach in 1918, and phenomenal success followed. During the 1920s, with his famous backfield players nicknamed "The Four Horsemen," Rockne made Notre Dame the first college football team to travel all over the country for intersectional games. A master motivator, he eventually amassed a record of 105 wins, 12 losses, and 5 ties. His teams won six national championships and were unbeaten for five of his thirteen seasons.

Under "The Rock," the Fighting Irish built a huge national following that remains fervent to this day. The coach's life ended tragically in an airplane crash in Kansas in 1931. Although details of the "win one for the Gipper" story were doubted by some (the coach told a mediocre team about Gipp's deathbed request in the locker room during halftime; inspired, the players returned to the field to beat Army in 1928), Rockne always insisted the tale was true.

Chris Schenkel—sportscaster

From Bippus to bowling—as well as the Olympics, football, golf and at least a dozen other sports around the globe.

That could be the slogan of smooth-voiced TV and radio sportscaster Chris Schenkel, who was born in 1923 and grew up on his family's farm near tiny Bippus in far northeastern Indiana. He studied at Purdue University, broadcast one of the first televised college football events (a Harvard game in 1947) and was the commentator for New York Giants' football games for thirteen years. Schenkel soon became one of the best-known sportscasters on TV, covering everything from boxing to rodeo and anchoring coverage of the 1972 Munich Olympics.

But he primarily is associated across the country with pro bowling. Schenkel served as the sport's commentator for thirty-six seasons for ABC-TV. Throughout his career, Schenkel and his wife, Fran, have lived on a farm on the banks of Lake Tippecanoe, about twenty miles from Bippus.

Wayne and Kim Seybold—Olympic figure skaters

The brother-sister pairs team of figure skaters from Marion, Indiana, drew international attention during the 1988 Winter Olympics because of their hard-luck story and the way their Indiana hometown rallied to support the athletes.

Wayne and Natalie "Kim" Seybold were born in 1964 and 1966, respectively, and graduated from Marion High School. Overcoming injuries and financial hardships—the Seybolds lived in a trailer during most of their years of training—Wayne and Kim were able to pursue their Olympic dreams thanks to donations from Marion residents and businesses. The Seybolds finished tenth at the Calgary Olympics. Kim survived surgery for a brain tumor in 1995 and has carved out a career with her brother in professional skating.

Active in his sport long past its conventional retirement age, pioneer gymnast Kurt Thomas executes a handstand at the top step of the Hoosier Dome (now the RCA Dome) in 1990.

Oliver P. Morton was Indiana's governor during the Civil War.

Sherman Minton, Indiana's Supreme Court justice.

Wilbur Shaw—race driver

He was born in Shelbyville in 1902 and grew up to dominate the Indianapolis 500 for several years. Wilbur Shaw won at the Indianapolis Motor Speedway three times—in 1937, 1939 and 1940, making him the first driver to earn back-to-back wins. He finished second in three other races.

Shaw also is credited with convincing Terre Haute businessman Tony Hulman to buy the deteriorating Speedway after World War II and restore luster to the facility. Hulman also named Shaw the speedway's president and general manager. A master showman, Shaw became America's premier racing promoter.

As a youth, Shaw had been an errand boy in Gasoline Alley at the Speedway. He became famous in the Midwest by winning dozens of dirt- and board-track races. In his first 500-Mile Race in 1927, he finished an impressive fourth.

He almost captured a fourth 500 victory. Shaw was in the lead in 1941 when a wheel hub broke on his Maserati; the car slammed into the wall, and Shaw fractured three vertebrae. He was killed in 1954 in the crash of a private plane in northeast Indiana.

Thomas Taggart—mayor and political boss

Thomas Taggart was born in Ireland in 1856, but emigrated as a child with his family. The Taggarts settled in Ohio. Thomas, who never graduated from high school, moved to Garrett, Indiana, in 1875. Two years later he came to Indianapolis to work at a restaurant in the Union Station railway center. Soon he owned a downtown restaurant and hotels.

By the mid-1880s, Taggart was active in Democratic politics and eventually became the party's state chairman. As mayor of Indianapolis from 1895-1901, he vastly expanded the public parks system. After leaving office, he became a major owner of the French Lick Springs Hotel in southern Indiana, one of the country's most popular upscale spas.

Taggart remained the state's top Democratic power broker for twenty-five more years and served four years as chairman of the Democratic National Committee. When a U.S. senator from Indiana died in office in 1916, Taggart filled out the term. He lost subsequent elections for the Senate and died in 1929.

Steve Tesich—screenwriter and playwright

The talented screenwriter who won an Academy Award for *Breaking Away* (1979), a lyrical movie filmed in Bloomington, wasn't a Hoosier by birth.

Steve Tesich was born Stoyan Tesich in Yugoslavia in 1942. To escape Communism, the family moved to East Chicago, Indiana, when Stoyan (Steve) was fourteen. His father worked as a machinist. Steve spoke no English, a fact that motivated him to start writing.

An avid bicyclist and an Indiana University graduate, Tesich based *Breaking Away* in part on his campus experiences. The movie—about a group of free-spirited teenagers who attempt to win the "Little 500" bicycle race—became an unexpected box office hit. After winning the Oscar for best screenplay, Tesich wrote *Four Friends* (1981), an autobiographical movie about an Eastern European immigrant who comes of age in northwestern Indiana during the 1960s. Although he became a New York-based playwright, Tesich always said he considered Indiana his "spiritual home."

He died suddenly of a heart attack at age fifty-three in 1996.

Twyla Tharp—choreographer and dancer

She was born in 1941 in Portland, Indiana, where she began piano lessons at two and dance training at four. Then Twyla Tharp moved with her family to California; she later came to New York and studied ballet and modern dance with many of the masters, including Martha Graham and Merce Cunningham.

Tharp spent a year performing with the Paul Taylor Dance Company, but left a promising career to form her own company in 1965. She won widespread praise for her choreography and created works for everyone from the Joffrey Ballet to professional ice dancers. She also has choreographed scenes for several movies, including *Amadeus* (1984) and *White Knights* (1985) with Mikhail Baryshnikov.

Kurt Thomas—pioneer gymnast

Like swimming legend Mark Spitz, gymnastics legend Kurt Thomas was not born in Indiana and has not lived in the Hoosier state since college. But also like Spitz, his greatest glory—and his pioneering efforts in his sport—came while Thomas lived in Indiana and represented a state university.

Kurt Thomas, generally considered the first truly great American male gymnast, was born in Miami, Florida, in 1956. A national high school champion in his sport, Thomas was lured to Indiana State University with a gymnastics scholarship in 1974. On the Terre Haute campus, he shared the national spotlight with classmate Larry Bird, sometimes reaping more attention than the basketball player. Thomas won the NCAA all-around championship in 1977 and repeated the feat in 1979.

In 1978, Kurt Thomas became the first American male gymnast to win a world championship in forty-six years. His explosive trademark routine on the pommel horse and the floor exercise—in which Thomas flared his legs in a flashy series of whirling, alternating, midair scissors kicks—is called the "Thomas Flair" to this day. In 1979, Thomas won the Sullivan Award as the country's top amateur athlete.

Lauded as the "Baryshnikov of the pommel horse," Thomas was considered a shoo-in for a gold medal in the 1980 Moscow Olympics, but lost the chance to compete when President Jimmy Carter ordered an American boycott of the games. Thomas starred in a movie *Gymkata* (1985), worked as a TV commentator and has carved out a career as a touring professional gymnast. Like Spitz's, a comeback attempt to make the 1992 Olympic team failed. Kurt Thomas lives in Texas, but says he always will consider Indiana "home."

Elton Trueblood—Quaker scholar, author, and Earlham College professor

Known as "Mr. Earlham" much the way Herman B Wells became "Mr. IU," D. Elton Trueblood was born in 1900.

Descended from a long line of Quakers—Trueblood's ancestors were imprisoned in seventeenth-century England for their religious beliefs—he wrote thirty-six books on spiritual and ethical topics. They include *The Philosophy of Religion*, *The Predicament of Modern Man* and *The Humor of Christ*. His insights, wit and poetry have been quoted in everything from "Dear Abby" advice columns to *Philosophical Review*.

In Richmond, Indiana, Trueblood founded Yokefellow International, a group of civic leaders devoted to using their Christian faith in daily life. Trueblood also was a professor at Earlham College for twenty years beginning in 1946; then he lived on campus another twenty years and wrote. An abbreviated version of one of his sayings that made its way into general use:

> *Man is the only animal who laughs, the only one who weeps, the only one who prays, the only one who can invent, the only one who is proud . . . the only one who is penitent, and the only one who needs to be.*

Trueblood died in 1994.

Will Vawter—painter and illustrator

He won fame as an artist in two ways—for his landscape paintings of rural Indiana scenes (particularly of Brown County) and his illustrations for the books of Indiana's best-known poet, James Whitcomb Riley.

John William Vawter was born in Boone County, Virginia, in 1871. When he was six years old, his family moved to Greenfield, Indiana, Riley's hometown. Will displayed a talent for drawing as a boy, and his mother encouraged his artistic interests. According to family folklore, she didn't even object too much when he set up an easel in the Vawter parlor and wiped his paintbrushes on the curtains and plush upholstered furniture.

His first professional work as an artist came with the *Indianapolis Sentinel* newspaper in 1891. Six years later, Vawter wrote and illustrated a series of verses for the *Cincinnati Gazette*. He also collaborated with his sister, Clara Vawter, on a children's book, *Of Such is the Kingdom* (1899).

Beginning in 1908, Vawter made his home in Brown County. Although about twenty years younger than Riley, Vawter became great friends with the distinguished poet. Most of Riley's books were illustrated by Vawter, whose style seemed to perfectly complement the poet's. Vawter's drawings also appeared in popular magazines of the era such as *Judge* and *Life*. He won many awards for his oil landscapes, particularly his winter scenes, which he painted in a hilltop studio. Vawter died in 1941.

"Mad" Anthony Wayne—Revolutionary War-era general and Indian negotiator

Anthony Wayne, who was born in colonial Pennsylvania in 1745, studied astronomy in his youth and worked as an assistant to Benjamin Franklin. During the Revolutionary War, Wayne took command of regiments known as the "Pennsylvania Line," survived the infamous 1778–79 winter in Valley Forge and pulled off the brilliant capture of a British fort near the Hudson River in New York. His bravery, often bordering on recklessness, resulted in the "Mad" Anthony nickname.

He retired to civilian life in 1783, but nine years later President George Washington asked Wayne to command a legion that would secure the "western front" (present-day Indiana, Illinois, and Michigan) from the British. The British were continuing to hold forts in the Northwest Territory and incite Indian attacks on American settlers.

Wayne took charge of soldiers, who were recruited among beggars and criminals from the streets and prisons of Eastern cities. He turned them into a precision force. In the Battle of the Fallen Timbers near the present city of Toledo, Ohio, Wayne and his men drove back the Miami Indians in 1794. The next year, the general built Fort Wayne to command the frontier waterways to Lake Erie; Wayne also negotiated the historic Treaty of Greenville with the Miami Indians. He died in 1796 in Pennsylvania.

"Mad" Anthony Wayne didn't spend much time in what is now Indiana, but he had a major impact on the future state. By securing the land from British forces and negotiating a treaty with the Miami Indians, Wayne helped open the Midwest to white settlers.

Dick Weber—pro bowler

Richard A. "Dick" Weber was born in Indianapolis in 1929 and started bowling at ten because his father managed a bowling center. When the Professional Bowlers Association (PBA) was organized in 1958, Weber was a charter member.

During the 1960s, Weber dominated pro bowling; he was named player of the year in 1961, 1963 and 1965. Weber is the only player to have won a PBA title in each of the last five decades.

Matt Williams—TV show creator, producer, and writer

Cited by *Esquire* magazine in 1993 as the Number One power in TV situation comedies, Matt Williams is a favorite son of Evansville, where he was born in 1951.

Williams, the son of a Whirlpool factory worker and a graduate of the University of Evansville, is the creator and executive producer of *Home Improvement*, one of the most popular TV sitcoms of the 1990s. He also was affiliated as a producer, creator or writer with a string of other hit TV shows in the 1980s and '90s, including *Roseanne*, *The Cosby Show*, and *A Different World*.

Maintaining his strong ties to his home state, Williams became a founder in 1986 of the New Harmony Project, an annual gathering of dozens of Hollywood screenwriters and playwrights in southern Indiana. In the historic setting, the writers work on scripts that "celebrate the human spirit."

Robert Wise—movie director

He has been involved in the making of a startling number of the all-time classics of the movie industry, from *Citizen Kane* (1941) to *West Side Story* (1961), and *The Sound of Music* (1965).

But before Robert Wise "went Hollywood," Indiana was his home. He was born in Winchester in 1914 and attended Connersville High School and Franklin College. Short on money, Wise left school during the Depression and followed his older brother, Dave, to Los Angeles. After obtaining an entry-level job at RKO Studios in 1934, Wise worked his way up to assistant editor on movies such as *The Hunchback of Notre Dame* (1939) and *Citizen Kane*, the legendary film directed by—and starring—Orson Welles.

After editing movies for several years, Wise yearned to direct. He began by directing low-budget films such as the 1944 thriller *The Curse of the Cat People* and *The Body Snatcher* (1945) with Bela Lugosi and Boris Karloff.

In the 1950s, Wise developed a reputation as one of Hollywood's most talented directors with films such as *Somebody Up There Likes Me* (1956), which made Paul Newman a star, and *I Want to Live!* (1958), for which Susan Hayward won an Academy Award.

His greatest success has come with two classic musicals, both of which received the Academy Award as Best Picture of the Year: *West Side Story*, a modern Romeo-and-Juliet tale involving New York City youth gangs, and *The Sound of Music*, the story of the real-life Von Trapp family of singers. *The Sound of Music* became one of the most popular movies ever made, setting box office records.

Wilbur Wright—aviator

Milton Wright, father of the legendary brothers Wilbur and Orville, was born in Rush County, Indiana, in 1828. Milton Wright was a bishop in the United Brethren Church and hoped his two sons would become ministers.

But the boys had other dreams—sky-high dreams. Wilbur, the older brother, was born in 1867 near the small town of Millville in eastern Indiana. The Wright family moved several times in the next few years, so Orville was born in Dayton, Ohio, in 1871. For a time during this period, the Wright family also lived in Fairmount, Indiana.

Despite their ties to Indiana and Ohio, the Wright brothers primarily (and rightly) are associated with North Carolina, where they spent most of their lives. In North Carolina, the Wrights opened a bicycle sales and repair shop, but devoted their spare time to studying flight and tinkering with gliders and airplanes. In 1903, the brothers' experimental plane with an engine survived a twelve-second flight over Kill Devil Hill near Kitty Hawk, North Carolina; it was the first time a motor-driven machine carried a man in free flight.

Wilbur Wright died in 1912, and Orville in 1948. A Wilbur Wright memorial birthplace near Millville is open to the public for tours.

Fuzzy Zoeller—professional golfer

Frank Urban Zoeller was born in New Albany in 1951. He has won two of the world's major golf tournaments—the Masters championship in 1979 and the U.S. Open in 1984. For several years after his prestigious wins, though, Fuzzy Zoeller's career was curtailed by back problems. He rebounded in 1993 and has been a contender in most major tournaments since then.

Fuzzy Zoeller is one of the great characters on the professional golf tour, a sunglasses-wearing wisecracker who whistles around the golf course no matter how well or poorly he is playing. Sometimes his humor gets him in trouble. In 1997, race-related jokes Zoeller made about young golf superstar Tiger Woods offended many Americans. Zoeller quickly offered an apology, which Woods accepted.

Zoeller and his wife, Diane, have three children. The family continues to live in southern Indiana.

Johnny Gruelle—cartoonist, artist and children's book author

Is the world's most famous rag doll a Hoosier?

Well . . . floppy, whimsical Raggedy Ann—and her brother Raggedy Andy—were created by a Hoosier, a gifted illustrator/story teller whose creativity was influenced by James Whitcomb Riley.

Johnny Gruelle, the creator of the Raggedy Ann book series and dolls, was born in 1880 in Arcola, Illinois. As a toddler, he moved with his family to the Lockerbie Street area of Indianapolis, where Riley was their neighbor and friend. Johnny's father, landscape painter Richard B. Gruelle, was one of the illustrious artists known as the "Hoosier Group."

In 1903, Johnny Gruelle was hired by *The Indianapolis Star*; his political cartoons regularly appeared on the front page. Reaping national acclaim, he became the cartoonist for *The New York Herald*; Johnny and his wife were living in the East when their thirteen-year-old daughter, Marcella, fell gravely ill.

According to Johnny's granddaughter, Joni Gruelle, the Raggedy Ann adventures originated as bedtime tales the cartoonist told to his dying daughter. Names and traits of Johnny's famous creations were inspired by blending his two favorite Riley poems: "The Raggedy Man" and "Little Orphant Annie."

Raggedy Ann Stories was published in 1918, and *Raggedy Andy Stories* in 1920. The dolls, handmade by Gruelle family members and mass-produced as marketing promotions for the books, were immediate sensations. The Gruelles moved to Florida, where Johnny and his son, Worth, illustrated and wrote dozens of books as well as Raggedy Ann proverbs syndicated to newspapers in the 1930s. Johnny Gruelle died from a heart attack in 1938.

Wes Montgomery—jazz musician

The legendary Hoosier born John Leslie Montgomery in Indianapolis in 1923 was married and nineteen years old before he ever picked up a guitar. Despite his late start, Wes Montgomery became an internationally-known musician with a reputation as one of the twentieth century's most innovative jazz guitarists.

A self-taught musician, Montgomery joined the Lionel Hampton Trio in the late 1940s and toured across the country, then became a central figure in his hometown's thriving jazz scene along Indiana Avenue. With his brothers Monk and Buddy, he released his first recording, *The Wes Montgomery Trio*, in 1959. Success followed success. In 1965, his album "Goin' Out of My Head," won a Grammy Award.

As he was preparing to tour Japan in 1968, Wes Montgomery died of a heart attack at age forty-five. An annual jazz festival and a park in Indianapolis are named in his honor.

Norman Norell—fashion designer

He was one of the first American fashion designers to become as revered as his European counterparts; as The New York Times phrased it, Norman Norell "made Seventh Avenue the rival of Paris."

His clients from the 1940s through the '60s included some of the world's most glamorous women; Marilyn Monroe, Babe Paley, Lena Horne, Arlene Francis, and Lauren Bacall were among them. Vanity Fair magazine hailed Norell as "the pioneering fashion icon . . . behind the first ladies' tuxedo, the first flash of sixties mod and the first U.S. designer perfume."

Norell was born Norman David Levinson in Noblesville in 1900. (When he changed his name as a young man, he explained "Norell" this way: "Nor for Norman. L for Levinson.

Another L for looks.") As a boy, he worked in his father's hat shop in Indianapolis; his big break came when he landed a job with New York designer Hattie Carnegie. Norell's sequined sheaths eventually became the most expensive dresses in America. He died in 1972.

Orville Redenbacher—popcorn king

The best-selling popcorn in America was developed by an Indiana farm boy who became a county agricultural agent—then a millionaire. "Popcorn King" Orville Redenbacher is credited with giving popcorn much of its mass appeal by creating a hybrid variety that was whiter, fluffier, and able to expand forty times its original size when popped.

Grandfatherly, bow-tied Redenbacher—who became famous by putting his image on the label of his product and by appearing in countless TV commercials—attended Purdue University when it was, as he put it, "on the cutting edge of popcorn research."

Born in 1907, Redenbacher grew up on his family's farm near Brazil, Indiana. At Brazil High School, he captured state championships in 4-H club contests; he paid for his tuition at Purdue by scrubbing hog houses and tending chickens.

After becoming an agricultural agent in Vigo County (he was the first county agent to broadcast live from fields), Redenbacher spent more than forty years crossbreeding three thousand popcorn hybrids before hitting the jackpot. In 1976, Orville Redenbacher Original Gourmet Popcorn became the number-one selling popcorn in the United States, a position it still holds today.

For years, Redenbacher lived in Valparaiso, which continues to hold an annual popcorn parade and festival even though the beloved "king" died in 1995. Among other distinctions, Redenbacher's popcorn leaves almost no kernels after popping.

"Do you want to know the secret?" he once asked an interviewer. "It is the exact moisture in each kernel—13.5 percent."

Redenbacher always ate his salted, no butter.

Bibliography

Alford, Steve with John Garrity. *Playing for Knight.* New York: Simon and Schuster, 1989.

Andretti, Mario. *Andretti.* San Francisco: Collins Publishers, 1994.

Andersen, Christopher. *The Book of People.* New York, Perigee Books: 1981.

Andrews, Andy. *Storms of Perfection*, Vol. II. Nashville, Tenn.: Lightning Crown Publishers, 1994.

Bailey, Damon with Wendell Trogdon. *Damon: Living A Dream.* Mooresville, Ind.: Backroads Press, 1995.

Barnhart, John O. and Dorothy Riker. *Indiana To 1816: The Colonial Period.* Indianapolis: Indiana Historical Bureau and Indiana Historical Society, 1971.

Blackwell, Earl. *Earl Blackwell's Celebrity Register.* New York: Celebrity Register Inc., 1986.

Blum, Daniel. *Great Stars of the American Stage.* New York: Grosset & Dunlap, 1954.

Bodenhamer, David J. and Robert G. Barrows. *The Encyclopedia of Indianapolis.* Bloomington and Indianapolis: Indiana University Press, 1994.

Brooks, Tim. *The Complete Directory of Primetime TV Stars.* New York: Ballantine Books, 1987.

Charles, Sol and Albert Wolsky. *The Movie Makers.* Secaucus, N.J.: Derbibooks Inc., 1974.

Cleaves, Freeman. *Old Tippecanoe: William Henry Harrison and His Times.* Norwalk, Conn.: Easton Press, 1939.

Clifford, Mike. *The Harmony Illustrated Encyclopedia of Rock* New York: Crown Publishers Inc., 1992.

Cusic, Don. *Sandi Patti: The Voice of Gospel.* New York: Doubleday, 1968.

Cwiklik, Robert. *Tecumseh: Shawnee Rebel.* New York: Chelsea House Publishers, 1993.

Dunn, Jacob Piatt, *Indiana and the Indianans.* Chicago and New York: The American Historical Society, 1919.

Foster, Harriet McIntire. *Mrs. Benjamin Harrison.* Indianapolis: Daughters of the American Revolution, 1908.

Girardin, G. Russell and William J. Helmer. *Dillinger: The Untold Story.* Bloomington, Ind.: Indiana University Press, 1994.

Hammel, Bob. *Beyond the Brink with Indiana.* Bloomington, Ind.: The Bloomington Herald-Telephone & Indiana University Press, 1987.

Hickok, Ralph. *A Who's Who of Sports Champions.* New York: Houghton Mifflin Co., 1995.

Hine, Darlene Clark. *Black Women in America: An Historical Encyclopedia.* Brooklyn, N.Y.: Carlson Publishing Inc., 1993.

Holley, Val. *James Dean: The Biography.* New York: St. Martin's Press, 1995.

Hoover, Dwight W. and Jane Rodman, *A Pictorial History of Indiana.* Bloomington, Ind.: Indiana University Press, 1980.

Langworth, Richard E. *An Illustrated Studebaker Buyer's Guide.* Osceola, Wisc.: Motorbooks International, 1991.

Layden, Joe. *Women in Sports.* Los Angeles: General Publishing Group Inc., 1997.

Lutholtz, M. William, *Grand Dragon: D. C. Stephenson and the Ku Klux Klan in Indiana*. West Lafayette, Ind.: Purdue Univesity Press, 1991.

Madden, W. C. *The Hoosiers of Summer*. Indianapolis: Guild Press of Indiana, 1994.

Madison, James H. *Eli Lilly: A Life*. Indianapolis: Indiana Historical Society, 1989.

Madison, James H. *The Indiana Way: A State History*. Bloomington: Indiana University Press, 1986.

Madison, James H. *Wendell Willkie: Hoosier Internationalist*. Bloomington, Ind.: Indiana University Press, 1992.

McClure, Col. Alexander. *Abe Lincoln's Yarns and Stories*. Chicago: The J.C. Winston Company, 1904.

McDonogh, Pat. *Hoosiers*. Louisville, Ky.: Scripps Howard Publishing Inc., 1993.

Minturn, Joseph Allen. *Frances Slocum of Miami Lodge*. Indianapolis: Globe Publishing Co., 1928.

Morrow, Barbara Olenyik. *From Ben-Hur to Sister Carrie: Remembering the Lives and Works of Five Indiana Authors*. Indianapolis: Guild Press of Indiana, 1995.

Morsberger, Robert E. and Katharine. *Lew Wallace: Militant Romantic*. New York: McGraw-Hill, 1980.

Neely, Mark E. *The Abraham Lincoln Encyclopedia*. New York: McGraw-Hill Inc., 1982.

Newton, Judy Vale. *The Hoosier Group: Five American Painters*. Indianapolis: Eckert Publications, 1985.

Ogden, Dale. *Hoosier Sports Heroes*. Indianapolis: Guild Press of Indiana, 1990.

Peckham, Howard H. *Indiana: A History*. New York: W. W. Norton & Company Inc., 1978.

Pitzer, Donald E., editor. *Robert Owen's American Legacy*. Indianapolis: Indiana Historical Society, 1972.

Reed, George Irving. *Encyclopedia of Biography of Indiana*. Indianapolis: Century Publishing & Engraving Co., 1885.

Ritchie, Andrew. *Major Taylor: The Extraordinary Career of a Champion Bicycle Racer*. Baltimore: Johns Hopkins University Press, 1988.

Rooks, Noliwe M. *Hair Raising: Beauty, Culture and African American Women*. New Brunswick, N.J.: Rutgers University Press, 1996.

Shanley, Mary Kay, editor. *When I Think About My Father: Sons and Daughters Remember*. Marshalltown, Iowa: Sta-Kris Inc., 1996.

Slide, Anthony. *Great Radio Personalities*. Vestal, N.Y.: The Vestal Press, 1982.

Spoto, Donald. *Rebel: The Life and Legend of James Dean*. New York: Harper Collins, 1996.

Talley, Steve. *Bland Ambition*. Orlando, Fla.: Harcourt Brace Jovanovich, 1992.

Thompson, Charles. *Sons of the Wilderness: John and William Conner*. Noblesville, Ind.: Conner Prairie Press, 1988 (originally 1937).

Wallace, Lew. *An Autobiography*. 2 vols. New York: Harper & Brothers, 1906.

Warren, Louis A. *Lincoln's Youth: Indiana Years, Seven to Twenty-One, 1816–1830*. New York: Appleton-Century Crofts Inc., 1959.

Williams, Bob. *Hoosier Hysteria: Indiana High School Basketball*. South Bend: Hardwood Press, 1982, 1997.

Winger, Otho. *The Frances Slocum Trail*. North Manchester, Ind.: The News-Journal, 1961 (original printing, 1933).